Entrepreneur.
MAGAZINE'S

LEGAL GUIDE

W. Rod Stern

Estate Planning, Wills, and Trusts

For Business Owners and Entrepreneurs

EP
Entrepreneur.
Press

Editorial director: Jere L. Calmes
Cover design: Desktop Miracles, Inc.
Composition and production: MillerWorks

This publication is designed to provide accurate and authoritative information in regard to
the subject matter covered. It is sold with the understanding that the publisher is not engaged
in rendering legal, accounting, or other professional services. If legal advice or other expert
assistance is required, the services of a competent professional person should be sought.

Library of Congress Cataloging-in-Publication Data

Stern, W. Rod.
    Estate planning, wills, and trusts: for business owners and entre p reneurs / by W. Rod Stern .
        p. cm.
    ISBN-13: 978-1-59918-094-6 (alk. paper)
    ISBN-10: 1-59918-094-4 (alk. paper)
        1. Estate planning—United States. 2. Family-owned business enterprises—
Succession—United States. 3. Businesspeople—United States—Handbooks, manuals, etc.
I. Title.

KF750.S743 2007
346.7305'2—dc22   2007003708

Printed in Canada

Contents

PART TWO

Estate Planning Goals

PART THREE

Estate Planning Tools

PART FOUR

Taking Charge of Your Estate Planning

Acknowledgments

T hank you to Jere Calmes, Helen Carasso, and Entrepreneur Press for understanding that the estate planning needs of the business owner are greater than, and diffe rent from, the needs of non-business owners. I appreciate the opportunity to address the issues from the perspective of a business/tax attorney who routinely guides successful business owners through the process.

Thank you to Dan Lathrope and Steve Lind at the University of California, Hastings College of the Law, for their kind sharing of information regarding the future of estate tax law. Any errors in the predictions set forth in Chapter 30 are entirely mine, but their input was invaluable in allowing me to guess—however incorrectly—regarding the future of the estate tax.

Dedication

To Bonita Kato Stern.
This book would have been written without you, but probably by a different author. Thank you for 40 years of friendship and direction (including 27 years of marriage, so far), marred only by the several months I spent too much time writing this book.

Preface

After more than 20 years as an estate planning attorney, I have developed three simple rules I try to convey to every client.

1. "No matter how good I am, I can't draft an estate plan that will bring your family closer together when you die."

2. "I can draft an estate plan that will blow your family apart, with both hands tied behind my back."

3. "We should never draft an estate plan that will blow your family apart, at least not unintentionally."

The point is simply this. Estate planning is not just about distributing your assets after you die. It is a roadmap for navigating through a complex set of financial, emotional, and social relationships to get to your goal. As a business owner, or successful investor, you must navigate carefully to avoid family disputes and to protect the life of the business that provides a stream of income for your family. The hardest part of designing an estate plan—and the part that you get to do since you are the one with the dual honor of paying the cost of preparing the estate plan, as well as being buried shortly before anyone else gets to learn the details of what is in the estate plan—is defining the family goals and business needs that are essential to meet your individual wealth-transfer goals.

> Your family is important. Protecting the life of your business is crucial to preserving your family's income.

Think of your estate plan as a vacation. The first step, and often the hardest part, is deciding where to go. If you talk to your friends, they will tell you about their trip to Disney World, or Hawaii, or visiting every cathedral and museum in Europe. All wonderful vacations, but each more or less suitable for you depending upon what you like to do and whether or not you have children. Moreover, despite the great popularity of all three vacations, you might simply prefer to visit Antarctica or trek up the Amazon. If your goal is an Amazon adventure, standing in line at Disney World may not be much of a vacation.

Your estate plan, like your vacation, should be tailored to fit you. If Hawaii is your dream vacation, that's fine. If your estate planning goals are fairly common—for example, providing for a spouse and then leaving what's left to be shared by your two college-educated children—then a fairly typical estate plan may work fine. But as a business owner, you must address special concerns about preserving the value—and income stream—of your business, in addition to any unique goals arising from your family circumstances. Therefore, your estate plan should be unique.

> Your estate plan, like your vacation, should be tailored to fit you.

In order to determine your unique goals, some of the issues you should explore include:

- Who do you want to benefit from your estate? A spouse? Children? Friends? Business partners or employees? Charity?

- What impact might your estate plan have on the relationships within your family, and do you want to design your plan in a way that minimizes potential harm to those relationships?
- What impact might your estate plan have on your business or investment assets, and do you want to design your plan in a way that protects the income stream coming from those assets?
- What concerns do you have about your children or other beneficiaries receiving too much money too soon, and do you want your plan to avoid creating a "trust fund baby"?

Once you define your unique goals, you will need to work with qualified professionals to implement a plan that addresses your concerns. This team will include an experienced estate planning attorney, your personal and/or business accountant, and possibly a financial advisor and a life insurance agent. This process is not about pulling a standard estate plan off the shelf and typing your name in the blanks. It is about understanding your personal goals as well as your business and family situation, and drafting documents that achieve those goals, protect the value of your assets for the benefit of your chosen beneficiaries, and minimize the administrative and tax burdens incurred in implementing your plans. Finding a team that can draft complex documents and navigate through state inheritance and probate laws, as well as estate tax rules, is easy. Finding a team that listens to your concerns and guides you through the process of defining your individual goals is harder.

> Put together a team that listens to you and explores your estate planning and business needs.

This book is designed to assist you in defining your estate planning goals, and to highlight for you some of the landmines to avoid. Chapters 1 through 4 are intended to give you background necessary to put the estate planning process in perspective. Chapters 5 through 9 start you down the path toward developing your estate planning goals. Chapters 10 through 13 are designed to help you review your personal situation in preparation for embarking on your estate planning adventure. Chapters 14 through 29 discuss various estate planning tools that may be of interest, depending upon your assets and your goals. Taken as a whole, the material in this book should help you crystallize your estate planning goals and prepare you to work with your estate planning team to achieve them.

PART ONE

Estate
Planning
Philosophies

What You Need to Know About Yourself

Estate planning is simple. Just fill out the questionnaire, check all the applicable boxes, and complete the forms. Your estate plan can be completed before you feel the pain of facing your mortality. It may even accomplish your goals ... but just as likely, a check-the-box estate plan won't. OK, estate planning is really an art, not a science. It is even more of an art when your estate includes a thriving (and likely, constantly changing) business that must be protected in order to provide for your family's needs.

There is a better approach than just filling in the forms, but it will take a little longer. And, of course, you run the risk of understanding yourself as a parent, spouse, friend, and human being. Worse yet, you may design an estate plan that addresses your financial, family, and emotional needs.

> Estate planning is not about filling out forms. It's about understanding your individual financial, business, and family needs.

Emotional needs? In an estate plan? You may be wondering if it's too late to take this book back for a refund and get the one-form-fits-all guide to estate planning. *Stop.* Before you go looking for your receipt, think about this. You probably don't drive a gold, 4-cylinder, diesel engine, Volvo station wagon. You should. They're safe, get good mileage, carry plenty of people and cargo, and the gold color never shows the dirt. If you do drive a 4-cylinder Volvo station wagon, have I got an estate plan for you! Minimizes estate taxes, protects your spouse and children from ever making a mistake after you die, and costs less to maintain than that fancy customized estate plan your neighbor chose for his family. So what if they seem happy. You're a gold Volvo station wagon kind of family. They're not. Right? Probably not.

So if you're still with me, let's explore some basic concepts so we can figure out a simple estate plan that works for you and your family. There are a few topics we need to explore. The list is almost endless, but some of the most important include:

- Who are you today? What life experiences—long term and short term—are influencing your choices?
- Who do you love? Who is in your family—immediate and extended—that you wish to take care of?
- Who do you trust? Are you the permanent protector of your family or simply a transitory player in fate's greater plan?
- What are your core values and goals? To what extent are they shaped by you, by your family, or by the community you call home?

The truth is, estate planning is simple if you understand a few basic things about yourself; some of them obvious, others a little less apparent. The key is asking the right questions and allowing yourself to give the answer you would give if nobody were listening and you'd never heard the words "politically correct." As you address the questions raised in this chapter, do not think about the "right answer" or the "safe answer." This is not about devising an estate plan that will amaze your friends with your sensitive and caring nature. Stop worrying about what anyone else thinks about your inner thoughts or estate planning choices. The fact is you'll be dead before anyone else gets to see your estate plan.

One last thought before you tackle the tough questions. No thinking at this stage of the game. You're searching for your gut reaction—emotions, not reasons. Asking yourself sterile theoretical questions won't work. Try to place each question into the context of your family and your life. Try to imagine your daughter spending your entire life savings on new purses and new shoes; your son spending your life savings on alcohol, a fast car, and even faster women; or your widow sharing everything you have with the tennis pro. It may not be a pleasant experience, but you'll come out of the process with a better understanding of your goals, a better-fitting estate plan, and maybe even a bad B-movie script. So let's get on to the questions.

Who Are You Today?

What life experiences—long term and short term—are influencing your choices? Deep-seated emotional reactions serve as a window to your core values and provide the insight necessary to develop your estate plan. You can be distracted from the path, however, by short-term emotional responses to recent unusual events. Before exploring your core values, try to understand what short-term experiences are influencing your thinking. Start with the simple question, "Why am I thinking about estate planning?" You probably weren't thinking about death and taxes when you were 20. There's a good chance you weren't thinking about death six months ago. Why now? Was it a gradual acceptance of adult responsibility, brought on by marriage and children? Or, was it something more dramatic? Gradual acceptance of responsibility is good; sudden shock isn't. More importantly, good news seldom triggers estate planning. Sad news often does—and carries with it fear that distorts your view of the world. The dark cloud that forms instantaneously when your doctor says, "The test results were a little unusual ..." The emotional

vacuum that begins with the words, "Jim was driving home late last night …"
The anxiety that sets in about three weeks before your first trip without the

> Sad news often triggers estate planning, but short-term emotional responses shouldn't be allowed to distort your thinking.

kids (especially if it involves airplanes traveling over large bodies of water). All trigger a protective streak so large that the life insurance salesman you didn't trust last week can probably build a 2,000 square foot addition on his house.

In addition, your short-term view of the world can be distorted by horror stories recently experienced by extended family or friends.

While there may be worthwhile lessons to be taken from your cousin Tito's fight with his formerly loving sisters, Delores and Tina, when Uncle Johnny passed away, don't let fresh wounds alter your plans for your family. Make sure you've had time to digest the circumstances, and time to determine which stories reveal universal truths and which stories are unique to Uncle Johnny's children. Remember, Delores and Tina used to take turns holding Tito's head under water in the bathtub. There's an excellent chance this fight would have broken out even if Uncle Johnny had found the perfect way to leave each of the kids an equal one third and "made up" for the fact that Tito got an extra two weeks of summer camp when they were growing up. If the fight happened in 1992, you've probably figured out the underlying causes of World War III. If it just happened two weeks ago, you may adjust your own estate plan for circumstances that have nothing to do with you or your immediate family.

Who Do You Love?

Who is in your family—immediate and extended—that you wish to take care of? This question can be quite simple, if you're boring enough. Take me, for example. Unlike many people who lived through the turbulent '60s, embraced the women's liberation movement in the '70s, and then went through two or three wives and an equal number of lifestyles in the '80s and '90s, I'm still rooted firmly in the 1950s. I'm Leave It to Beaver, without the excitement. Still on stay-at-home wife number one (married for more than a quarter century, knew her more than a dozen years before that, grew up together in the same small suburb of Los Angeles), two daughters (both from this relationship), and my siblings and my parents have all achieved varying degrees of financial success (nobody is relying on us for support or help). If something happens to us, all we need to do—or want to do—is make sure the girls get through college and use the money that's left after that to get a good start on their adult lives (first house, save for their kids' education, maybe start a modest business—Leave It to Beaver, Part Two). Maybe throw in a token piece of jewelry, china, or silver for my favorite cousin, Michelle, possibly a few dollars for charity. It's a pretty simple estate plan. I'm boring.

Some "families" are a little more modern and a lot less boring. Mark never did get married, but he did live with Ashley—and her young son from a prior marriage, Alex—for several years in the 1980s. Even after Mark and Ashley went their separate ways, Mark stayed close with Alex. Alex is family; Mark wouldn't have it any other way.

Louise got married and had three boys of her own. That didn't change the maternal relationship she had with her brother, Vince. Vince was born with Down Syndrome. Louise's mom worked hard all her life to take care of Vince, but Mom couldn't do it alone. Vince was part of the family— her fourth boy—and Louise wanted to take care of him.

> Estate planning is usually about taking care of family. Family, however, doesn't always mean people related by blood or marriage.

Jeff is a retired medical professional whose children are grown. He wants to leave some financial legacy to his children. At the same time, he is concerned about a broader family. Nearly one half of his estate is earmarked for charity. A portion is dedicated to research to find a cure to the disease that took his wife, some will fund medical research in the specialty area in which Jeff practiced his entire career, and the rest will support an organization that fights disease and war around the world.

Cecelia has been "alone" since her husband died 15 years ago. They never had children. She hasn't been completely alone, however, since she's active in her church, has many friends, and lives on one of those old-fashioned streets where neighbors often stand outside and visit, and always look out for each other. She doesn't feel the need to track down long-lost, blood relatives. Her family is a network of friends and neighbors.

Once again, the question is, "Who do you love?" While you are alive, who do you want to help? Do you need to provide supplemental income for mom who is living on a fixed income? Do you worry that your sister will be living on the street if she stops taking the medication for her bouts of depression? Are you concerned that your niece who is always reading books won't be able to go to college because your brother has an injury that limits his earning potential? Are there charities that have helped you or your family in times of need or that do work that you consider important to your community or the world?

Who Do You Trust?

Are you the permanent protector of your family or simply a transitory player in fate's greater plan? The vast majority of people fear the results of leaving children too much money, too fast. Ignore the fact that most 18-year-olds lack the financial expertise to prudently invest several hundred thousand dollars, or even the experience to pick honest financial advisors. The problem is scarier than that. It's easy to imagine colorful images of wild parties, fast cars, and who knows what else. Beyond that, some people cannot envision that their children will ever be ready for such financial responsibility without advice from their dear old parent.

When designing an estate plan, you need to clearly understand where you fall on the control spectrum. Will you simply hand the kids the money all at once and let them worry about picking up the pieces three years from now when they've spent every penny? Or, are you so certain that the kids will muck it all up that the only sensible thing to do is have a professional trustee distribute a cash "allowance" to each kid for the rest of their lives? There's probably a "politically correct" answer to this questions, but the truth is, the only right answer is the one that is carefully thought out to fit the strengths and weaknesses of each of your children, and also enables you to sleep well at night while you're still alive.

What Are Your Core Values and Goals?

To what extent are they shaped by you, by your family, or by the community you call home? Don't ask yourself, "What are my values and goals?" Instead, try to explore the values that are being expressed to your child every day. Start with the easy ones. How does your extended family view college? Should college prepare you for a job (such as accounting, business management, or teaching) or is a degree in political science or art (with little possibility of gainful employment) every bit as valid as a high-paying job-related degree? How many years do people in your family typically go to school? What degrees do you, your spouse, your parents, and your siblings have? These are the people who have the greatest direct influence on what your children may want to achieve educationally.

Next, look around your neighborhood. Where you have chosen to raise your children reflects your values and determines your children's values. What percentage of kids from the local high school go on to four-year colleges? How many go to state schools and how many go to elite private schools? Beyond educational values, what are the social values and spending habits in your neighborhood? The attitudes of your community will influence who your children become.

Finally, don't forget to look at each of your children individually. Outside influences are important, but internal, hard wiring is important, too. Determining what you need to save for your child's college education, and how to structure distributions from your estate plan, requires you to make your best guess about each child. Just remember to leave enough flexibility to compensate in the event that your guess isn't 100 percent accurate.

As you explore these basic questions, and the concepts discussed in this book, you will begin to develop an estate plan that will satisfy your economic situation and your retirement goals. Properly designed, it will help you achieve your expectations for your children, and facilitate the transfer of wealth to your children in a manner that is consistent with each child's level of maturity and responsibility (or lack of both).

Horror Stories You Need to Hear

As I stated in the introduction, it is almost impossible for me to draft a will or trust that will bring your family together after you are gone, but I can draft one that will blow your family apart with one arm tied behind my back. Making sure your kids continue to get along with each other after you're gone is the result of years of hard parenting decisions and of random genetic mix. This book won't help you accomplish that. A good psychologist may or may not.

When you're gone, the family will read a will made up of black letters on an aging sheet of paper. Unless the words are drafted carefully, years of "Mom always loved you best" can morph into "Jimmy

> Years of sibling rivalry can evolve into costly litigation over your estate plan. Careful exploration and planning can minimize the risk of attorneys receiving the bulk of your children's inheritance.

tricked Mom into leaving him everything of value and cheated me out of my fair share!"

Over the last 15 years, hundreds of people have sat in the gray and black checkered chairs on the other side of my desk. Each has come in for the same reason, "I need a trust." While I try to be more diplomatic about it, I'm usually thinking, "I'll be the judge of that!" More accurately, I'll let them be the judge of that *after* we both learn a lot more. I need to understand why they are thinking about estate planning, what their personal and family goals are, and what types (and value) of assets are involved. They need to understand all of that and also learn what estate planning tools are available to satisfy their objectives. Perhaps they will decide on a trust after all, but we need to sort through the possibilities first.

Who Has Sat in the Checkered Chairs?

Each estate plan begins with a family story and personal concerns. Here are some of the families, and a short summary of their concerns.

Keith and Sue have left three-year-old Chelsea with a babysitter. Four months from now, Chelsea will become a big sister when her baby sister is born. Their biggest concerns include deciding who will raise Chelsea One and Chelsea Two if something happens to both Keith and Sue in the next 18 years. What about paying for college educations? Chelsea's already showing signs of brilliance and she'll probably want at least a master's degree in psy-

> A three-year-old child, and a three-year-old business, must both be nurtured by your estate plan.

chology like her mother or an MBA like her father. How will Keith's 8 percent interest in the growing business he and his partners started turn into cash if he isn't around to bring home a paycheck?

Steve and Fay don't have a three-year-old at home and haven't in over 30 years. They do have seven adult children. Some are very successful; some are paying their bills but not a whole lot more. Of greatest concern today, however, are the two who started a business with Steve three years ago. If something happens to Steve, what happens to his three-year-old—the business—and to his two sons who are dealing with the struggling cash flow of a start-up business?

Scott is a retired doctor. His wife, Beth, was a doctor, too, prior to her death several years ago. Beth left each of their three daughters a considerable sum; enough so that Scott thinks more money will not significantly impact his daughters' lives. He wants the girls to know that he loves them, but he wants his money to make better lives possible. Ultimately, he decides to split the majority of his assets between three charities: one that searches for treatments and cures related to the cancer that took Beth's life, one that researches cures for diseases that Scott treated as a medical professional, and a third that fights diseases in third world countries.

Ted and Sharon built a successful business and raised two daughters. Margie still runs the family business and Nancy runs a business of her own. Both are successful, but Nancy is the one who can afford to buy herself a new yacht. Before setting out on a six-month cruise with Nancy and her husband, Ted and Sharon want to review the details of the estate plan they signed more than ten years ago.

Sam started a small industrial company 40 years ago. Sarah stayed home and raised their four sons and one daughter. As the company grew, so did Sam's dream that his four sons would jointly run the company (back then most people didn't realize daughters could run businesses). As the years went by, Sam came to realize that son number three could run the business, but sons one, two, and four lacked either the interest or the ability, or both. Sam wants to provide for all five children, but he also wants to make sure the business survives under the watchful eye of son number three.

What Stories Have the Checkered Chairs Told?

Not every occupant of the Checkered Chairs has come in search of an estate plan. Some have come in search of a solution to correct a bad estate plan—at least, an estate plan that they are unhappy with.

Yes, despite your careful efforts to be "fair" to each child—whether splitting your assets into equal shares or allocating more or less assets to adjust for special needs or to make up for the down payment you gave Susie for her first house—one child may misunderstand or misinterpret the cold words of your estate planning documents in the context of 40 years of family history. Understanding the kinds of disputes that can arise can help you design an estate plan that will minimize the risk of family explosions. The examples below are real, but they are the extreme cases that ended up in an attorney's office, with each child willing to spend tens of thousands of dollars to settle real disputes or perceived resentments. Keep these examples in the back of your mind when designing your estate plan, try to look at your family objectively for warning signs, and adjust your plan to reduce the risk of your assets being split equally between your children and their attorneys.

The Manipulative Child

Children come in all ages. Don was 76 years old when he came into my office. His father had recently died and the will left 90 percent of everything to his two older sisters. Don knew this wasn't really what Dad had wanted. He knew because ten years ago Dad's will left everything in three equal shares—one third to each child. More recently, four years ago to be specific, Dad wrote a new will leaving two thirds to Don and one sixth to each of his sisters. Two years after that, Dad changed things again to leave 80 percent to Don and 10 percent to each sister. Surely, Dad couldn't have had a sudden change of heart in favor of Don's sisters.

After contacting Dad's attorney—the one who drafted last year's will leaving 90 percent to the two sisters—the truth came out. When Don's mom passed away 10 years ago, Don began pressuring dad to change his will. Don made every argument imaginable: "They don't need the money as much as I do." "They are irresponsible with money and your lifetime of hard work will be spent frivolously in a few months." "I've taken such good care of you since Mom died and they haven't done a thing."

Although Dad changed his will twice to favor Don, he never felt right about it. When dad told his daughters what Don had convinced him to do, they helped Dad find a new lawyer. The result was the 90 percent will. Dad would have liked to leave one-third to each child—and more importantly, for his children to be friends and get along—but not after what Don did.

Despite his manipulative behavior, Don got lucky. His sisters didn't really want 90 percent of dad's money; they just wanted to teach their little brother a lesson (at age 76!). Ultimately they agreed to give Don 25 percent (not quite his full one third). Of course, out of his reduced share, Don paid tens of thousands of dollars in attorney's fees.

Lesson: Listen to your heart, not your children. If Dad had stuck with his own wishes—not Don's—his 70-something-year-old children would have had to find something else to fight about. Remember, even a brilliantly drafted estate plan can't bring your children closer together, but a poorly drafted one can blow them apart.

> Allowing your children to manipulate your estate plan can create hard feelings and invite litigation. If you don't want your children spending your estate on attorneys, be careful not to let your son or daughter manipulate your plans.

Big Sister/Little Sister

Linda was three years older than Kathy. Mom always took pride in the way that "big sister" watched over little Kathy. Sure, they fought sometimes, but that's just the way sisters are. Kathy didn't really mean anything bad when she called Linda "bossy."

Since Linda was older, and always more responsible, when Mom created the family trust she appointed Linda as the sole trustee. When the time comes, Linda will sell Mom's house, pay Mom's last expenses, and divide the remaining cash with Kathy. It was the perfect plan. After all, Linda had been taking care of her little sister all her life.

One problem. Mom died three years ago and Kathy still hasn't received a penny. Linda won't tell Kathy how much the house sold for, or how much money is in the trust. In fact, all Linda will say is that there's only a few thousand dollars left. More specifically, "Take this check for $9,200, sign this release, and we'll be done."

Kathy doesn't want to sign, or to settle for $9,200. She knows that houses in mom's neighborhood are selling for over $350,000, and that Mom didn't believe in owing people money. How did half of $350,000 become only $9,200? Why won't Linda share information about the sale of the house or account for the money after the escrow closed?

After nearly a year of asking for escrow papers and bank statements, Kathy hired an attorney. By the time the judge ordered Linda to account for the money from the sale of Mom's house, Kathy and Linda had spent more than $25,000 each in attorney's fees, and their 20-something-year-old children had taken to calling each other names that sailors don't use until after the fifth drink.

What Mom hadn't noticed was that Linda and her husband seemed to need more toys—and increasingly expensive ones—every year. If Linda's neighbor bought a new Lexus, Linda bought one with a navigation system and the designer interior. Family vacations stopped being about relaxing and exploring, and became more about pictures of exotic locations and unusual activities. Mom never stopped to think about how Linda was paying for it all. Mom raised the girls not to go into debt for anything except a house. If Linda was spending so much on fancy toys and travelogue vacations, then it must be because she and her husband were incredibly successful. The same success that was so much fun for Mom to brag about to the ladies at church was one of the reasons Mom thought Linda was such a good choice to be the trustee of mom's trust.

Mom's mistake was in not asking to see Linda's financial statement. OK, maybe that's a little unrealistic, but Mom should at least have done a little reality check. Linda's husband was one of the project managers for his company. That had to pay a better than average salary. But, Linda only worked part-time since quitting her teaching position to raise the kids. Considering how often they bragged about their new toys and trendy vacations, it seems unlikely that they would have forgotten to mention winning the lottery. The disparity between Linda's likely income level and her spending habits should have been a red flag.

> Be realistic about your children's strengths and weaknesses. Don't put a "big spender" in charge of distributing your assets to the family.

Linda never intended to spend all the money that Mom left in the trust. It was just a coincidence that the bill for last summer's $25,000 vacation came in the same month that Linda received the kids' orthodontic bill and the lease expired on the Lexus RX 330. Why not lease the new Lexus hybrid since there was plenty of money available from the sale of Mom's house? Without stopping to think, Linda had spent her share of mom's trust and "borrowed" Kathy's share. She always intended to pay it back, at least until Kathy started being so belligerent. Ever since Kathy was born, Linda was looking out for her little sister and if something went wrong, no matter what happened, Kathy never got in trouble. It was always Linda's fault. Now that she thought about it, the money Linda had spent from the trust didn't even come close to compensating her for the work she put in as trustee, much less all the work of being a big sister for 42 years.

Kathy decided not to spend tens of thousands of dollars to get a "paper judgment" against her big sister. Given Linda's spending habits, the chances of ever collecting her half of Mom's trust seemed slim. Being in debt to an attorney for legal fees would not make that any better, and being at war with her sister's family for two years would not be the best way to honor Mom's memory. Kathy might never have a close relationship with her sister again, but as Kenny Rogers says: "You've got to know when to hold 'em, know when to fold 'em, know when to walk away."

Lesson: Blinders are better worn by horses than by people creating estate plans. Especially when picking a trustee or executor, you need to be objective. As a parent, it's easy to see your children's strengths and successes. Before you choose one of your incredibly successful children to serve as trustee, take a step back and try to be objective. Does your daughter live in a mansion or a house of cards? Do her siblings respect her opinion and trust her to be fair with everyone, or simply love her because she's been their big sister all their lives?

Protecting the Troubled Child: Jim

Jim was 45 years old and hadn't been steadily employed for several years. Health problems seem to flare up every time he started a new job. When Jim was growing up, it wasn't like this. Good grades, a college degree, and a good career in the financial industry. But something had changed.

Dad worried that Jim might end up homeless, or worse. His brother and sister, Joshua and Julie, cared too, at least at first. After several years of problems, his siblings still cared, but didn't have the energy left to deal with Jim's repetitive pattern of downward-spiraling behavior and, while they didn't admit it at first (even to themselves), they were a little afraid Jim would harm them or their children.

No one understood what triggered Jim's problems. From Dad's point of view, "cause" didn't matter. If Jim needed rent money, Dad was always there. Same for car repairs and other "emergencies." Before long, Julie was concerned. Dad was 78 and living on a fixed income. Other than the family home—a 40-year-old house in the San Fernando Valley now worth almost a million dollars and paid off 15 years ago—and Social Security benefits, nothing about Dad's economic future was certain. Financially speaking, these weren't the "Golden Years;" "Bronze" at best, and some days they looked more like "Tin." Jim needed to straighten up and take care of himself. Julie talked to Josh, and they both talked to Dad. Same response no matter what they said: "I'm not going to turn my back on your brother. I'll be fine."

Nothing changed, at least financially. Two things did change, however. First, Julie and Josh became increasingly suspicious toward, and resentful of, Jim, although they were careful not to show it in front of Dad. Second, Dad began to worry about protecting Jim after he was gone. Dad went to the family attorney and changed his trust. Each child would still receive one-third of dad's estate, but Jim's share wouldn't be in cash like Josh's and Julie's. After Dad died, Josh would become trustee of Dad's trust and would be responsible for dividing the family memorabilia fairly, selling Dad's house, and then using one third of the money to buy an annuity for Jim's benefit. Dad was smart enough to know that Jim couldn't handle getting $350,000 all at once. Jim would need monthly income for life. With the lifetime annuity Josh would buy for him, Jim would never be without rent money again. His annuity would provide him a monthly income of more than $2,000.

Dad died last year knowing that everything would be OK for Jim. However, Dad didn't know that Jim would develop serious eye problems six months after Dad died. Jim lost most of the vision in his left eye, and the operation at County Medical (paid for by the state) did nothing to help. In fact, Jim says the operation made things worse. When the doctors wanted to operate on his right eye to prevent further deterioration, and possible blindness, Jim ran as fast as he could away from County Medical and state-paid medical care. With $350,000 due to him from the trust, Jim figured $20,000 to pay for doctors he trusted was well worth it. Preventing blindness and still having $330,000 to buy the annuity sounded like a no-brainer to Jim. So what if his monthly income would be only $1,800?

Providing Jim with money for the operation was a no-brainer for Josh's attorney, too; it wouldn't happen. The trust said everything was to be used to buy Jim an annuity, and said nothing about providing money for medical bills. The trust wouldn't—couldn't—pay for the operation, is what Josh had to tell his big brother. It was too late to get medical insurance to cover the operation since Jim now had a diagnosed, pre-existing condition. Jim had only one choice: go back to County Medical. But Jim was sure the doctors at County Medical were the reason things went so badly with his left eye. So Jim chose the other option: Go untreated and hope to figure out something else before blindness took over. Dad's plan to make sure the money was always there when Jim needed it is the reason Jim can't get the money he needs to save his eyesight!

> Controlling from the grave can have grave consequences. Be careful when imposing restrictions that outlast your lifetime.

Lesson: Controlling from the grave can have grave consequences. Family circumstances sometimes require strict limits—maybe even a lifetime of control—but even rules that are etched in stone require some built-in flexibility. Strict controls should be carefully thought-out and designed. Fully appreciating the consequences of lifelong restrictions requires the help and insight of an experienced professional who has dealt with the complexities arising from dealing with ill-conceived restrictions.

Protecting the Troubled Child: Ron

Ron's story is remarkably similar to Jim's. Ron has two brothers, Robert and Fred. He has all of Jim's job-stability problems and financial needs. Fortunately, Ron hasn't had any eye problems. However, over the past 20 years, Ron has been in and out of the hospital for psychiatric observation.

The other difference between Jim and Ron is that Ron's dad knew a fixed annuity designed to pay Ron income for life wasn't the solution. Dad knew that someone who was still alive would need to look at Ron's circumstances and decide when to give him money—and how much. That person would also need to decide when to pay Ron's bills directly rather than giving him the cash to pay his own bills (after all, when Ron was off his medication, he sometimes donated all his belongings to charity and lived out of his car). In fact, whoever became the new "Dad"—that is, the one responsible for deciding when and how Ron would receive money from his inheritance each month—would occasionally need to tell Ron he couldn't have anything. Dad wouldn't want Ron using the money for alcohol, drugs, or worse.

Not surprisingly, Robert wasn't exactly thrilled when he was appointed trustee of the trust their dad set up for Ron. Robert loves his big brother, and wanted to honor dad's wishes, but being the financial keeper for your older brother rarely brings families closer together. In the 18 years since Robert took over managing Ron's financial welfare, he's done an incredible job protecting

> Consider corporate trust companies to limit distribution to troubled children after your death. The professional trustee fees can be less costly than the toll on family relationships.

him. Ron doesn't always see it that way. I'm not the only attorney Ron has consulted, but I still get calls every few years looking for ways to "break the trust" and give Ron control of his own money. The strain on Ron's relationship with Robert is substantial. Some years, their only communication is the checks that Robert sends to Ron. Both have expressed an interest in returning to the comfortable relationship they had before Dad died, but that can't happen unless Robert turns control of Ron's money over to Ron. The change of control can't happen under the legal terms of the trust, and without ignoring Dad's wishes. For 18 years, Robert has been the jail keeper, and Ron has been the financial prisoner. They're still brothers, too, but just barely.

Lesson: Difficult situations require difficult decisions that strain family relationships. When such decisions become necessary, you need to weigh the benefit of extra flexibility that comes with appointing a family member or friend as financial gatekeeper against the fees and institutional inflexibility inherent in appointing a bank or trust company to enforce the necessary financial restrictions. Neither is a perfect solution, but institutional trustees can help avoid family tension—and breakups—after you are gone.

Blended Family Blues: Who Owns What?

When Grandpa remarried, everyone was happy. It had been many years since Grandma passed away, and Martha was a good companion who was about Grandpa's age. No trophy wife for Grandpa (and none of those strained, trophy-wife relationships for the rest of the family).

Certainly, Martha wasn't marrying Grandpa for his money. He had a modest home in a nice neighborhood in Southern California, and so did she. Grandpa had some cash in the bank, and so did she. Martha used her extra money to help out her dentist-son. He never seemed to make quite as much money as he spent. Grandpa gave a little money now and again to his daughter. She never seemed able to earn quite enough, either. No problem though, Grandpa and Martha seemed happy, and they always had plenty of money for themselves.

Grandpa and Martha kept their houses, and other property, separate. Martha's will left everything she owned to her boys, and Grandpa's will left all of his property to his daughters. As time went on, however, Grandpa realized that money would be tight for Martha if he died first. Wanting to make sure that his wife was provided for, Grandpa transferred one half of his house into Martha's name. That way, she could live in the house after Grandpa died. Grandpa knew Martha would do the right thing and leave his house to his daughters when she died.

No one ever found out if Grandpa was right about trusting Martha to do the right thing. A year after he put one-half of the house in her name, Martha's health started to decline rapidly. Realizing that he was going to outlive Martha, Grandpa went to the stationery store and bought a blank real estate deed. Months before Martha died, they signed and recorded a deed transferring the house back into Grandpa's name. When Martha died, her house went to her two boys, and Grandpa kept living in his house.

Grandpa didn't see Martha's boys very often, but when he did neither one acted like they owned half of Grandpa's house. That changed about two days

When blended families are involved, don't "blend" the assets you want to leave to your own children.

after Grandpa died. The dentist led the charge. Apparently, money had been tight during the five years since Martha died. According to his attorney, Grandpa's homemade deed—signed when Martha was showing symptoms of dementia—might not have succeeded in putting Grandpa's house back into Grandpa's name. Martha's dentist-son wanted to extract one-half of Grandpa's house like a bad wisdom tooth.

Grandpa's two daughters weren't too happy with the idea that nearly one-half of Grandpa's estate would go to the two boys who were never all that close to Grandpa. They weren't any happier when their attorney explained that what Grandpa did was less than perfect and that the title company wouldn't let them sell Grandpa's house without either the boys' signatures or a ruling from a judge determining that the deed successfully put the house back into Grandpa's name. If the boys fought the efforts to get a court ruling, the attorney's fees incurred to put the house back in Grandpa's name could exceed $100,000. Since the boys weren't willing to sign off for free, getting their signatures could cost just as much—in the form of a settlement paid to the boys.

Lesson: Spouses and children from prior relationships don't always mix well. The natural conflict between providing for a second (third, fourth, or fifth?) soul mate, while making sure that your assets ultimately flow down your bloodline, is complex. It must be carefully thought out and even more carefully implemented. Like the death-defying stunts on the silver screen, you should leave the tricky estate planning stunts to the professionals.

Blended Family Blues: How Long Is a Lifetime?

As Rob was approaching retirement, his wife of nearly 40 years died unexpectedly. With the help of his three adult children, he worked through the grieving process. After several years, he regained his joyful outlook, began dating a local widow, remarried, and began to enjoy his golden years.

Rob's new bride, Lois, had assets from her first marriage, including real estate. Rob had the family home where his three children grew up, and sufficient assets for a comfortable, but not extravagant, retirement. After five years of marriage, Rob updated his estate plan. He made sure that his assets would go to his children, just as Lois' assets would go to hers. To be fair to Lois—who had now lived in Rob's family home for five years while her house had been rented out—Rob gave Lois the right to live in his house the rest of her life. If Rob passed away, his kids wouldn't mind their nearly 70-year-old step-mother living in the family home the last few years of her life, or until she chose to move back to her own house.

Several weeks after Rob signed his amended estate plan documents, he passed away quietly in his sleep. Undoubtedly, Rob was at peace knowing he had provided his wife with a comfortable home for the final years of her life, while protecting his assets for the benefit of his children.

> Beware: Family homes and second spouses raise thorny issues.

Now, ten years later, nearly-80-year-old Lois still lives in Rob's family home while she prepares a quiet celebration for her mother's 100th birthday. Meanwhile, Rob's oldest child is only a few short years from retirement and has still not received any value for her one-third of the family home. Rob never anticipated that Lois might stay in the family home long past the time when the equity (paid for by Rob and his first wife) could provide an economic cushion for his children's retirement. While the kids always got along with Lois, they can't help but notice that she has lived in their family home twice as long *after* dad died as she did while he was alive.

Lesson: Step-families, family homes, and life estates all carry large emotional price tags. When dealing with any one of these—let alone all three—remember, your desire to take care of a second spouse must be balanced carefully against your desire to take care of your children. Rob isn't the first widower to carefully set up an estate plan to protect his children's inheritance only to find out his legacy may get handed down directly to his grandchildren instead.

Blended Family Blues: What's Love Got To Do With It?

Sam's life could be a movie. Successful executive with a large, national corporation. Great wealth. Cold, distant relationships with his wife and children.

Divorce. Heart attack. Soul-searching. Remarriage to a younger but grounded woman named Kate. Tenuous reconciliation with his children, largely orchestrated by his new wife.

Sam always loved his children more than anything. If you ask them, however, Dad never loved anything but power and money. That's why his kids approached the reconciliation cautiously. To Sam, it seemed the kids came around less to see him than to visit his wallet. Years of expressing love through money became an unbreakable pattern. That's why the reconciliation was never really complete.

Wife number two was never part of the money-as-love pattern. She had a well-established income of her own by the time she met Sam, and he was a (slightly) changed man after the divorce and heart attack. Because Sam knew she loved him—and not his money—he left everything to her.

Kate wasn't surprised when the kids wanted a piece of their dad's estate. After all, she had told him to leave most of it to them, not her. She was surprised, however, that they never called and spoke to her about it. Instead, before she could even make a call to them, they spoke to an attorney. Until the lawsuit was served, Kate thought she had a good relationship with her stepchildren. A year or two later, Kate and the kids divided dad's estate four ways (with one share going to each of their attorneys). Amazingly, the kids got the share they wanted (reduced only by the share taken by their attorney), but less than Kate had wanted to give them before the lawsuit was filed. Because the kids' attorney came out with "guns blazing," Kate's desire to help the kids diminished before serious settlement talks began.

Lesson: Bad estate plans set off conflicts. Families—even extended ones—can sometimes reduce the fallout by an open discussion. Lawyers have their place but, like exotic spices, should be used sparingly.

The Financially Troubled Child

Diane's grandmother passed away leaving a clean estate plan, part of which left Diane $200,000. The money would help her incredibly. She hadn't found her way financially since her husband left her. Unfortunately, Grandma didn't know that when Diane's ex-husband left, he hadn't paid taxes in three years. With penalties and interest, the balance due was now over $250,000. After the divorce, Diane's ex-husband filed bankruptcy. Diane didn't. Now the tax burden was all hers.

Instead of helping Diane regain her financial footing, Grandma's money all went to satisfy an IRS levy. And Uncle Sam didn't even send a thank-you note.

> The best estate plan won't work if it doesn't take into account the financial circumstances of those you intend to benefit.

Lesson: Good estate planning takes into account the financial and personal strengths and weaknesses of those who you intend to benefit. If your loved ones have trouble handling money, tax problems, a tendency toward drug or alcohol abuse, or other human frailties, your estate plan should include safeguards to make sure the money will truly benefit the ones you love, rather than benefit only their creditors or subsidize your loved one's self-destructive vices.

Death and Divorce

Alan built a $10 million business. He wasn't nearly as good at building a marriage. When his relationship fell apart, it fell apart in style. With $10 million to divide, the divorce proceedings dragged on for years.

Alan died in a tragic car accident less than two weeks before his final divorce hearing ... the one where the judge signs the final order terminating the marriage. After the funeral, Alan's brothers and sisters searched his office and home, but they never found a will. Under state law, Alan's almost-ex-wife—whom he separated from years before—was still legally his wife. Because there was no will saying otherwise, state law required that everything Alan owned be split between his son and his almost-ex-wife. Alan's relatives have five million reasons why

> Divorce and other changes require changes to your estate plan. Don't delay.

Alan would never want his business broken up this way, but Alan's ex-wife has the $5 million.

Lesson: When things change, change things! If you decide to get divorced, or a child develops a substance-abuse problem, or your attitude about your estate plan changes, make changes to your documents immediately. No judge will distribute assets based upon what you probably would have done, or even on what you told someone you wanted to do. Put it in writing, now!

Even Businesses Can Die Prematurely

By his 60th birthday, Art had built a successful architectural firm employing numerous professionals. In addition, he had finally reached the stage where he was thinking about retirement.

Several years earlier, the last of the children had moved out of the house. Art and his wife wanted to retire while they were both in excellent health and young enough to enjoy activities together. He began to make plans to sell the firm to two of the firm's more promising young architects. Working closely with his accountant and attorney, Art negotiated an agreement with the two future owners that would allow them to buy the company over the next five years. Knowing the agreement would be finalized and signed in the next several weeks, Art left for a weekend trip to celebrate his 60th birthday.

> Planning the sale of a business or professional practice takes time—sometimes five to ten years. Begin planning now to preserve the value of your business (and your family's wealth).

No one had reason to expect that Art would die of a sudden heart attack that weekend. Within weeks of burying Art, his widow had to deal with selling the business. The two young architects weren't interested in buying the firm without Art around to help with a five-year transition. Suddenly, the business was worth $1 million less, and Art's widow was $1 million poorer.

Lesson: Business transitions—internally to young partners or externally to third-party buyers—take years to plan and implement. Begin your transition early to avoid losing business value and the security it can provide for your family.

Blind Faith

During 50 years of marriage, Jack and Joan's church became their family. They never had children of their own. As the years went by and Jack's business grew, they continued to donate time—and substantial money—to the church. As Jack's wealth and status in the community increased, so did the size of his financial contributions to the church. At least one of the many buildings on the church grounds was built primarily with Jack's money. It gave the two of them great joy to know that their financial good fortune benefited the congregation of the church they loved.

They got even more back from the church than they put in. They developed deep and lasting relationships with numerous caring people. Among them was Floyd, a church member and employee of the church's trust department, who looked out for Jack and Joan as if they were his own parents. When they expressed a desire to create an estate plan, he not only helped them find an attorney, but he arranged for the church's trust department to provide them assistance free of charge. It gave them peace of mind to know that when their earthly lives were over their several-million-dollar estate could provide more than $1 million to fund the good work of the church, in addition to distributing over $2 million among their many nieces and nephews.

When Jack was widowed 15 years ago, his church-family—Floyd among them—provided emotional support and helped ease the pain. As time went by, Jack gradually recovered from the loss of his beloved wife. About five years after Joan's death, Jack became reacquainted with Eileen, a recently widowed woman that Jack had known as a child in his small, midwestern hometown. When Jack and Eileen married, Floyd helped Jack amend his estate plan to provide $600,000 for Eileen (who had substantial assets of her own from her first marriage). In addition to providing for Eileen, the new estate plan shifted most of the rest of Jack's money away from his nieces and nephews and to the church instead. Jack was pleased that his lifetime of earnings would do so much to further the good work of the church.

Jack and Eileen remained active in the church, and Jack continued to be a major financial supporter of the congregation. After many years, however, Jack began to have doubts whether his generous contributions were being properly managed by the church's leaders. Further, he was concerned that Floyd may not have Jack's best interests at heart. Eileen suggested that Jack discuss his concerns with the estate-planning attorney that she had used to set up her trust.

At the meeting Jack explained his concerns, and also told the attorney that he wanted to leave about one-half of his estate to his nieces and nephews, rather than to the church. After the meeting, Jack's new attorney wrote to Floyd at the church's trust office, and asked for Jack's estate planning documents so he could advise Jack regarding possible amendment. Rather than sending the documents, Floyd went to see Jack. Floyd explained how much the church loved Jack and wanted to help him. He also explained that it wouldn't be possible to continue helping Jack—financially or spiritually—if he went to a new attorney. As a result, Jack abandoned his efforts to change his estate plan.

A few months later, when Eileen fell and broke her hip, Floyd was right there to help. While Eileen was in the hospital recuperating, Floyd came by the house to visit Jack. He offered to take Jack for a ride to visit his sister in an Alzheimer's facility 30 miles away. While visiting with his sister, Jack had no idea that Floyd was in the front office signing paperwork to have Jack admitted to the locked Alzheimer's facility. Floyd didn't ask Jack's permission. He didn't ask Eileen's permission. He didn't even tell Jack's nieces and nephews what he had done. Worst of all, Jack didn't even have Alzheimer's disease.

It took awhile for Jack's family to learn what Floyd had done, and it took many more weeks before Jack's family sought legal advice and learned that that Floyd's position as a cotrustee of Jack's trust did not give him the right to force Jack to stay in the Alzheimer's facility. Once they understood, they picked Jack up and took him home. Not surprisingly, a few days after coming home Jack was adamant that he wanted to amend his trust to leave all his money to his family, and nothing to the church. Compared to what some might have done in response to Floyd's misconduct, Jack's response was mild. Within days, Jack met with an attorney and amended his estate plan. Jack rested easier knowing that his assets were no longer being left to the church, and that his former friend, Floyd, could no longer attempt to take control of Jack's money.

Jack's feeling of well being lasted only a week. That's when he learned that Floyd had secretly gone to court to have Jack declared incompetent, and to take control over all of Jack's assets. Although state law normally required Floyd to give Jack and Jack's family notice before seeking court intervention,

Floyd didn't give notice to anyone. Instead, Floyd told the judge that Jack was incompetent and his family was trying to steal his money. Ignoring the rules—after all this is the same Floyd who surreptitiously locked Jack in an Alzheimer's facility—Floyd argued that the court needed to put him in charge before the family could disappear with Jack's assets. Somehow, Floyd got the judge to go along with his request.

Over the next several months, Jack's family spent several thousand dollars to get Jack's money out of Floyd hands. Because the judge didn't know who to believe, and he didn't want anyone disappearing with Jack's money, he didn't put the money back in Jack's hands. Instead, the judge appointed an independent administrator (called a conservator) to handle Jack's money. When Jack died a little over a year later, he was frustrated that he didn't have control over his own money, and that he had spent tens of thousands of dollars to have a stranger control it for him. He drew some comfort, however, from the knowledge that Floyd wasn't handling his money and that his family—rather than the church—would receive the money when he died.

> When selecting trustees and executors to carry out your estate plan, honesty is crucial. Select from trusted family members and friends, or consider a bank or corporate trust officer.

Jack would roll over in his grave if he knew that the church sued his family to overturn the amendment that Jack had signed after he "escaped" from the Alzheimer's facility. He would probably come back from the dead and seek vengeance if he knew that the church's lawsuit dragged out for over two years and cost more than $500,000 in legal fees before the trial judge ruled that the church did not have any evidence to support its allegations against Jack's family members.

Lesson: In an honest poker game, the dealer has no stake in the outcome. To be safe, however, the players still cut the cards before the game begins. In devising an estate plan, take great pains to select advisers who don't have an interest in the final outcome. Once Floyd's employer, the church, stood to receive millions from Jack's estate, the dark side of human nature took over. While most people doing God's work don't give in to such earthly temptations, if it does happen—as it did with Floyd—imagine how easily things can spin out of control if you don't choose your advisors carefully.

Common Myths You Need to Ignore

Myths and misunderstandings dominate the public consciousness when it comes to estate planning. Some are the result of incomplete media reports, while others arise from half-truths and exaggerations put forth by "advisors" interested in generating a quick fee or commission. Further, labels such as "death tax" and other politically charged mischaracterizations are given life by politicians "spinning" estate-planning issues to stimulate political support in close elections. Your estate plan should be motivated solely by family considerations and sound legal analysis, not by imaginary monsters under the bed. A brief description of these myths is set forth below. By reading them, and then forgetting them once and for all, you can find your way to an estate plan that is based on reality and meets your goals and your family's needs.

Myth: Probate = High Cost and Long Delay

"Even if you know nothing about estate planning, you probably know that your failure to do the 'right' estate planning will result in your heirs being bogged down in a lengthy and costly preceding called probate." Not true.

The probate process does cost money in the form of attorney's fees, court filing fees, and miscellaneous costs. Most methods of avoiding probate cost money as well. You need to understand the real costs of probate, and the real costs of avoiding probate, before you make your choice. Taking cash out of your monthly budget today (and, in some cases, every year for the rest of your life) to avoid probate many years from now may be a greater burden than the impact of letting your heirs pay probate costs out of the inheritance you leave them. If you are on a tight budget and/or a fixed income, the impact of spending a small number of your dollars now may mean a major sacrifice in your lifestyle. Most likely, your children wouldn't want you to make that sacrifice just to leave them slightly more money later (and if they do want you to make that sacrifice, maybe they don't deserve any inheritance at all).

In order to compare the costs of probate with the costs of avoiding probate, you need to understand the probate procedure. While the procedure varies f rom state to state, in general terms, a probate proceeding is opened upon your death to make sure that all of your debts are fully paid, and to distribute any remaining assets to the people you have designated in your will. If you did not leave a will, then each state has its own set of rules defining which of your relatives will be entitled to receive your property. Under these rules, your surviving spouse and children are very high on the list and likely to share everything (in proportions that depend on the rules of the state where you were living at the time of your death). On the other hand, if you have no surviving spouse or children, everything will pass to your nearest living relatives (or "next of kin"), possibly your brothers and sisters, or nieces and nephews, or even a great nephew in Minnesota whom you have never met. The probate process begins when a person designated in your will—called the executor—files the initial probate papers with the court. If you did not have a will, or did not designate someone in your will to handle the probate, then a friend, relative, or the public administrator (a local-government agency that serves when there are no friends or relatives willing to do so) can file the initial papers.

A simple probate will remain open somewhere between 6 and 18 m o n t h s, during which time the executor follows court-mandated procedures to:

- provide notice to interested parties ("beneficiaries" named in your will to receive your property and "heirs" who may receive your property under state law if not left elsewhere by your will—for example, your spouse, children, grandchildren, parents, grandparents, or brothers and sisters);
- permit beneficiaries and heirs to challenge the validity of your will or some provision contained in it;
- provide a formal inventory and valuation of each of the assets in your estate;
- sell any assets that need to be liquidated (such as real estate or a business);
- pay your burial expenses and debts;
- pay any estate taxes, if your estate is large enough; and
- provide a detailed accounting and distribute the assets to the people, and in the manner, provided in your will.

> While assets are in probate, your family can still operate the family business, sell assets as necessary, and draw a reasonable income, without undue court interference.

The formal probate procedures provide protection to your beneficiaries and heirs, and ensure that your assets are properly handled and distributed to the people you have named in your will. The procedures are not nearly as burdensome or restrictive as they seem at first glance. Most transactions—such as liquidating stocks, selling real estate, or continuing to operate your business while a buyer is located—can be performed without advance permission from the court. Necessary transactions are simply carried out as needed and accounted for in reports given to the heirs and beneficiaries, and simultaneously filed with the court. Perhaps more importantly, your executor will likely be able to provide reasonable living expenses for your family during the probate process.

There is an economic cost to probate that should not be ignored. The cost includes attorney's fees, executor's fees, court filing fees, and other miscellaneous costs. Many states set the attorney's fees and executor's fees as a percentage of the value of the assets in the estate (typically with a decreasing percentage applied as the size of the estate increases). Other states allow the attorney to charge fees based on an hourly fee and the actual number of hours necessary to handle your probate, subject to court approval based upon "reasonableness."

But the cost of fees should not be viewed in a theoretical vacuum. Don't listen to promoters of "trust mills" that inflate probate fees to their largest theoretical amount simply to scare you into paying for an off-the-shelf trust package designed to avoid probate (and put money in the wallet of the promoters). In California, for example, the attorney and the executor are each entitled to receive a statutory fee based on a percentage of the value of the assets in the estate. The statutory fee starts at 4 percent *each*. That's 8 percent in addition to court filing fees starting at about $300 (and going up substantially with the value of the estate), plus incidental expenses of hundreds of dollars. If the real cost of probate is 9 or 10 percent of value of the estate, then of course you need to avoid probate. But the real cost is nowhere near 10 percent. First, in most instances the executor is a relative or family friend who is willing to serve without fee. In addition, while the attorney's or executor's fees start at 4 percent, that number is only applied to the first $100,000 of value in the estate. The percentage drops to 3 percent for the next $100,000, 2 percent for the next $800,000, and then to 1 percent or less. For most probates in California, the actual cost will be in the neighborhood of 2.5 percent of the value of the estate. On a $1 million estate—in California that's an average house, a retirement account of a few hundred thousand dollars, a nice car and a handful of miscellaneous investments—expect probate to cost about $25,000.

While this cost is substantial, the analysis shouldn't end there. The cost of probate—which will be paid after you are gone and no longer need your monthly income to pay monthly living expenses—must be weighed against the direct economic cost of an estate plan designed to avoid probate. These costs include additional fees paid to prepare the estate plan and any additional costs that may be incurred as a result of the estate plan after you are gone. Professional fees will vary by locality and by complexity of the estate plan, but rarely are they less than $1,000, and they often exceed several thousand dollars. In addition, certain types of estate plans may result in accounting fees being incurred each year to prepare a separate tax return. Finally, while the cost of administering a trust at the time of your death is likely to be less than the cost of probate, that million-dollar estate that might cost $25,000 to probate in California will still cost several thousand dollars in legal and accounting fees to implement and administer at the time of your death.

Myth: Without a Will, the Government Will Seize Your Property

"If you die without a will or trust, the government will take all of your property." Wrong.

If you die without a will or trust, the laws of the state you called home just before you died will determine who will receive your assets. In some states, your surviving spouse will receive everything. In others, your spouse will share your assets with your children or parents. Without a will or trust, however, your assets will generally not go to a live-in significant other, or to stepchildren that you raised like they were your own flesh and blood. (Although, some states are beginning to grant inheritance rights to registered domestic partners, which may include nonmarital relationships with same-sex or opposite-sex partners.)

> State laws protect your spouse and children even if you don't have a will or trust. If you desire to leave assets to anyone else, make sure you have a written estate plan.

In very rare cases, such as when there you have no living relatives of any kind—not even a fourth cousin, twice removed, for example—your property will go to the state. By having a will or trust, you can avoid his outcome and leave your assets to close friends or charities that you care about.

In general, state law will not take your money away when you die, and for many people, it actually leaves property exactly where you would want it to go.

Myth: You Must Have a Trust to Avoid Estate Taxes

"Estate taxes—sometimes called inheritance taxes or death taxes—will take one-half of everything you have, unless you have a trust or a will." Simply wrong. For more than 98 percent of us, the estate tax will be far less than 50 percent. In fact, it will be zero.

At the risk of oversimplifying, there is no estate tax on the first million dollars (or more) in your estate. In 2007 and 2008, you can leave up to $2 million completely free of estate tax. In 2009, that amount increases to $3,500,000. In 2010, there is no estate tax no matter how much you are worth. To keep things confusing, if the law does not change before January 1, 2011, the estate tax will apply to everything over $1 million in assets. This quirky, roller coaster estate tax system is the result of political accounting—and accountability—that was applied in the mid-1990s when the current law was passed. Most estate planners expect these rules to change—and hopefully become a little smoother—before 2010. For a guess as to how the rules may change in the next few years, take a look at Chapter 30.

> More than 98 percent of Americans will pay zero estate tax. Period.

For purposes of this myth, what you need to know is that the estate tax is not affected by whether or not you have a will. It may be affected, however, by having a trust, if you are married. Properly designed, the trust may allow you to double the amount that can be left to your children (or friends) free of estate taxes. In 2007, for example, that means a married couple using a trust can leave $4 million to their children (or friends) free of tax.

Generally speaking, there is no estate tax when assets are left to your spouse or to a charity, no matter how big your estate may be.

> Most business owners pay zero estate tax.

It is important to note that as a entrepreneur you may be able to structure your business ownership in ways that can reduce taxes. A well-crafted buy-sell agreement, limited partnership, or limited liability company may allow you to protect the existence of the business upon your death and reduce the estate taxes for your family.

Myth: Without a Will, My Kids Will Lose the Family Farm (or Business)

"The family farm—or family business—that Mom and Dad hoped to hand down from generation to generation will need to be sold to pay the 'death tax.' " Not true, for several reasons.

First, remember the first $2 million is tax free ($4 million with a family trust). That increases to $3,500,000 (and $7 million) in 2009. Some family businesses, or farms, may be worth more than that. Most aren't. There f o re, no tax. The family will inherit the business tax free, and your children can continue to run the family business.

Second, even if you are fortunate enough to own a family business worth more than $7 million, the tax code actually has special provisions to protect your family business—and even more special provisions to save the family farm. If your estate is greater than $7 million, and the family business accounts for more than 35 percent of the value, any taxes due on your estate can be the paid over 14 years. If that isn't help enough, your children can pay interest only for the first five years, at interest rates in the 1 percent or 2 percent range, and then pay off the balance over the next nine years at an interest rate of about 4 percent. Even when the Federal Reserve Discount rate was below 1 percent in the year 2004, you couldn't get that low an interest rate on a first mortgage on your house!

> Businesses large enough to incur an estate tax may be eligible to pay the tax over 14 years, at interest rates between 1 and 4 percent.

Finally, if you don't want your family to payoff a 14-year, low-interest loan, as a business owner you can buy life insurance to provide funds to pay any estate taxes that may become payable. By holding this life insurance policy in a special life-insurance trust, you provide a tax-free source of funds to fully pay the taxes due on a family business worth tens of millions of dollars, or more.

Myth: Trusts Always Reduce the Cost of Dying

"Probate is expensive. A living trust will avoid probate and save money." Avoid probate, yes. Save money, maybe.

Whether a living trust will save money when compared to probate depends upon your unique circumstances. Remember, probate and living trusts are two different methods to transfer your assets to your family or friends. It's true that a trust will do that at a lower direct cost than probate will. However, unlike most probates, trusts commonly distribute your assets over many years. For example, a trust may provide lifetime income to your surviving spouse and then continue distributing income to your children for many years (until they become mature enough to handle the money themselves). These distributions can last 10, 20, or 30 years, or more. In each of those years, your family trust will incur accounting fees to prepare an additional income tax return (although additional income tax usually will not be due), and in some years additional attorney's fees will be incurred to resolve administrative issues related to the trust. Finally, if a family member is not serving as trustee, the fees paid to a private trustee over several years will exceed the cost of probate. Simply put, you need to evaluate the costs and benefits of a trust over the entire anticipated lifetime of the trust. Frequently, the benefits of a trust are great and the cost comparison to probate is favorable, but the analysis needs to be done on a case-by-case basis.

Myth: The Estate Tax is an Unfair "Death Tax"

> The estate tax is not an unfair double taxation on death. Most estates subject to the estate tax are comprised of appreciated businesses, real estate, and stocks that were not subject to income tax during the decedent's lifetime.

Politicians often refer to the estate tax as an unfair "death tax." You work hard, you pay income tax your entire life, and then when you die, the government taxes the money you already paid taxes on, just because you died. Sometimes this is true; often it is not. Most estate tax is imposed on income that has never been taxed. How can that be?

There are two basic kinds of income tax in the United States. The most common is "ordinary" income tax on things like wages, interest earned on savings accounts, dividends on stocks, rent received on property, and the like. The other is "capital gains" income tax on the increased value of things you invest in such as stocks, real estate (including your house), and your family business. You pay tax on your ordinary income every year, whether or not you actually receive the money. If you earn $1,000 in interest on your savings account this year, you will probably pay around $300 in income tax even if the money you earned is still in your bank account. Capital gains are different. If the value of a stock you own goes up $1,000 this year, you pay no tax unless you choose to sell the stock. If you have built a successful family business, either from the ground up or by buying an existing business, you haven't been taxed on the increase in the value of business. If you have used the profits of your business to buy stocks, real estate, and other investments, the growth in those investments may not have been taxed as of the time of your death. While most Americans receive the bulk of their income as "ordinary" income—and are fully taxed every year—if you have accumulated enough value to be subject to the estate tax, much of what you own is likely to be "capital gains" investments that have not yet been taxed: investments in your business, your family residence, and your brokerage account. Under our tax laws, these investments will go to your family or friends free of income tax and free of capital gains tax. Without the estate tax, these assets that have grown to be worth several million dollars (remember, the estate tax doesn't even start until $2 million—or $3,500,000 starting in 2008) can completely escape taxation. The result is either a well-deserved tax shelter for the most productive (and economically fortunate) members of our society, or simply "welfare for the rich." In any event, the estate tax is not an additional tax on death.

Myth: Estate Planning Is Asset Protection

You read about it in the newspaper and see it on the television news. A lawsuit filed because coffee is too hot. Fraudulent auto accidents staged to extract money from drivers of late-model, luxury cars. The list is endless and the message is clear. You need to take steps to protect your wealth from frivolous lawsuits. However, estate planning is not asset protection. A family trust does not shield your assets from lawsuits or business risks. Under most state's laws, a living trust or family trust is "transparent" and your assets are subject to the same risk of lawsuits or other loss as before you established the trust.

There are ways to protect your assets, but estate planning isn't the way. Some ways are simple, such as auto insurance and homeowner's liability insurance. Others are incredibly complex and require the help of highly-trained specialists. This book does not address asset protection planning, other than to point out that estate planning is not asset protection.

Estate Planning Philosophies You Need to Know

In more than 20 years of designing estate plans and guiding families through the financial and personal transitions that follow a death, I've seen more than my share of family battles and other disasters. On a more reassuring note, in the vast majority of cases I've seen families come together and deal with the financial and emotional adjustments necessary to move forward.

The successful estate plans—those that bring families together (or, at least, don't blow them apart) and result in an orderly distribution of the estate assets, rather than a costly and nasty litigation battle—have one thing in common: the plan was designed

41

to implement a clear philosophy that is based upon an honest understanding of the family involved. A carefully thought out estate plan will implement a transition of wealth in a way that embodies the views that the parent has believed, and tried to live, her or his entire life. The consistency with Mom's or Dad's view of life will ring true to the surviving family members. The comfortable this-is-what-Dad-would-have-wanted feeling helps to avoid family disputes and allows the survivors to move more quickly into the grieving—then healing—phase, without an unnecessary diversion of intra-family economic battles.

Of course, philosophy cannot be implemented in a vacuum. Just as well-intentioned advice given to children during life is often rejected if not presented in a way that the child is ready to hear, a well thought out estate plan only works if the plan takes into account the surviving family members' personalities and their character strengths and weaknesses.

This chapter is intended to share some common, and not so common, estate planning philosophies, and discuss the possible impact on survivors of various personality types. Your estate plan will likely draw from several different philosophies, and should be adaptable to meet issues raised by strengths and weakness in your family. Don't expect to simply pick Plan A or Plan B. Instead, use the examples in this chapter to raise questions and develop your personal philosophy. When you successfully do this, working with a qualified professional to put the plan on paper becomes the easy part.

One last reminder: You're not looking for the "right answer," or the estate plan that most pleases your children. You're developing your philosophy and understanding the strengths and weaknesses of your family. Keep your eyes—and mind—wide open, and be willing to consider that your family members may have some of the strengths and weaknesses of the people in the following examples.

Philosophy One: "Leave It to Beaver" … and Wally

June and Ward Cleaver probably started dating in high school, when she was the head cheerleader and he played football. They probably never kissed anyone besides each other, and that may not have happened the first time until the Reverend said, "I now pronounce you man and wife." All speculation aside, however, we know they only married once and did not part until death (or cancellation for low ratings). They had two children, Wally and Theodore ("The Beaver"), and certainly had no children from any prior relationships. In fact, if it weren't for neighbor child Eddie Haskell, the Cleavers' life would be pretty darn near perfect.

In American mythology, the Leave-It-To-Beaver, 1950s family is the ideal. And the Leave-It-To-Beaver estate planning philosophy is simple: The best inheritance you can leave your children is instilling in them the philosophy that "hard work and honesty are more important than money." Ward's hard work at the office has earned him the right to sit comfortably in his favorite chair in the evening, while June deals with the day-to-day adventures of Wally and the Beav. More importantly, Ward's job has generated a tidy nest egg for the Cleavers' golden years. And that fact is the first, and most significant, component of their estate plan philosophy. Their primary goal is to provide for Ward and June. If anything is left over it can go to the boys, but only if it's left over. The boy's real inheritance was the wisdom coming from those short talks around Ward's chair at the end of each episode that ended something like this:

> Ward: "Well, I hope you boys learned a lesson from this."
> Beaver or Wally: "Yes, sir."

If you are a Leave-It-To-Beaver family, then your estate plan can be as simple as your life. A simple will or trust that puts everything in the hands of your surviving spouse, and later distributes everything in equal of shares to your children, should do the trick. In fact, the only thing you need to worry about is the thing Ward and June worried about every episode: Did the boys learn the lesson delivered lovingly from Ward's easy chair? Remember, your modest bank account (and IRA or 401(k)) will provide a comfortable (but not opulent) retirement for your golden years. But if the boys already have families and homes of their own, your modest, three-bedroom ranch style home will add another $1 million to the pot. As long as life lessons—including financial responsibility—have been taught along the way, the extra cash can simply be divided equally and go a long way to putting

> Leave-It-To-Beaver estate plans provide for your surviving spouse and dependent children first, and your adult children (or others) only if something is left over after your spouse dies.

your grandchildren through college or providing an economic cushion for your children's retirement. If you're not sure if all the armchair lessons have been fully absorbed yet—or if your daughter married Eddie Haskell instead of Wally Cleaver—you may want to spread out distribution of the money over several years or more (in the hope that maturity will come with time), but otherwise the Leave-It-To-Beaver estate plan works fine.

Philosophy Two: "The Brady Bunch"

I recently took an informal survey of my neighborhood and determined that very few of the families are as openly dysfunctional as the family headed by Marge and Homer Simpson. My survey also disclosed that only a small percentage of the neighbors fit the Leave-It-To-Beaver mold. I'm beginning to suspect that few families really fit the Leave-It-To-Beaver mold even in the 1950s and early 1960s. Even fewer of us fit that mold today.

Despite my own belief that I grew up in a traditional 1950s family, here I am at age 51 with two brothers, four stepbrothers, one stepsister, and one half sister (adopted). What's my point? First, life is always more complex than it seems. Second, the powers of self-delusion are great. Seriously, most of us view our lives, and our children, through rose-colored glasses. Take those glasses off while you're designing your estate plan. The success of the plan depends on being objective about your family's strengths *and* weaknesses. And, third, many of us need to be aware of the Brady Bunch estate planning philosophy. I'll leave points one and two for Dr. Phil, and move straight to point three.

You may recall the Bradys were what we now call a "blended family," with three boys from Mike's prior marriage and three girls from Carol's earlier relationship. I imagine that the non-television version of the Brady Bunch family is comprised of two kids from Mom's first marriage, two kids from Dad's first marriage, and two kids from Mom and Dad's current marriage. In popular culture, we refer to the three sets of kids as "yours, mine and ours." The perception that Mom and Dad favor one set of children over the others—whether or not having any basis in reality—is a significant consideration in the Brady Bunch philosophy. Remember, the only inviolate goal of estate planning is

"Do not draft an estate plan that blows up your family—at least, not unintentionally." Meeting this goal is somewhat more complex for Mike and Carol Brady than it was for Ward and June Cleaver.

But how does the Brady Bunch philosophy differ from the Leave-It-To-Beaver philosophy? Not that much. Mike and Carol still want to take care of each other first and then what's left, if anything, can be divided among the kids. Now, here's the difference. The kids may not get equal shares. Instead of equal *shares*, the Brady Bunch philosophy strives for equal *treatment*. The Brady Bunch estate plan may distribute a greater or lesser share to each child to "make up" for past economic differences. Perhaps Greg needs a little extra help because the economic hardship of Mike's divorce kept Greg out of a good college (the unintended results of two years attending public schools without the benefit of private tutors). Or, perhaps Marsha's chances of a successful singing career were jeopardized by those years when Carol's child-support check couldn't pay for music lessons. Perhaps for reasons as silly as those set forth above, or perhaps for more serious reasons, the Brady Bunch estate plan often attempts to compensate for perceived differences among each child (or each group of children).

> Brady-Bunch-type estate planning for a blended family requires sensitivity toward differences in the relationship with each child—both real and perceived.

Here's a real-life example of one Brady Bunch family solution to perceived differences. Faced with two "his," two "hers," and two "ours," this family took into account the possibility that the "his" and "hers" kids may inherit assets from the other parent in the first relationship—an assumption that may or may not be true depending upon the ex-spouse's level of financial responsibility and the number of children resulting from the ex-spouse's next relationship. Not wanting to treat the "his" and "hers" kids better than the "ours" kids—as would be the outcome if each received one sixth of the estate and then the "his" and "hers" kids inherited additional assets from their other parent—the estate was instead separated into eight shares; one for each "his" or "hers" and two for each "ours." The result would be "equalized"—so the theory goes—when each "his" or "hers" inherited additional assets from their biological parent.

Depending upon the stability of the other parent, this plan may work brilliantly to equalize the economics. The big unknown, however, is how each of the kids will perceive the "equalization plan." Particularly in light of the frequent misperception that "ours" children are favored over "his" or "hers," the awarding of two shares to each "ours" child may drive a wedge between the children—a direct violation of our only inviolate rule. (Remember, "Do not draft an estate plan that blows up your family—at least, not unintentionally.")

One final note on the Brady Bunch. Aside from the blended-family issues, you may recall that Mike was a self-employed architect. As such, Mike faced the same estate planning challenges as every business owner. First, how to transition or sell his business to new owners so Carol (and ultimately, the kids) can benefit from the cash value of the business. Second, how to minimize the liability (i.e., malpractice) risks inherent in the business so that an unanticipated lawsuit doesn't reduce a lifetime of savings to three trash bags of belongings kept in a shopping cart under the freeway overpass. (If you are a visual person, you may wish to pause here and visualize Carol Brady as a bag lady.) If your estate includes any kind of business holding, spend a little time with the issues of business ownership and professional malpractice raised in Chapter 6.

Philosophy Three: The Ewings of Dallas

When Jock Ewing died, his wife, Miss Ellie, continued on as the matriarch of the family. It wasn't easy. Not only was she a grieving widow, but she also had to deal with sons who didn't always get along. Family infighting is difficult in any family, not just in TV soap operas. It can be even more disastrous when a family business is involved.

Simply put, Miss Ellie's post-Jock years would have been easier—both emotionally and financially—if Jock had implemented an ownership transition plan years in advance. By the way, "years in advance" means "starting today," since life has a way of randomly dishing out death or disability without advance warning. You may recall that Jock died when his helicopter crashed into a lake in South America.

The lack of a clear ownership-transition plan at Ewing Oil didn't leave Miss Ellie, or any of the Ewing kids, destitute. The Ewings, however, were financially better off than most business owners. More frequently, the family business is the main family asset—the golden goose, so to speak—and disruptions in business mean disruptions in the family's income. A fight among heirs, or an ill-conceived transition plan that puts the business decisions in the hands of a child lacking the skills necessary to run the family business, can kill the golden goose.

Let's recap the Ewing family situation, and then talk a little about yours. Jock and Miss Ellie had been married forever and had two sons, J. R. and Bobby. Oh, wait. They had three sons if you count Gary, the alcoholic black sheep of the family who moved to California (Knots Landing, to be specific) and had little to do with the Ewing clan or Ewing Oil. Come to think of it, they had four sons if you count Jock's illegitimate son, Ray Krebbs, who worked as the Ewing's ranch foreman both before and after Miss Ellie found out about him. The Ewing fortune traced back to Jock's wildcatting days in Central Texas, and was enhanced each year by Jock's strong management of Ewing Oil. Any given season, Bobby and J.R. would be more or less involved in the family business, and depending upon whether J.R.'s ruthless business scheme had generated billions or brought the wrath of government regulators, the heir apparent of the day could be either J.R. or Bobby. Jock knew either boy had the brains to run Ewing Oil, but he never seemed sure whether the modern incarnation of the business needed J.R.'s cutthroat instincts (so very similar to Jock's wildcatting days) or Bobby's more ethical (and sometimes less profitable) management skills. This vacillation between two distinct views of Ewing Oil's future left the golden goose at risk—instead, there should have been a clear direction for the company, and a clear designation of either J.R. or Bobby as the guiding light.

> Your business—whether it's the neighborhood dry cleaners or Ewing Oil—can provide your family with income after you are gone if you begin your ownership transition planning now.

If the writers of "Dallas" had been more concerned with Jock's estate plan and protecting the Ewing family wealth (rather than TV ratings), Jock would have spent the first two seasons identifying the long-term business plan for Ewing Oil, determining the management skills that would be necessary to execute the business plan, and identifying the individual or team that would be best suited to accomplish these goals. Next, Jock would consult with his company lawyers to determine the best corporate structure to accomplish a gradual transition of power to the designated successors. This might involve giving one or more of the Ewings (perhaps J.R. and/or Bobby) voting control of the company, while giving others (perhaps Gary and/or Ray) a share of profits but no say in running the company. Wisely, the writers of "Dallas" avoided this storyline, as the lack of conflict and resulting dip in ratings would have negatively impacted their own personal estate plans.

> If you want to pass lasting value to your family and other beneficiaries, your estate planning philosophy must be this: Survival of the business is crucial and depends upon a sound ownership transition plan implemented over a five- to ten-year period.

Even if it will never make great television, the lesson is simple and important: As a business owner, your estate plan must be designed to protect the value of the family business—the golden goose. Simply leaving equal shares of the business to each of your children may guarantee that the golden goose will be buried in the burial plot next to yours. A dead goose isn't much of an inheritance. If you want to pass lasting value to your family and other beneficiaries, your estate planning philosophy must be this: Survival of the business is crucial and depends upon a sound ownership transition plan implemented over a five- to ten-year period. Remember, if no one in the family shows the interest or ability necessary to run the business, your ownership transition plan may include putting nonrelative managers in place so that the business can be sold for a fair value (either to the nonrelative managers or to a third party).

Philosophy Four: "Family Ties"

Alex and Mallory grew up in a Leave-It-To-Beaver family. They were born to the same parents, who were still in a long-term, first-marriage relationship (and, like Ward and June, dispensing sage advice on a weekly basis). Sure, Steve and Elyse were politically more liberal than Ward and June, and they may have indulged in a few youthful indiscretions that Ward and June never even fantasized about, but otherwise they were indistinguishable. Alex and Mallory, however, were not Wally and the Beav. (Yes, I remember Alex and Mallory's younger sister, Jennifer, and their much younger brother, Andrew, but I'm trying to make a point here and I don't think Jennifer and Andrew are crucial to making it.) You see, Wally and the Beav were practically interchangeable. Sure, Beaver was more mischievous, but by the time they each reach 23 years of age, they are each likely to have accounting degrees from the state university and be settling into a safe career with a firm not far from Ward's office.

Alex and Mallory, however, were not headed for similar lives or careers. No doubt, Alex is now considering retiring early from his incredibly successful Wall Street career. When his liberal-minded, public-television parents pass away, his share of the inheritance may finance a two-week vacation to some uncharted portion of the planet or may simply cover the cost of a dinner party for six close friends at Manhattan's trendiest new restaurant. In any event, the money won't impact his life one way or the other. On the other hand, Mallory is either a highly successful fashion designer or, quite possibly, an incredibly energetic PTA mom making far less money. She and her husband (probably Joey from "Friends"), like Mallory's parents, care more about family relationships and social causes than about money. They are raising two remarkable children who are incredibly close to all of their quasi-aunts and uncles who used to live with Joey in New York. Mallory is deeply involved in the kids' lives and has helped bring out the free spirit that she believes resides every human being (except, possibly, her brother Alex). Despite Mallory and Joey's hard work and careful spending habits (the latter having come to Mallory late in life), they have never been able to save enough money to buy their first house. Inheriting money from Mom and Dad could have a much bigger impact on Mallory than it would on Alex.

When Steve and Elyse sit down to develop their estate plan, they may consider the each-according-to-their-needs philosophy. Some parents decide that inheritance is not a birthright. Instead, they weigh each child's needs—as impacted by physical and/or mental limitations, personality, and even by social consciousness. An Alex—who has amassed his own

> Different children achieve different degrees of financial success, despite equal efforts. You may consider leaving more assets to a hardworking child who has chosen important but low-paying work—such as being a stay-at-home parent. However, remember that your financially successful child may equate "less money" with "less love."

fortune worth more than 10 times his parents' estate—may benefit from the money far less than Mallory, who has chosen an equally (or more) important but less lucrative career path. The hard part of this need-based estate-planning philosophy is conveying to Alex that less money doesn't mean Mom and Dad love you less. OK, Alex may never quite understand that, but with proper disposition of family heirlooms, and some token amount of money, the message may get across to your child.

One final note, Steve and Elyse may blend this need-based philosophy with the charitable estate planning philosophy discussed below.

Philosophy Five: "Taxi"

Jim Ignatowski, or Reverend Jim, as he was sometimes called, may have been the strangest character on "Taxi." Being stranger than Louis DePalma, Tony Banta, Latka Gravas, and the rest was no easy task. How was it that Jim was able to get way out in front? It may simply have been good upbringing … or it may have been a bad estate plan.

You may recall that Jim is the burned-out ex-hippie who could be the poster child for the this-is-your-brain-on-drugs commercials. Every so often, TV viewers were given a brief glimpse of Jim's high level of intelligence, and his privileged past as a child of incredibly wealthy parents. What is abundantly clear is that Jim had access to unlimited money most of his young life. At least, he did until his family realized how the money allowed Jim to engage in self-destructive behavior that, no doubt, came close to killing him on more than one occasion. Opting for "tough love," Jim was cut off from the family fortune in hopes his self-destructive behavior would end. On one or more occasion, Jim's family offered to open the door for reentry to the family fold (and access to the family money) if Jim would return to proper, upper crust behavior. To his credit, Jim's loyalty to his principles and his friends prevented him from selling out. Sadly, Jim's loyalty to principles cost him his family relationships— and access to his vast inheritance.

You may remember the "Taxi" episode first aired on Wednesday, May 18, 1983, where Jim decides to buy Mario's, the bar across the street from the Sunshine Cab Company. In the course of 30 minutes, Jim has to talk his brother, Tom, into allowing him access to his trust fund to buy the bar, and then proceeds to nearly lose his inheritance twice; first because the bar has few customers other than the gang from Sunshine Cab, and then again (after the bar is saved by all the taxi drivers telling tourists that Mario's is New York's newest hip night spot) when Jim almost sells alcohol to an undercover liquor authority officer after closing hours. Happily, in one of his moments of brilliance, Jim has actually sold the officer nothing more than a bottle of seltzer.

> Inheritance should improve, not destroy, the lives of those receiving it.

What, you are no doubt wondering, is the estate-planning philosophy buried deeply in this obscure "Taxi" episode known as "Jim's Mario's?" I'm glad you asked, because it is one of the most important philosophies of all. Simply put, it is this: inheritance should improve, not destroy, the lives of those receiving it.

Jim Ignatowski illustrates two major concerns behind the "improve, not destroy" philosophy. First, too much money, too soon, equals too much access to evil. Throughout the five years that "Taxi" aired on primetime television, we are led to believe that if Jim's access to vast wealth had been more limited, his brain might be far less fried. If Jim had been less able to afford vast quantities of drugs, alcohol, and who knows what else, his innate intelligence might have led him to a more positive—and lucrative—career. Second, too large a trust fund can result in too little motivation. Here's a chicken-and-egg question for you. Was Jim Ignatowski's lack of motivation the result of his substance abuse, or was his substance abuse the result of his lack of motivation? More to the point, did Jim's awareness that he was a trust-fund baby deprive him of the drive to succeed that is often associated with the need to pay the rent and to put food on the table? Even if a large trust fund doesn't drive your child to drugs and alcohol, do you see a large inheritance as freeing the next generation from unnecessary economic worries so they can accomplish greater things (think John F. Kennedy, Nelson Rockefeller, or George W. Bush, depending upon your political leanings), or only as freeing them to jet set and party with the beautiful people (think Ted Kennedy, Paris Hilton, or

George W. Bush, depending upon your political leanings)? Either result is okay, if it's okay with you. But before you finalize your estate plan, you need to decide which philosophy fits you—and your children—so you can design your plan to accomplish your goals.

One final thought about Jim. Remember, the Mario's episode starts with Jim approaching his brother Tom for money from the trust fund. In determining your personal philosophy, keep in mind the stories of Jim and Ron in Chapter Two. Big (or small) trust funds managed by other family members (especially siblings or stepparents) create tensions that may or may not be acceptable to you. Consider the impact on your "Jim" and "Tom" and decide if it feels right to you. If not, consider using a bank or corporate trustee in place of Tom to avoid the family tension.

Philosophy Six: "The Andy Griffith Show"

Who wouldn't want to be Opie Taylor? Start with an idyllic childhood in Mayberry, North Carolina, then move to Milwaukee, Wisconsin, change your name to Richie Cunningham and spend your teen years in an even more perfect family. The only thing that could make it better would be growing up and becoming a highly paid director in the movie business.

But I don't want to talk about Opie. I'm more concerned about Sheriff Andy Taylor, Opie's dad. Widowed at an early age with a young child to raise, he was certainly lucky that his Aunt Bee could move to Mayberry to help with Opie. But if Andy is reading this book, he is probably a little disappointed that none of the estate planning philosophies we've covered so far make much sense for him (unless, of course, Opie develops a cocaine habit after landing that big Hollywood job—something I just don't see happening). Is there an estate planning philosophy that might work for Sheriff Taylor? Not surprisingly, there is.

When Andy Taylor takes a look at his somewhat untraditional family, he sees at least two people he wants to care for if they are living at the time of his death: Opie and Aunt Bee. If Andy were to die young—as did his sainted wife—Opie would need a guardian to raise him, and Aunt Bee would likely need a place to live (and probably some source of income to supplement her fixed income). That's why Sheriff Taylor needs to understand two basic philosophies:

1. Shared values make the best guardians (or, as I like to say, "No one can raise my child as well as I can, but someone who shares my values will try")
2. Parents deserve respect … and support.

Philosophy One addresses the issue that is often the strongest motivation for parents of young children to draft their first will. What will happen to your children if you are not around to finish raising them? Will aunts or uncles—who are usually too strict or too liberal or simply don't understand what is really important in life—raise your children the way you would? Would your best friend do a better job? Worse yet, if you haven't drafted a will selecting who you want to raise your children, some judge who has never met your family will choose the person to finish your most important job (probably from your extended family). Are you comfortable leaving that decision to an anonymous judge?

Let's think this through. If you were Andy Taylor, who would you pick to raise Opie? Aunt Bee is a good possibility. Opie's used to her, and they might be able to stay in the same house they've been sharing with Andy. Continuity is probably a good thing when your dad just died. Don't forget, however, just before the show went off the air, Andy married Helen Crump. Assuming Andy didn't get divorced (something I like to think didn't happen to people from Mayberry) maybe Helen should finish raising Opie. But then there's that whole stepmother thing to deal with. Maybe Andy shouldn't pick Aunt Bee or Helen. After all, doesn't Opie need a male influence in his life on a daily basis? If Andy thinks that's important, perhaps he could choose Barney Fife. Okay, Barney may not look like a good choice on the surface, but you're forgetting that Barney is Andy's cousin (did you miss those three references to the family relationship during the first season?).

Quite frankly, if it were my choice, I would pick Aunt Bee. But that's not the point. The point is Andy needs to consider "shared values," geographic location, family relationship and a dozen other intangibles in order to select a guardian for Opie. Then, just like the rest of us, Andy has to pray that he lives long enough so that Opie never finds out whether or not Andy made a

> If you die prematurely, someone will need to finish raising your children. Choose a guardian who shares your life values, is geographically desirable, and meets your other intangible criteria.

good choice. Note, by the way, that I said "a good" choice, not "the right" choice. There may be many good choices. Try your best to identify the good choices, and don't lose sleep over whether or not you've selected the perfect choice.

The second philosophy—parents deserve support—is an equally big issue for many families. Of course, as illustrated by Aunt Bee, it applies more broadly than just to parents. It can apply to any relative (or even close friend) who may be on a fixed income. We don't know for sure if it really applies to Aunt Bee since the writers never chose to explore Aunt Bee's economic situation. For all we know, Aunt Bee might have cashed in a $10 million life insurance policy when her first husband died (if she had a first husband). The point, however, is that you need to consider the economic situation of the people you care about, including parents, grandparents, aunts and uncles, or anyone else, and decide if you would like to supplement their income if something happens to you. What you choose to do will depend upon your personal philosophy and your economic ability. If there is barely enough money to provide for your spouse and children, you may not be able to provide supplemental income for your parents. If there is extra money, you may choose to assist your parents. In that case, you'll need to consider how best to help out. Sometimes the best help is providing a home to live in rent free. Other times it's a lump sum of money to provide a cushion; maybe $100,000 or more. And sometimes, it may be a chunk of money set aside to provide monthly income for life, with the balance left in the account to go back to your children upon your parents' death. The options are endless once you understand the philosophy and decide what you want to accomplish.

Philosophy Seven: "Newhart" (Larry, Darryl, and Darryl)

I always enjoyed "Newhart," the Bob Newhart television series set in an inn in Vermont. I liked everything about it, but I especially enjoyed Larry, Darryl, and Darryl, the three quirky brothers who lived somewhere in the neighborhood. Every time the three brothers entered the room, Larry would deadpan, "Hi, I'm Larry, this is my brother Darryl and this is my other brother Darryl." The two Darryls never said anything.

The show never made it clear how Larry and his brothers made a living, but it was quite clear they weren't rocket scientists or brain surgeons. If their cumulative IQs exceeded 100, it was probably only because Larry's IQ was 85. He was the brains of the family. If anything ever happened to Larry, the two Darryls would have walked into the next Newhart episode and just stood there. Neither one would have known to say, "Hi, I'm Darryl, and this is my brother Darryl." More importantly, neither Darryl would have known how to kill, skin, and cook a possum (or whatever it was Larry, Darryl, and Darryl killed and ate in Vermont).

If Larry died, assuming he had any assets, he certainly could leave things outright to Darryl and Darryl. If he left them cash, they'd probably bury it in the woods or given it to someone less fortunate than themselves. Your brother might not be as strange as the two Darryls (or maybe he makes them look normal), but perhaps he has a physical or mental condition that limits him in some fashion. Even if he could handle the funds you want to leave him, the fact that he receives $20,000 from your estate might make him ineligible for the government benefits he needs in order to live a better life. If your "Darryl" is in that position, you need to be aware of something called a "special needs trust." Maybe this isn't, purely speaking, a philosophy, but it is an essential tool when one of your estate planning goals is to supplement government benefits for someone you care about. Special needs trusts must be carefully drafted in order to work. If you have a "special needs" situation, have a trust prepared by a qualified, estate-planning attorney.

Philosophy Eight: "The Jeffersons" (Fantasy Version)

You may remember George and Louise Jefferson as the industrious, working-class neighbors of Archie and Edith Bunker. Their years of industriousness paid off and George and Louise moved from working-class Queens to a penthouse in Manhattan. George did his best to hide it—and the screen writers never wrote an episode dealing with it—but I've always imagined that George and Weezie (as George called Louise) were grateful for their good fortune and generous toward others. In my rich fantasy life, George Jefferson contributed generously each year to support the church that Weezie attended every Sunday, and also to the United Negro College Fund (at his son Lionel's urging), and to Easter Seals Disabilities Services (because of the wonderful things Easter Seals did to integrate Weezie's disabled niece into the general community and enable her to live independently and hold down a part-time job). In addition, I fantasize that George and Weezie carved out 15 percent of their estate to be split between the church, the United Negro College Fund, and Easter Seals Disability Services.

The Jefferson's overriding philosophy was that good fortune should be shared in a way that provides opportunity to others. Charitable giving—both during their lifetimes and as a part of their estate plan—was as important as passing money down to Lionel. Further, by carving out assets to go to charity upon their death, George and Weezie were sending one final message to Lionel: "You are part of a larger community and must give as much as you take." Their generosity through their estate plan directly funded good work in the community. Equally valuable was the message and legacy they left for Lionel.

By the way, I know that episode after episode Lionel tried to explain to his dad the concept of charity and giving back to the community, while George

> Charitable giving in an estate plan funds good work and reminds your children of the need to be a part of a larger community.

played the role of narrowly focused, free-enterprise entrepreneur. I choose to believe that storyline was played up for comic effect, and that George was just as community minded as his son. I know I've distorted the storyline that you remember, but I hope my fantasy helped to illustrate the concept of charitable giving in estate planning.

One last thought about charitable giving. It can be combined with the Taxi "trust fund baby" philosophy discussed above. Remember, "Too much money equals too much evil" and "Too large a trust fund results in too little motivation"? You may have noticed in the newspaper that people like Bill Gates and Warren Buffett, Jr., are giving away more money than everyone you know, combined, will earn in a lifetime. I am sure that part of their motivation is altruistic and charitable.

I am equally certain that part of their motivation is a belief that there should be some limit on the amount of money that they leave their children. If your philosophy includes a belief that each generation should be motivated to earn its own way, at least in part, then maybe your estate plan should limit the amount of money going to your children by leaving some portion of your estate to charity. Depending on your philosophy, this can be a specified percentage of your estate, or it can be every penny after your children receive a certain amount (for example, $5 million per child).

Making the Philosophies Work for You

The eight philosophies discussed above illustrate the most common approaches to estate planning. You may have other philosophies that are more unique to you. In addition, these common philosophies interact with each other based upon your specific family circumstances, economic situation, and personal beliefs. The art to estate planning is to explore your situation and beliefs in sufficient depth so that your distinctly blended philosophy can be developed and implemented. With the guidance of an experienced estate planning professional, you should be able to define your goals and philosophies, and then implement a written estate plan that navigates the maze of state inheritance laws and federal tax laws.

PART TWO

Estate Planning Goals

Questions to Help Define Your Estate Planning Goals

Now that you've heard the horror stories, busted the myths, and explored common estate planning philosophies, you can begin to effectively explore your personal estate planning goals. The process requires an honest and objective exploration of hopes, plans, and values that involve you, your life partner, your children, your grandchildren, your extended family members, and possibly your religious institution and other charities. The exploration demands open discussion with your spouse regarding your goals for yourselves and for others (for example, children, elderly parents, disabled siblings, etc.).

To be successful, your initial exploration should ignore outside influences. Do not consider what your children want or what others will think. The goal is to determine what you want. Later, after your goals are clearly defined, you may choose to factor in the expectations of your children or others who are important in your life, not because they have any right to determine your estate plan, but only because you decide that one of your personal goals is to meet the expectations of certain people that you care about (or avoid the tension caused by failing to meet such expectations). Whether or not you decide to take that path is entirely up to you.

For the exploration process to succeed, you need to respond honestly to open-ended questions designed to evoke emotional responses. The starting questions, and some common follow-up questions, are explored in this chapter. Allowing yourself to respond intuitively, without consideration for getting the answer "right" and without caring what others may think, will start you down the path to understanding your estate planning goals. In most cases, however, your estate plan can be more carefully tailored to meet your personal estate planning goals by an experienced estate planning professional who observes your body language, verbal hesitations, and furtive eye movements, and formulates narrow follow-up questions based upon your specific situation. Never forget, your estate plan requires careful exploration of your personal values and should result in a unique set of documents designed to meet your specific financial and emotional goals.

The answers to many of the questions posed in this chapter may seem obvious to you. That's okay. That just means you have a clear view of your goals and philosophies on that particular issue. Other questions may be more difficult. That's okay, too. If necessary, take time to ruminate and return to the issue later. You may or may not find the answer on your own. If the answer remains elusive, an experienced estate planning professional may be able to help you dig deeper and uncover your objectives. In any event, by first exploring these issues on your own, you will be further along in the exploration process and better equipped to work with an estate planning professional in a more efficient (and hopefully less costly) manner.

Providing for a Spouse

Of course, you want to leave everything you have to your spouse. By "spouse," I mean life partner. The issues are the same no matter what type of relationship you are in. After all, you've been partners—both emotionally and financially—for so long. What could be more important than taking care of them?

Wait! Stop! Were you paying attention? The whole point of this chapter is to explore *your* estate planning goals, not to accept conventional wisdom or meet other people's expectations. It may be true that your primary concern is providing for your spouse—for many people it is—but you need to look carefully at your situation, explore your emotional response, and then decide.

> Your estate planning goals depend upon a complete picture of your life. Most likely, your goals—for example, providing support for your spouse, protecting inheritance for children from your first marriage, and supplementing income for your aging parents—will pull you in several directions at the same time.

First, let's put your marriage in the context of your life. Do you or your spouse have any prior marriages? Do either of you have children from prior relationships? Are you childless? Are there others in your life (besides children) that you may wish to assist financially, such as aging parents on a fixed income, or a sibling with a physical or mental disability? Do you feel strongly about leaving some part of your estate to charity? When you understand these possible competing interests, you are ready to explore your goals for your spouse.

Providing for a Traditional-Family Spouse

If you have no children, from this relationship or any other one, and you do not wish to provide support to extended family or charities, then defining your estate planning goals for your spouse is relatively simple. You won't need to leave some percentage of your estate to your spouse and the rest to your children, or design a trust to make sure that your assets go to your children after providing lifetime support to your spouse (who may not be their other parent). You will, however, need to evaluate how much you wish to, and can, leave to your spouse. You need to explore the financial relationship that you have with your spouse. Do you both work? Is one of you a homemaker who has been out of the work force for many years? Do you wish to guarantee that your spouse can continue to live in the family home, and maintain your current lifestyle, even if your salary is no longer available?

Once you decide what you hope to leave for your spouse, you need to figure out how to pay for it. If your spouse is already in the work force, include that income in your calculation. If not, decide whether it's reasonable to expect your spouse to return to the work force, and determine how much he or she can reasonably expect to earn. Next, review your bank accounts, retirement accounts, and other investments. Determine what income your assets can reasonably generate. Use a 5 percent rate of return if the assets are likely to be kept in bank accounts and certificates of deposit. Use a higher rate of return if your spouse has the sophistication—and a trusted financial advisor— necessary to invest more aggressively. In any case, be realistic. Don't assume a 10 percent rate of return if 6 percent is all you've ever gotten. Compare your spouse's anticipated monthly income to your mortgage payment and other living expenses. If the anticipated income exceeds your expenses, great. Congratulations, you've reached the point where you can provide for your spouse. If the expenses exceed your income, you may wish to consider purchasing life insurance (assuming you are healthy and the premiums are affordable). Or, you may decide that your spouse will need to reduce expenses to make ends meet. The choice is yours and should be made after you explore these questions and determine your goals.

Providing for a Blended-Family Spouse

Not surprisingly, defining your goals becomes more challenging if you have children from a prior relationship, or desire to assist aging parents or disabled siblings. Do you wish to provide for your spouse first, and others only after your spouse is gone? Would you rather provide funds to assist your parents immediately, even if it affects your spouse's lifestyle? Should your children from your first marriage receive something when you die, or should they wait until your spouse passes on? Are the assets that go to your spouse his or hers to spend or to leave to others as he or she pleases—even if that means it all ends up in the hands of a 23-year-old gold digger or a handsome tennis pro—or should there be restrictions to ensure that whatever is not needed to support your spouse's lifestyle will come back to your children after he or she dies?

Most likely, your goals—for example, providing support for your spouse, protecting inheritance for children from your first marriage, and supplementing income for your aging parents—will pull you in several directions at the same time. For most of us, there will not be a solution that satisfies every aspect of every goal. With careful planning, however, most of your goals can be met, at least in part.

Every solution will be different, but here is one example. A trust can be established with 10 percent of your assets segregated to provide supplemental income to your parents if and when financial help is needed. Whatever is left of the 10 percent will be returned to a trust for the benefit of your spouse after your parents pass away. The rest of your estate can be held in trust to provide funds as needed to support your spouse. When your spouse dies, whatever is left can go to your children. This addresses most of the issues—assuming there is enough money to support your spouse and supplement your parent's fixed income. You may have noticed, however, it doesn't provide money to your children from your first marriage until after your spouse dies. That may be okay if your second spouse is your high school sweetheart who you've reconnected with after your first spouse passed away. It may not be acceptable if your second spouse is a high school classmate of your children. By asking the right questions, and defining your goals, you should be able to come to a solution that works for you.

Rich Spouse, Poor Spouse

Defining your goals is not just an exploration of your desires and your assets. Equally important is developing an understanding of your spouse's financial need. Particularly in second marriages, or later-life first marriages, spouses often bring established wealth into the relationship. If your spouse is already worth $10 million or more in his or her own right, providing financial support may not be a concern. Emotional issues may be more important. Often, inheritance—or lack of inheritance—is interpreted as a measure of love. My wife accuses me of making this same irrational link between "love" and "cooking me dinner." She's probably right, but that doesn't mean my irrational feelings aren't real. Keep this silly example in mind when dealing with the emotional side of estate planning. You need to decide if emotional issues exist for your spouse, and then decide whether or not your goal includes catering to your spouse's emotional needs after your death. Try not to think about what your spouse or others will think of your decision. Don't forget, you'll be dead before they start badmouthing you. Besides, I like to think that if you have been attentive to your spouse's emotional needs during your lifetime, the posthumous comments will be largely positive. If you haven't been very attentive while you were alive, I doubt that a few dollars parceled out in your estate plan can change the tone of your obituary. (Realize, of course, that people less naïve than me have a different view regarding the use of inheritance to change one's reputation. Some cite the Nobel Peace Prize, created by the estate of the inventor of dynamite and nitroglycerin who was known during his lifetime primarily for increasing death and destruction in the world, as an example of successful, posthumous public relations.)

Protecting the Kids' Inheritance

Protecting your children's inheritance usually comes up in the context of second marriages and blended families. But it can also arise in the context of a traditional family if one spouse is irresponsible with money due to drug or alcohol abuse, gambling, or an attraction to get-rich-quick schemes that drain the bank account with little or no probability of success. The subject may also arise when your surviving spouse has serious health problems that can result in substantial medical bills and/or long-term care costs. Finally, the need for protection may arise because one child is particularly good at living off of, and manipulating, your surviving spouse such that anything not protected will end up in the manipulative child's hands (rather than being distributed among multiple children), either as gifts during your spouse's lifetime or after your death via a will coerced by the manipulative child. Note that in the context of the manipulative child, protection should be in place both for the benefit of your other children and for the benefit of your surviving spouse.

Is "protection" part of your estate-planning goal? Are you content to let your surviving spouse and children fend for themselves (utilizing the philosophy that "inheritance is not a right")? Alternatively, do you believe that each child is entitled to receive a predetermined share of your estate (either for economic or emotional reasons)? If a family fight erupts over your estate, are you content to let the family work it out, even if it means two years of litigation followed by a lifetime of not talking to each other?

What protection makes sense for you? What is the relationship between the parties competing for your inheritance? Did your children grow up in a household that included your spouse? What kind of relationship do your children have with your spouse? Did the potentially competing children grow up in the same household? Do the children get along with each other or have they always been like oil and water? Do your children trust each other personally and financially? Do any of the children display signs of irresponsibility, drug or alcohol abuse, or blatant dishonesty?

> You may choose to carve out some portion of your estate—either specific assets or a percentage value—and leave those assets directly to your children.

Answering these questions can help you decide what tensions between stepparent and stepchild, or between your children, are acceptable and which should be avoided. Based on your answers, you may choose to carve out some portion of your estate—either specific assets or a percentage value—and leave those assets directly to your children. If you choose the "carve-out" option, your spouse will have less money to live on. If there is plenty of money to provide for your children and still support your spouse in the manner to which he or she is accustomed, then no problem. If there's not enough money to do both, you need to decide if you are OK with your spouse adjusting his or her lifestyle or needing to get a job to supplement his or her income. If you're not OK with that idea, then you need to reconsider carving out assets for your children.

Instead of carving out assets for your children while your spouse is still alive, you can create a trust that allows your spouse access to all of your assets for the rest of his or her life as necessary to maintain his or her lifestyle. The trust can limit your spouse's use of the assets to the amount needed each year to maintain the lifestyle that you and your spouse shared when you were alive. Upon your spouse's death, some or all of the remaining assets can go to your children. Your spouse will not have the option to leave your assets to someone else. Your children's inheritance will be protected. Keep in mind, however, if your spouse needs every penny to live on, your kids will still receive nothing (just as they would receive nothing if you needed all your money to meet your own living and medical expenses). In addition, your children may have to wait many years before your spouse passes away. Think about whether or not these risks are acceptable to you.

One final observation. If you have assets that do not produce income (other than your personal residence), you may be able to leave these assets to your children immediately, without reducing your spouse's lifestyle. You may have family heirlooms such as jewelry, furniture, artwork, or even a vacation home, that can be handed down immediately, and satisfy your emotional need to protect your children's inheritance. Consider whether you have such assets, and whether or not you would like to leave any of them directly to your children (or someone else).

The solution for each family situation will be different, but once you have carefully explored the issues and defined your goals, a reasonable solution can be designed to meet your needs.

College and Other Economic Hurdles

Sixty years ago, not everyone went to college, and the parents of those who did go were not viewed as some form of scholarship fund. Today, college is viewed by a large segment of the population as required education. If you bought this book, you are very likely a member of that segment of the population. You are also probably planning to contribute toward some portion of the cost of your child's college education. While college education is not, strictly speaking, an estate planning issue, it is a family goal that deserves some attention in the estate planning process. Further, college education can serve as a placeholder for other similarly large expenses that should be considered while defining your estate planning goals.

Families differ on the purpose of college. Some see a four-year education as preparation for a job, such as an accounting degree or a teaching credential. Others view a liberal arts education as a foundation unrelated to job preparation. Understanding where you fall along the spectrum can help you put your estate planning goals in perspective. Although no direct correlation exists, those with a job-related view of education tend to be less concerned with providing tuition money for their children in the event of an untimely death. A child with a clear focus on their job goal, so the reasoning goes, will find a way to finance his or her own education if circumstances require it. Those with an education-for-the-sake-of-education attitude tend to be more concerned with providing tuition money. In determining your goals, you need to explore how important it is to you to finance your child's college education (or even graduate school) if you die prematurely. If providing for your child's education is important to you, then you need to review your assets and liabilities to determine if the money will be there to assist with college if your salary comes to an abrupt end. If you don't have sufficient assets to cover the cost of your children's college education, then review your life insurance policy and consider adding additional coverage to provide for educational expenses.

While you are reviewing the college-tuition issue, you should also consider other big-ticket items from the same perspective. The most obvious big-ticket item for most families is the mortgage. If something happens to you prematurely, do you want your family to continue living in the family home indefinitely (and keep paying the family mortgage), or should your family move to a smaller home or different community to reduce the mortgage commitment in light of the loss of your income? As with the college expense, determine your goals, evaluate your current assets and liabilities, and then explore whether or not you need to increase your life insurance coverage.

Leaving a Legacy

Bill and Melinda Gates have a foundation doing good works in their name. So do Jimmy and Roslyn Carter (The Carter Center). As of this writing, they are all alive and well. They are able to establish a legacy while they are still alive due to their unique wealth and/or positions of respect. You and I may have to wait longer to establish our legacy, and do so on a more modest scale. Many Americans build a legacy within their families and communities by contributing time or money to local community causes. This legacy—in the form of providing a living example of community involvement for our children—may be more important than anything else discussed in this book. Although this book focuses on the financial aspects of estate planning, do not lose sight of the importance of your non-financial legacy. Leading by example, and providing insight and advice based upon your years of life experience, is an important part of your legacy.

With respect to your economic legacy, however, you need to explore whether your goal includes a desire to leave some portion of your estate to charity. Most of us will not have enough money to warrant starting our own foundation, or to have a building named after us at the local university. However, most of us should at least decide if one or more charities should be a part of an estate plan. If you have any charity you care passionately about, consider leaving some percentage of your estate—1 percent, 10 percent, whatever works for you—to continue the good work you have admired. Or, perhaps you are more comfortable with setting a specific dollar amount that goes to your family first, and then sharing some portion of the excess over that amount with charity. Whether or not you choose to leave anything to charity, at least take some time to consider how it makes you feel, and whether or not you want the example of giving to charity to be one final legacy you leave to your family.

One last thought. Your charitable goals may align with your financial self interest. In certain circumstances, tax advantages can permit you to increase your income during your lifetime in exchange for transferring assets to charity upon your death. Look at Chapter 22 for further explanation.

Implementing Your Goals

After you spend some time thinking about the issues raised in this chapter, take time to discuss the ideas with those you trust—family, friends, and experienced estate planning advisors. Then, use the approach in Chapter 11 to reach some conclusions regarding your personal goals and move toward the implementation phase of the estate planning process.

Special Considerations for the Business Owner

Your estate plan, no matter how complex, can be implemented any time before you die (as long as you are still legally competent). It's probably a good idea to begin planning sooner rather than later, since you may not receive advance warning of your impending death.

If you own a business, or a professional practice, it is even more important that your estate planning begin today. As a business owner, it's quite likely that a significant portion of your wealth (and your family's source of income after your death) is tied up in the family business. The success of your estate plan is dependent upon the business being transitioned to

> Develop your business philosophy as a first step toward protecting the value of your business to provide well for your family.

the next generation, or sold to someone outside the family for a fair price. Either result takes years of planning and preparation, sometimes as much as ten years.

Start thinking about these issues today, and talk with trusted business advisors such as your business' accountant or lawyer. Begin your ownership transition plan now so that the value of the business will be preserved upon your death. This chapter will introduce you to many of the concepts necessary to preserve the value of your business and provide a smooth transition of ownership. It is not, however, intended as a complete guide to ownership transition. Successful ownership transition requires careful evaluation of the unique characteristics of your business, and development of a plan specifically designed for your business. I strongly suggest that you work with an attorney or other consultant with experience in developing and implementing ownership transition plans. Use this chapter as an introduction to assist you in working with your advisors.

Understanding Your Business Philosophy

The first step toward developing a successful ownership transition plan is gaining an understanding of your business management philosophy. You likely fall into one of three broad categories:

1) owner dependent,
2) multigenerational, or
3) marketable.

A brief discussion of each model follows.

Owner Dependent

Many businesses are started and run by one strong individual, and then close when the founder retires or dies. For those businesses, the guiding philosophy is to generate the best income possible each year and allow the founder to take out the profits as current income and retirement savings. There is no expectation that the business will continue past the founder's involvement.

Therefore, less money is reinvested in the business each year and no effort is made to develop a strong management team to continue on after the founder leaves.

Often doctors, dentists, architects, lawyers, accountants, and other service providers choose to operate their businesses under the owner-dependent model, as do many general contractors, local restaurant owners, and countless other businesses. The decision to be an owner-dependent business should be a conscious choice, not an accident. With proper planning, and an investment of time and energy, most businesses can become multigenerational. As the owner of a small business, you should investigate all options and choose the model that best fits your personality, business plan, and estate planning goals.

If your business is operating under the owner-dependent model, you are likely to have centralized control, with all decisions requiring your direct involvement. All elements necessary to make the business succeed—for example, marketing, professional services, operations, etc.—are in the sole control of the owner. All other employees, if any, are essentially clerical support.

> The decision to be an owner-dependent business should be a conscious choice, not an accident.

The owner-dependent business can be highly profitable during its existence since little is spent on payroll, training, or other infrastructure. The fact that the business will literally die with its owner is offset by the potential for increased profitability while the business is in operation.

The fact that the business will end when the owner retires or dies does not mean the business can be ignored for estate planning purposes. During the years the business is in existence, steps must be taken to minimize the risk of liability arising from the business activity. This will likely be accomplished through a combination of careful attention to quality, adequate liability insurance, well-drafted contracts dealing with issues of liability and indemnification, and possibly the formation of a corporate entity or limited liability company to shield the owner from personal liability. Upon termination of the business, the owner (or his surviving family) should look into the cost of continuing liability insurance for a reasonable period of time. If the termination of the business results from the death of the owner, the family should consider appropriate procedures to limited liability by reducing, to the extent possible, the applicable statute of limitations (the period during which clients or customers can sue for alleged harm caused by the business). An estate planning or trust administration attorney should be consulted regarding formal trust administration or probate procedures to achieve this goal.

Finally, while the business is in existence, steps should be taken to document the intent to terminate the business upon the owner's death or retirement. Although the business may, in fact, become worthless upon the owner's death, estate tax may theoretically be imposed on the value of the business on the day before the owner died. If the owner's death is unexpected—for example, due to a sudden heart attack—the business may be thriving immediately prior to the owner's death. To minimize the risk of the surviving family members owing estate tax on a business that no longer exists, you should document the business plan and the business' characteristics that act to limit transferability of the business. Your ability to prove the limited value of the business is crucial to avoiding estate tax on a business that no longer exists.

Multigenerational

For many business owners, simply closing the doors upon retirement or death is not an acceptable option. For them, the business is a legacy to be carried on as a tribute to the founder's efforts. For others, the motivation is purely economic; an acknowledgment that the business can continue to be operated by the family and generate income, or be sold to someone outside the family for a chunk of money that can be invested for the family's benefit.

Ewing Oil, from the "Dallas" TV series, is an example of a multigenerational business. As Jock Ewing established his successful oil business, he realized that the business could continue to flourish, and even grow stronger, after his involvement in the business ended. Much of the business operation fell into a routine that could be successfully carried on by Ewing Oil's scores of well-trained employees. Beyond that, Jock understood that the long-term success of Ewing Oil was dependent on nurturing a talented management team that could develop and implement the constant adjustments to Ewing Oil's business plan that were necessary to keep pace with the changing marketplace, the frequent power struggles within the Texas oil cartel, and the obstacles imposed by government regulators and politicians.

Jock Ewing's view of a multigenerational business was quite literal. If you were a member of the next generation of Ewings, you were a candidate for top management. Jock's ownership transition plan was for his boys to learn the business, continue to operate Ewing Oil successfully, and provide income for the entire Ewing family to live comfortably. Jock did many things right in implementing his ownership transition plan. First and foremost, his vision was clear. Jock and everyone around him knew the next CEO of Ewing Oil would be a Ewing. Ambitious employees and outsiders need not apply. Whatever harm came from limiting the talent pool that could provide the next CEO was offset by the resulting certainty and stability from knowing the clear direction of the business organization.

Of course, Jock's vision for the company would work only if one or more of his children possessed the talent necessary to run the business, took an active interest in participating in the family business, and was trained and tested long before it became necessary for him to take the helm. Again, Jock seems to have done everything right. Long before the boys were old enough to be involved in the business—and years before the first episode of "Dallas" premiered—Jock consciously and subconsciously set up conflicts that would test his sons' strengths and expose their weaknesses. By the time "Dallas" became a prime-time hit, Jock (and every viewer) knew that Gary lacked the cutthroat instincts to succeed in the Texas oil industry. One almost wonders whether the writers left Gary in the script simply in hopes of developing the "Knots Landing" spin-off. Gary was never destined to rise to the helm of Ewing Oil, and was barely equipped to survive the personal infighting of the Ewing family.

After determining that Gary's sole role within Ewing Oil would be to cash dividend checks after J.R. or Bobby took over the company, Jock set out to train his two stronger boys to run the family empire. Jock realized that J.R. had more of Jock's ruthless Ewings-against-the-world mentality, and that Bobby was far better equipped to deal with the outside world when less combative tactics were called for. Perhaps by design, or perhaps because Jock was never able to decide whether J.R. or Bobby was better equipped to lead Ewing Oil into its next phase, when Jock died J.R. and Bobby were left to battle each other for control of the company from roughly equal positions (subject, of course, to intervention by Miss Ellie—who had inherited the bulk of Jock's shares of the company—when necessary to keep the business, and family, on track). In any event, when Jock died J.R. and Bobby were both well versed in the operation of Ewing Oil, and well established within the business organization. Because Jock began to implement his ownership transition plan years before he died, Ewing Oil was in a position to survive as a second-generation, family-run business.

> For your multi-generational business to succeed, you must develop a clear picture of the skills necessary to successfully operate the business, and search for the right team of individuals to provide future leadership.

Not every multigenerational business stays in the family when the next generation takes over. Frequently, the next generation is comprised of one or more key employees who have successfully participated in the company's management for many years. Ewing Oil could have been such a company in an alternative script. To illustrate the point, let's fall asleep and dream about a slightly different Ewing Oil.

In our alternative "Dallas," Gary still moves to "Knots Landing," J.R. never gets married and decides to become an astronaut, and Bobby moves to another network and marries Suzanne Somers. Having no children interested in carrying on the family business, Jock decides to groom an internal management team to buy the company upon Jock's retirement. With the help of a team of advisors experienced in management structure and ownership transition, Jock develops a clear picture of an ideal management team with the skills necessary to successfully operate Ewing Oil into the future and he conducts a search for the right team of individuals to complete the transition. Combining existing Ewing Oil employees with key individuals from outside the company, Jock puts a team in place that he hopes can successfully operate the company and gain the confidence of Ewing Oil's bankers (so massive sums of money can be borrowed to buy Jock's shares of the company when he retires). Then, over several years, Jock tests the new management team both for competence and for compatibility with each other. As soon as Jock develops a team talented and cohesive enough to take Ewing Oil to the next level, his advisors design a detailed ownership transition plan to be offered separately to each member of the team. Jock initially offers each key employee a small ownership interest, with the promise that those members of the management team who develop as leaders will be given the opportunity to acquire greater ownership in coming years.

Years later, when Jock retires (or passes away) the new generation of owners—hand-selected by Jock—is in place to buy the remaining shares with a combination of bank financing and personal promissory notes payable to the Ewing family. The specific details of the Ewing Oil ownership transition plan will have been worked out by Jock with the assistance of his lawyers, accountants, and ownership transition consultants. The plan will fit the unique circumstances surrounding Ewing Oil, just as every ownership transition plan must be designed to meet the unique needs of the company involved.

The bottom line is that successful ownership transition takes years to implement. As a business owner interested in preserving the value of a multigenerational business, you need to begin now. Without a carefully thought out ownership transition plan in place, your family may be forced to sell the family business for pennies on the dollar, or possibly watch the business fail entirely due to inadequate management.

Marketable

Some ownership transition plans involve the outright sale of your business to a third party. Like the multigenerational plan, this requires years of planning. Like each of the prior ownership transition plans, the planning begins with determining a clear vision. Most sales of marketable businesses are sales to competitors or others closely involved in related businesses. Some "sales" involved the more complex transition of taking your company public. Whichever option you choose for your marketable company, planning must begin early and be guided by experienced advisors. The details of preparing your company to be absorbed by a competitor who wishes to increase volume in your regional territory, or to issue shares on a public stock exchange, involve far more than can be dealt with in one chapter of an estate-planning book. Simply realize that both require proper analysis of your company's management needs, proper recruiting of key personnel, and compensation packages designed to retain key management. Further, they require clean financial information and banking relationships. None of this can be developed overnight. If your ownership transition plan involves marketing your company to third parties, work closely with qualified advisors to develop your plan early on. The financial rewards of such a plan can be great, but only if you begin early.

Understanding Estate Taxes

Understanding estate taxes is an important step in developing your estate plan. Most importantly, as stated earlier, you need to remember that less than 2 percent of Americans ever pay an estate tax. Consequently, estate tax considerations should take a back seat to personal and family issues discussed in prior chapters. Even if you are in the tiny minority of Americans who pay an estate tax, an estate plan that would reduce the taxes paid but fails to provide adequately for your spouse, or that puts money in the hands of children who are not yet mature enough to properly handle it, would be a disaster. Review this chapter to get a basic understanding of the estate tax laws, but do not allow tax considerations to overshadow the family issues raised in prior chapters. Also, as you read this chapter, keep in mind that this is only a summary, and not a detailed analysis, of the estate tax. Many estate tax laws come into play and they are complex and often convoluted. While it is helpful to have a basic understanding of the rules, you should work with an experienced estate planning professional to design an estate plan that minimizes the potential impact of estate taxes while at the same time achieving your personal and family goals.

> Less than 2 percent of Americans ever pay an estate tax.

To make it more difficult for you to understand the estate tax rules—and almost impossible for me to write this chapter—the estate tax laws are currently in a state of flux. As recently as 2002, estate taxes could be incurred if your estate was valued at more than $1 million. In 2007 and 2008, your estate will be completely free of tax so long the value is under $2 million. If you die in 2009, there will be no estate taxes as long as your estate is under $3,500,000. Should you be lucky enough to die in 2010, and assuming that Congress does not change the rules before then, there will be no estate tax no matter how large a fortune you accumulate. Then, beginning in 2011 (again, assuming Congress does not change the rules), your estate could be subject to estate tax if the value is over $1 million. By the way, the repeal of the estate tax for one year in 2010 is somewhat of an illusion. Take a moment to review the example set forth in Figure 7-1.

> In 2007 and 2008, your estate will be completely free of tax so long the value is under $2 million. If you die in 2009, there will be no estate taxes as long as your estate is under $3,500,000. In 2011, the law reverts to its earlier upper limit and your estate could be subject to estate tax if the value is over $1 million.

In addition to the $1 million, $2 million, or possibly as much as $3,500,000, depending upon the year of death, that can be left free of estate tax to anyone, any amount left to your spouse who is a United States citizen is also free of estate tax (as is anything left for the benefit of a non-citizen spouse using a specially crafted, qualified domestic trust). On top of that, any amount you decide to leave to a 501(c)(3) charity—such as your church or temple, organizations like the American Heart Association or Easter Seals Disability

FIGURE 7-1. **Small Business Owner Tax Increase Lurking in Estate Tax Repeal**

Assume your Mom dies leaving an estate comprised of the family home (purchased for $280,000 and now fully paid for), a one-third interest in a small business (with a tax basis of $300,000), a savings account, and some miscellaneous assets such as a car, some furniture, etc. Today, in many parts of the country, Mom's estate would look something like this:

House	$ 600,000
Business (1/3 interest)	700,000
Savings	360,000
Automobile	20,000
Miscellaneous	120,000
Total Estate	**$1,800,000**

Because the total value of Mom's assets is less than $2 million, the assets can be left to Mom's children completely free of estate tax. Under applicable estate tax rules, the children are allowed to "step up" the tax basis in Mom's house and her share of the business, to the $600,000 and $700,000 that each was worth on the date of her death. If the kids sell the business to Mom's partner and then sell Mom's house, they pay no income tax on the sale. Consequently, the kids will share $1,800,000.

If the kids inherit Mom's assets in 2010, they get a limited step up in basis (under complex basis-allocation rules), since there is no estate tax. As a result, when they sell the house they will pay capital gains income tax on a portion of the sale price. And the worst part is that they don't even get to protect $250,000 from being taxed the way Mom did when she sold the house as her primary residence. When the kids sell Mom's house and business, the capital gains income tax will be computed as follows:

	House	Business
Sale price	$ 600,000	$ 700,000
Less tax basis	433,333	505,556
Taxable gain	$ 166,667	$ 194,444
Federal capital gains tax (15%)	$ 25,000	$ 29,167
State income tax (5%)	$ 8,333	$ 9,722
Total tax	$ 33,333	$ 38,889
Net cash after tax	**$ 566,667**	**$ 661,111**

The assets available to the kids after selling Mom's house will look like this:

Cash from sale of house	$ 566,667
Cash from sale of business	661,111
Savings	360,000
Automobile	20,000
Miscellaneous	120,000
Total Estate	**$1,727,778**

Amazingly, when the estate tax repeal takes effect in 2010, many small business owners will find the after-tax inheritance available to their families reduced; in this example by more than $70,000. At the same time, the wealthiest families will pay no estate tax at all. So much for tax fairness!

> Any amount left to your spouse who is a United States citizen is completely free of estate tax.

Services, and countless other public charities active in your community—will be free of estate tax.

The value of your estate—and the determination of whether or not your estate is large enough to be subject to estate tax—includes everything you own; the current fair market value of your house and any other real estate, your ownership interest in your business, retirement accounts or annuities, stocks, bonds and other securities, cash in the bank, artwork, jewelry, and anything else you own. In addition, any life insurance benefit that is not carefully structured to avoid inclusion in your estate (by use of a carefully designed life insurance trust) will be added to the value of your estate. Finally, a detailed set of rules require you to add to the value of your estate any asset you gave away less than three years before your death, and assets over which you have effective control (but not ownership). Because these rules are highly technical, extremely nuanced, and change over time, they are beyond the scope of this book. An experienced estate-planning attorney will explore these issues with you in the course of developing your estate plan.

> Any life insurance benefit that is not carefully structured to avoid inclusion in your estate will be added to the value of your estate.

As a general rule, inherited assets are not subject to *income* tax (whether or not your estate is subject to *estate* tax). However, certain types of assets derived from transactions that would be taxable during your lifetime may be subject to income tax under a principal known as "income in respect to a decedent." Examples of these types of assets are retirement accounts (such as IRAs, 401(k)s, or profit-sharing plans) or interest payments due under promissory notes or other contractual rights.

Another form of the estate tax, known as the Generation Skipping Tax, can come into play if you are leaving your assets directly to your grandchildren or great-grandchildren (or grandnieces and grandnephews), or to non-relatives who are more than $37^1/_2$ years younger than you. This tax is designed primarily to prevent extremely wealthy families from paying estate tax only every second or third generation simply by leaving assets directly to grandchildren or great-grandchildren. It is designed to approximate the tax that would be payable if the assets had been left first to the children, and then the children left the assets to the grandchildren as part of the children's taxable estate. The Generation Skipping Tax does not apply to the first $1 million left to your grandchildren (or great-grandchildren), so that the tax does not interfere with middle-class grandparents helping their grandchildren go to college or buy their first house. Rather than spend time trying to explain in detail a very complex tax that, quite frankly, may not be fully understood by the majority of estate planning professionals, suffice it to say that if you intend to leave substantial assets to grandchildren or great-grandchildren (or non-relatives in that age group) you should work closely with an experienced estate planning professional to avoid or minimize the Generation Skipping Tax.

Finally, a close relative of the estate tax is a separate tax known as the "gift tax." Together, the estate tax and gift tax are sometimes referred to as "transfer taxes," since they are imposed upon transfers of wealth from one person to another. Like the estate tax, the gift tax is not imposed until a certain minimum threshold is achieved. In the case of the gift tax, no tax is imposed upon the first $1 million of cumulative gifts given during your lifetime. However, to the extent such gifts are given during your lifetime, the amount that you can later leave free of estate tax in your estate will be reduced dollar for dollar.

Like most other taxes, an exception to the gift tax exists. Specifically, during each calendar year you are allowed to give gifts up to $12,000 each to any number of individuals, without using any of your $1 million lifetime gift exemption. If you are married, you and your spouse, jointly, may give up to $24,000 to each individual.

Now that you have a very basic understanding of the estate tax rules, let's take a minute to consider some of the most basic methods of reducing estate taxes. Each of the techniques will be discussed in more detail in the overview of estate planning tools (see Chapters 14 through 22). The discussion here is simply to introduce the concepts.

Family Trust

Perhaps the most common method of minimizing estate taxes is the creation of a family trust by a married couple. Without a family trust, when one spouse dies, all the family assets would be left outright to the surviving spouse. Upon the surviving spouse's death, everything over the estate tax exemption amount

> The most common method of minimizing estate taxes is creation of a family trust by a married couple.

(in 2007, for example, it would be $2 million) is subject to estate tax at approximately 45 percent. For a married couple with $4 million in assets, this would result in estate tax of approximately $900,000 when the surviving spouse died. By creating a family trust, upon the surviving spouse's death assets will be treated as if they are being inherited partially from the husband and partially from the wife. Since each spouse can leave $2 million to the children free of estate tax, the entire $4 million can go to the children tax-free, a tax savings of $900,000. See Chapter 15 for further discussion of family trusts.

Irrevocable Life Insurance Trust

Another common tax savings tool is known as an "irrevocable life insurance trust." Properly structured, this specialized trust can literally move life insurance proceeds outside of your taxable estate. If your estate is large enough to be subject to estate tax, and you did not have a life insurance trust, the proceeds

> A properly structured life insurance trust can literally move life insurance proceeds outside of your taxable estate.

of any life insurance policy that you own will be subject to tax at 45 percent. With a life insurance trust, your estate will not pay a single dollar of estate tax no matter how large the insurance policy, even though the policy proceeds will still be available to support your family. If you have a $1 million insurance policy, your family will receive the full $1 million, rather than $550,000 after paying a 45 percent estate tax. It is worth pointing out that whether or not you have a life insurance trust, the life insurance proceeds will always be free of income tax.

Other estate tax savings can be achieved through the use of lifetime gifting of assets, or numerous specialized techniques that may apply depending upon your personal circumstances. Many of the techniques are discussed in the overview of estate planning tools (Chapters 14 through 22). Take a look at the discussions in those chapters to see if any of these techniques are worth considering for you.

CHAPTER 8

Coordinating Your Estate Plan with Retirement Benefits

In order to reduce income tax and accumulate wealth more quickly, many Americans have taken advantage of tax-favored retirement accounts such as IRAs, 401(k)s, defined contribution pension accounts, profit-sharing accounts, and the like. It is not uncommon to accumulate several hundred thousand dollars, or even more than a million dollars, in your retirement account. While this is a good thing for providing a comfortable retirement, it can present a difficult problem in implementing your estate plan. Because the funds in your retirement savings account were not subject to income tax when the money was earned, every penny that accumulates tax free until you retire is subject to income tax when you begin taking funds out of the retirement account (starting sometime after age 59½, and no later than age 70½).

The problem arises when you die with substantial money still in your retirement account. Until the Pension Protection Act of 2006 was signed into law on August 17, 2006, if you left your retirement account to anyone other than your surviving spouse, your heirs would pay income tax on all of the accumulated retirement money in a relatively short period of time—usually at the highest income tax rates (very likely, 31 percent or more, plus whatever income tax imposed in the state where you lived). If your retirement account balance was $400,000, the federal income tax due would be nearly $125,000 (plus an additional $40,000 in state income tax in states like California). Consequently, your $400,000 retirement account would be worth only $235,000 to your heirs—even if your estate is not large enough to incur estate tax. Imagine how little of your retirement money would be left if your estate was worth several million dollars and you also incurred estate tax at the 45 percent rate.

> Many Americans have taken advantage of tax-favored retirement accounts such as IRAs, 401(k)s, defined contribution pension accounts, profit-sharing accounts, and the like. This can present a difficult problem in implementing your estate plan.

The estate tax law allows some reduction of the combined income tax and estate tax when your estate is large enough to incur both taxes, but even with the slight adjustment the tax impact on your retirement account is huge. Your $400,000 retirement account might be reduced to approximately $130,000 after payment of both income taxes and estate taxes.

Paying Income Taxes on Retirement Accounts

It is common thinking that while you are alive, your retirement account grows each year, tax free. But more accurately, it grows tax deferred. (One type of retirement account, called a Roth IRA, actually grows tax free. Unlike other types of retirement accounts, the contributions you make are not tax deductible. As a result, the money you or your heirs take out of a Roth IRA account will be tax free. In addition, a Roth IRA is not subject to the minimum distribution rules applicable to other retirement accounts.) When you retire and start withdrawing money from the retirement account, those withdrawals will be subject to income tax at whatever tax bracket is then in effect for your total income level. Any funds remaining in your retirement account at the time of your death will be subject to income tax when withdrawn by your beneficiaries. Unless an exception delays the required withdrawal, your beneficiaries will be required to withdraw funds from your retirement account, and pay the applicable income tax, no later than the following times:

- If you are at least $70\frac{1}{2}$ years old at the time of your death (the required beginning date for distributions from your retirement account), your beneficiary can continue to receive distributions based upon your remaining life expectancy (set forth in IRS tables) determined using your age at the time of your death. For example, if you are 80 years old at the time of your death, the IRS-determined life expectancy would be approximately 10 years, and distribution could be made over 10 years. If you are 95 years old, distribution would be required over four years.

- If you are less than $70\frac{1}{2}$ years old when you die, your designated beneficiary—the person named in your retirement account documents to receive the funds—must withdraw the funds over his or her remaining life expectancy (based upon the same IRS tables).

- If you are less that $70\frac{1}{2}$ years old when you die, and you have identified a trust (such as your family trust) as the designated beneficiary, the funds must be withdrawn over the remaining life expectancy of the oldest beneficiary who may receive funds under the trust (even if the retirement funds are actually being distributed to a much younger beneficiary).

- If you are less that $70\frac{1}{2}$ years old when you die, and you did not properly identify a designated beneficiary with your retirement plan administrator, the funds must be withdrawn over five years.

In order to avoid these mandatory distribution rules, and further defer the payment of income tax on the retirement account funds, a designated beneficiary can roll your retirement account over into his or her own IRA. This can only be done if you have identified your designated beneficiary in the manner required by your retirement plan or IRA prior to your death. Make sure that you keep your beneficiary designation current on all of your retirement accounts. In

> A designated benefici-
> ary can rollover your
> retirement account into
> his or her own IRA if you
> have identified the ben-
> eficiary in the manner
> required by your retire-
> ment plan or IRA prior
> to your death.

certain circumstances, you may choose to avoid these distribution rules by converting your retirement account to a Roth IRA
account prior to your death. Each method is discussed below.

Retirement Account Rollover

Prior to August 2006, only your surviving spouse could "roll
over" your retirement account into his or her own IRA. This
would avoid immediate income tax, and permit your surviving
spouse to continue to enjoy tax-deferred growth in a retirement account until he or she became required to begin distribution when he or she turned $70^{1}/_{2}$ years old. However, when
your spouse died and left the remaining retirement money to
your children, the harsh rules requiring payment of income tax on the full
amount in a relatively short period of time came back into play.

As a direct result of the Pension Protection Act of 2006, the ability to "roll
over" your retirement account—thereby avoiding any immediate income tax—
was extended to all beneficiaries. Now, your children, your significant
other/domestic partner, or any other beneficiary you choose, can elect to
deposit the retirement funds into their own retirement accounts and avoid current payment of income tax. This avoids the payment of income taxes within a
few short years after your death, and allows the retirement funds to continue
to grow tax deferred for any beneficiary you chose.

> Your significant other/
> domestic partner, or any
> other beneficiary you
> choose, can elect to
> deposit the retirement
> funds into their own
> retirement account and
> avoid current payment
> of income tax.

Converting Retirement Accounts to Roth IRA Accounts

In the right circumstances, you may consider converting your
retirement account to a Roth IRA. The down side of doing
this is that every penny you move into a Roth IRA will become
immediately taxable as current income. You will pay income
tax on your entire retirement account in the year that you convert it to a Roth IRA. The up side is that all future growth on
your new Roth IRA account will be income tax free, forever. It
will be tax free if you withdraw funds during your retirement,

and it will be tax free if your heirs take money out after your death. Moreover, you will entirely avoid any minimum distribution rules that would require you or your beneficiaries to begin withdrawing funds from the account. Therefore, if you don't need the funds to pay current living expenses—whether for necessities or just for fun—you can leave more money in the retirement account earning income tax free.

> If you convert an existing IRA to a Roth IRA all future growth on your new Roth IRA account will be income tax free, forever.

If you will be using money from the retirement account to pay any income tax incurred as a result of converting to a Roth IRA, the conversion probably doesn't make sense. Even though future earning will be tax free, the fact that the account will shrink by approximately one-third (to pay the income tax) means that you will have less money invested for your retirement. The net dollars available to you each year may be about the same, since the earning on the smaller account can be distributed to you tax free. Although the distributions from your original retirement account will be larger, the net amount will be about the same after you pay the income taxes due on the distribution. For example, if you have $400,000 in your retirement, at 8 percent you are earning approximately $32,000 each year. If you take that amount as a distribution and pay approximately 35 percent in combined federal and state income tax, your net distribution after tax will be $20,800 ($32,000 less $11,200 in taxes). By comparison, if you convert to a Roth IRA and pay the 35 percent tax immediately, then you will have $260,000 available in your new Roth IRA ($400,000 less $140,000 in taxes). Your $260,000 Roth IRA, invested at the same 8 percent, will generate $20,800 ($260,000 x 8 percent). Since the $20,800 can be distributed to you free of income tax, you have the same money after taxes. However, in years that you don't withdraw all of the current earning, the reduced balance in your Roth IRA will generate less pre-tax income. As a result, there will be less earnings to compound and grow quicker.

On the other hand, if you have sufficient assets available outside your retirement account to pay the income tax due on the conversion, you can end up with increased income available for retirement and less estate tax due upon your death. For example, if you have a $400,000 retirement account, and you have other assets available to pay the $140,000 tax cost of converting it to a Roth IRA, you can keep the entire $400,000 earning for you tax free. If the retirement account ($400,000) and the outside money ($140,000) were both earning an 8 percent return, you would have $43,200 available each year, before tax. After paying taxes at 35 percent, your net after-tax return on the $540,000 would be $28,080 ($43,200 less $15,120 in taxes). After you convert to a Roth IRA, the outside money will be gone (used to pay taxes). The Roth IRA, however, will earn $32,000 ($400,000 x 8 percent). You will receive the entire $32,000 free of income tax and your net income available will have increased almost $4,000; an increase of nearly 15 percent. In addition, the $140,000 paid in taxes on the conversion is out of your estate, and your heirs will pay approximately $63,000 less in estate taxes ($140,000 x 45 percent). Not a bad result for paying $140,000 in taxes.

Just one note of caution: Withdrawals from a Roth IRA won't be entirely tax free if made before you turn age $59\frac{1}{2}$, or within five years of putting money into the account. Don't convert your retirement account into a Roth IRA if you expect to need to withdraw the funds prematurely.

Creditor Protection

Before making any decisions regarding your retirement account, you should take into account the fact that funds maintained in a "qualified" retirement account, as opposed to an IRA or Roth IRA account, are protected from attachment by your creditors, even in bankruptcy. Once you roll the funds into an IRA or Roth IRA, your creditors may be able to attach the funds to satisfy judgments or other debts that you owe, depending on applicable state law where you live. Particularly if you have been engaged in business, professional, or investment, activity that puts you at greater risk of being sued, think very carefully—and seek legal advice—before you roll funds from a qualified retirement plan into an IRA or Roth IRA account.

> Funds maintained in a "qualified" retirement account, but not an IRA account, are protected from attachment by your creditors, even in bankruptcy.

Recognizing When to Change Your Estate Plan—Fast!

Developing your estate plan takes a lot of emotional energy, time, and money. Worse than that, it cannot be accomplished without admitting that you are mortal. If you're going to go through what can be an emotionally draining experience and spend more in attorney's fees than you spent on many of the pieces of furniture in your house, the estate plan you develop should outlast the sofa that you bought two years ago. The good news is that a carefully thought out estate plan can last a lifetime. The bad news: even the most brilliantly drafted estate plan won't last a lifetime if things in your life change.

The subject of recognizing when to change your estate plan—fast! is broken out as a separate chapter for a very good reason. This is the one chapter you should re-read every few years after you complete your estate plan. Everything else in this book is intended to help you understand estate planning philosophy and the tools that are available to implement an estate plan. Once your estate planning is done, if you and the professionals who assisted you have done your jobs well, you shouldn't need to open this book ever again—except for this chapter.

I'm not big on "rules of thumb," but there are some I try to follow. One example is that each spring when I set the clocks forward and each fall when I set the clocks back, I change the batteries in the smoke detectors. I'm going to suggest a rule of thumb for reviewing your estate plan: *Re-read chapter nine of this book every time there's a presidential election.* OK, I'll admit it's not snappy, but I think it's a good rule of thumb.

> A simple rule of thumb—review your estate plan every time there's a presidential election and update it if necessary.

It's important to check from time to time to make sure that nothing significant has changed that affects your estate plan; four years is probably a good interval for checking. I think tying it to the presidential election is a good reminder since, like it or not, most of us know when there's a presidential election going on. So at the next presidential election, it is my hope that all you responsible citizens will reread this chapter.

The other rule of thumb—hey, you have two thumbs—is don't wait for a presidential election if something significant changes in your life! Try to commit to memory the circumstances discussed in this chapter, and rush to change your estate plan if any of these occur in your life. So get your bottle of gingko, ginseng, or whatever it is that enhances your memory, and read on.

> A second rule of thumb: Don't wait for a presidential election to reread this chapter and review your estate plan if something significant changes in your life!

"I'm Getting Married in the Morning"

In most states, if you get married and have a pre-existing estate plan that doesn't provide something for your new spouse, the law simply assumes you would have changed your will or trust if you had stopped to think about it. To make sure that you don't inadvertently omit your new spouse from your estate plan, state law will likely leave some portion of your assets to your new spouse. The exact percentage varies by state, but the point is you need to review your estate plan and decide exactly what you want to leave to your new spouse. Particularly if this is a second (or later) marriage and you have children from a prior relationship, you may not be happy with the rules that apply by default in your state. Therefore, if you are about to get married, take the time to review your estate plan and decide how much (and what) to leave your new spouse.

> If you are about to get married, take the time to review your estate plan and decide how much (and what) to leave your new spouse.

"I'm Gonna Wash That Man Right Outta My Hair"

Remember the $10-million-man in Chapter Two ("Horror Stories You Need to Hear")? You know, the one who died several years after he filed for divorce, but two weeks before his divorce was final? He died without a will, and since he was still legally married, state law left millions to his (soon-to-be) ex-wife.

> If you are getting divorced, modify your estate plan immediately unless you want to leave your assets to your almost ex-spouse.

The result could be just as bad if the old estate plan—the one leaving everything to your spouse—is still in place. While many states have laws protecting your new spouse from being inadvertently left out of your will, they don't automatically disinherit your ex-spouse, at least not before your divorce is final. Why take a chance? If you're "gonna' wash that man right outta your hair," review your estate plan and rewrite your will so that your money doesn't go down the drain right after him.

"Wake Up Maggie, I Think I've Got Somethin' to Say to You"

Rod Stewart said it best. His lyrics captured the emotion and his message was clear; love hurts, relationships fail, and breakups happen. You don't have to be

> Nonmarital partners, of whatever shape or size, don't get anything from your estate unless you sign a document that makes it happen.

married to go in and out of relationships. But if you are in a good relationship that doesn't include the gold ring and the marriage license, then you need to update your estate plan. Nonmarital partners, of whatever shape or size, don't get anything unless you sign a document that makes it happen. Just as important, if your good relationship turns into a nightmare, you need to check your estate plan ASAP. If your gold-ring relationship ends up in divorce court, there is at least a chance that state law will disinherit your ex-spouse after the divorce becomes final. No state, however, will automatically disinherit your former live-in lover. Ironically, if your relationships are less traditional, you need to spend more time dealing with traditional estate planning issues and monitoring your personal estate plan.

"Ding, Dong, the Witch Is Dead"

OK, dancing Munchkins and ruby slippers on green feet have absolutely nothing to do with marriage or estate planning. I just love the line from the song, and I think it's a great way to remind you that if your spouse (male or female) passes away, you need to review your estate plan. It may or may not need updating, but you need to look it over just to be safe. Oftentimes, a married couple's estate plan is designed to provide for the surviving spouse, and then leave everything to the couple's children upon the second spouse's death. That

> If your spouse passes away, you need to review your estate plan.

type of estate plan may not need to be amended when the first spouse dies. However, don't just assume that's the case even if you have a very simple, and incredibly traditional, estate plan. When your spouse dies, take some time to talk with an experienced estate planning professional, and make sure that your estate plan still works for your new circumstances.

"Workin' at the Carwash Blues"

You may remember Jim Crocc for his beautiful love songs. But I remember Jim Croce for songs like "Workin' at the Carwash Blues." That song was filled with characters who were down on their luck or simply not living up to their potential.

When you first developed your estate plan, you probably identified several goals for your family. Often, one of those goals is to provide inheritance to your children in a manner that does not impair their own initiative or desire for success—which you probably hope has nothing to do with washing cars. If this happens to be one of your goals, you need to recognize that it is based upon the assumption that your child *has* initiative or a desire for success. When your son was a junior in high school and excitedly talking about going to college, your assumption made sense. When he drops out of school and takes a job at the carwash, you need to step back and look at your assumptions. This is no easy process. Sometimes the carwash job or other career diversion—mine was a couple of years spent first as a bank teller and then as a stereo salesman before regaining rationality and becoming a tax attorney—is nothing more than a brief reassessment period. Other times, this loss of former ambition is a symptom of greater problems, such as physical or mental health issues, drug or alcohol abuse, or who knows what.

> If your child shows signs of loss of ambition from physical or mental health issues, drug or alcohol abuse, or whatever, you should review your estate plan immediately.

Any time that you see a change in your child's (choose one):

- ambition
- drive
- focus
- responsibility
- sobriety
- physical or mental condition
- level of financial responsibility

or virtually anything else you can think of that could call into question any of the assumptions built into your estate plan, it's time to consider whether a change to your plan may be appropriate. If your son is maturing at a slower rate than you assumed, you may consider delaying or extending the distribution from your trust to limit the risk that your life savings are dissipated in six short months of beer, girls, and fast cars (unless, of course, that's acceptable to you). If your daughter's fashion "budget" exceeds the gross national product of most Third World nations, delaying or extending the distribution to her may be equally appropriate. If either child displays physical or mental limitations that suggest an inability to manage money or investments, or the need for the assistance of government programs, then more extensive rewriting of the estate plan may be necessary to protect that child's long-term interests.

Finally, remember that the term "child" is used here to mean any person you have chosen to be a beneficiary of your trust. You should remain aware of substantial changes in personality or value structure of any of your chosen beneficiaries, so that your estate plan remains properly designed to enhance or improve their lives, and does not become a vehicle that finances a downward spiral.

"Material Girl"

Madonna got it right; we are living in a material world. There's a good chance that your children spend money more freely—and on more material objects— than you did. Now you know how your parents felt.

"Free spending" isn't the problem. "Out of control" is the problem. If you see signs of debt problems, out-of-control spending, or get-rich-quick "investing," then it's time to review the estate plan, and consider restricting access to money. Get-rich-quick investing is easy to recognize when your son talks extensively about "scratching bubbles" to see if his investment paid off, he can explain the difference between thoroughbreds and quarter horses (and he's not a veterinarian), or he tells you about his internet pen pal whose father used to be a general in the Nigerian army. It can be a little harder to recognize when it involves speculative land investments, penny stocks, or starting a business with his two fraternity brothers (who will contribute their share of the cash just as soon as they are able). If you are comfortable with the concept of letting those who inherit from you spend as quickly as they like—even if the spending continues after the inheritance is gone (so that your beneficiary is

further in debt as a result of receiving money from you)—
that's fine. If you prefer to restrict distributions to protect the
financially impaired from their own behavior, then rewrite
your estate plan to provide those protections. The point is, if
the underlying assumptions about your child's financial maturity change, you should review your estate plan to decide if it
should change as well.

> If you see signs of debt problems, out-of-control spending, or get-rich-quick "investing," then it's time to review the estate plan, and consider restricting access to money.

"Taxi"

I think I've outgrown most of Harry Chapin's songs—I was
never very fond of "Cat's in the Cradle"—but I'm still intrigued
by "Taxi," which is the account of a random encounter between a taxi driver
and his passenger, whom he had dated in high school. You may (or may not)
remember that after high school, they parted ways to pursue their separate
dreams. She was going to become an actress and he was going to learn to fly.
The tragic irony, recognized by the taxi driver, is that his former high school
lover is now acting only to pretend she is happy, while he is flying only with the
help of mind-altering drugs.

Leaving a few hundred thousand dollars to a son who wants to go to flight
school, or who is already a pilot, is one thing. Leaving a few hundred thousand dollars to a son who flies only with the use of drugs is quite another. If
your child exhibits any signs of drug or alcohol dependence, or other addic-
tive behavior, immediate review of your estate plan is essential. Leaving assets
outright to someone who is unable to control self-destructive behavior is dangerous. Enough said.

"Get Off of My Cloud"

I never quite understood the song, but it was quite clear that Mick Jagger no
longer wanted anything to do with whomever it was he was singing to. I'm
assuming that sometime before the song was written, Mick actually invited
this person on to his cloud. Obviously, something changed. It's not clear to me
from the song exactly what changed. More importantly, it may not have been

something objective. It may simply be that Mick's attitude toward this particular cloud-intruder changed.

In your life, relationships may change as well. Sometimes, parents and
children decide to live entirely separate lives and never speak. More often,
relationship changes involve friends or more distant relatives who, at one
time, may be included as beneficiaries in your will or trust. Simply put, if the
relationships between you and the people who are scheduled to benefit from
your estate plan change, then you should consider changing your estate plan.
As long as you keep your eyes open, you'll know it when you see it.

Selecting an Estate Planning Team

Or Deciding to Go It Alone

O nce you decide you need an estate plan—and you absolutely do if you own a business, have small children, have enough assets that you may be subject to estate tax (in 2007 and 2008 that's $2 million or more), or simply wish to leave your assets differently than they would pass under state law—you must decide whether or not to seek professional help. If your estate is modest in size (under $1 million), your family situation is uncomplicated (for example, you are single with no children, or you are married and have children only from your current marriage relationship), and there are no "special needs" to be planned around (such as physical or mental disabilities, financial irresponsibility, or substance-abuse problems), then it may make sense for you to prepare your own will without the assistance of an estate planning professional. As long as you are the type of person who is careful with paperwork, careful with following procedures, and willing to do your homework, you can save thousands of dollars. However, keep in mind that in most states, if you do not follow the procedural rules, your estate plan won't work. For example, in California if you prepare and sign your will, but do not sign it in front of two witnesses, neither of whom is receiving anything under the will, it may not be a valid will. Similarly, if you undertake to prepare your own family trust, your estate will avoid probate only if you then take the steps necessary to transfer all of your assets into the trust. While none of these procedures are conceptually difficult, if you are not a detail-oriented person, it will be safer to work with an estate planning professional.

> In most states, if you do not follow the procedural rules, your estate plan won't work.

If you feel comfortable preparing your estate plan on your own, spend a little time reviewing the discussions of simple wills (Chapter 14), family trusts (Chapter 15), advanced health care directives (Chapter 23), and durable powers of attorney (Chapter 23). You will need to research the specific technical rules that govern execution of wills and limitations on trust agreements in your state to make sure that your estate plan is effective and does not run afoul of any restrictions imposed by state law. Be very careful to understand and address each of the issues raised by your chosen estate plan, and carefully follow the implementation procedures. Remember, unless you follow the signing procedures—including having the appropriate number of witnesses—to the letter, and follow through on any and all funding requirements, your estate plan will not achieve the results you desire.

If a do-it-yourself estate plan is not right for you, you will need to select the right estate planning professionals to assist you. The first step is to determine who should join you on your estate planning team. Certainly, you will want to locate an experienced estate planning attorney. In most cases, your team should also include a reputable life insurance advisor. Finally, in some situations, you may want to involve your accountant, your financial advisor or stockbroker, and a bank or trust company. The remainder of this chapter discusses the possible role of each advisor, suggests qualities to consider when selecting each type of advisor, and points out situations that may indicate the need for a particular type of advisor to be involved.

> Your estate planning team should include an experienced estate planning attorney, a reputable life insurance advisor, and possibly your accountant, financial advisor, or a trust company.

Selecting an Attorney

Conventional wisdom is that less than half of all Americans have no formal estate plan because they are afraid to face their mortality. I believe that it's because they're afraid to face an attorney! In any event, the concept of dealing with death and lawyers at the same time is overwhelming. The truth is, however, if you select an attorney carefully, the experience can be less painful and possibly even downright pleasant. To increase the likelihood that your experience is a good one and results in a well-thought-out estate plan carefully tailored to meet your needs, I suggest you consider the following approach to selecting an attorney.

First, accumulate referrals for estate planning attorneys. Start by asking attorneys, accountants, financial advisors, and life insurance agents that you already know. Get names and phone numbers, but also ask what direct experience, if any, the referral source has had with the attorney they are recommending. Referrals based on direct experience are likely to be more valuable than those based solely upon reputation or word-of-mouth. In addition to asking for referrals from other professionals, talk to family, friends, and business associates whose judgment you respect. Again, ask not just for names and phone numbers, but also ask them to tell you what it was like dealing with the attorney they are recommending and what makes them recommend that particular professional. Did they feel the attorney listened to their concerns and designed a plan with them in mind? Did they return phone calls promptly and provide accurate estimates of fees? Finally, if advice from professionals, family, friends, and business associates does not yield at least two or three solid referrals, consider contacting your County Bar Association for a referral. Be aware, however, that while local Bar Association's may set minimum experience levels (having drafted at least 10 estate plans, for example) in order to be listed on the referral panel, they rarely, if ever, investigate the quality of the attorney's work or the satisfaction level of the attorney's clients. A Bar Association referral may work out well, but be cautious.

> First, accumulate referrals for estate planning attorneys. Next, set up interviews with up to three of the most promising referrals.

Next, set up interviews with up to three of the most promising referrals. But what will you ask at the interview? How will you approach the interview process? First and foremost, the interview should be about you. After all, it's your estate plan. You need to know that the attorney will listen to you, hear your concerns and issues, and help you develop a plan that fits your needs. If the meeting is mostly about "how we do estate plans here" or "what works best for most people," I suggest you move on to the next interview.

When a prospective new client comes into my office, the interview is different every time. Often, however, one of the early questions I ask is, "What motivated you to come in here today?" My question is open ended because I want to find out what is in the client's mind, even if it's not directly relevant to the estate planning process. Just as importantly, I want to know why the client is thinking about estate planning. The topics that I will explore, and the resulting estate plan, will be different depending upon the circumstances. One approach works for the client who has just been diagnosed with cancer, a different approach may work better for a client who has just become a parent for the first time. An entirely different approach may be better if the client has recently experienced a nasty will contest following the death of her father. Simply put, estate planning is not about formulas, it's about people. The estate planning attorney you hire must know all the state inheritance rules, tax laws, and other "formulas" that are necessary to make your estate plan work, but when she is talking to you it must be entirely about "people." You need to find an attorney who can look you in the eyes, ask open-ended questions, and then sit back and listen. Further, when the attorney explains estate-planning principles, or answers your specific questions, she must speak plain, simple English. No matter how brilliant the attorney is, if you cannot communicate comfortably with her—so that she understands you, and you understand her—you will not get the estate plan you want.

By the way, don't bother to ask an attorney how many estate plans he's done in his career, or how much of his professional time is spent on estate planning. We are professional advocates, and we know you're not interested in hearing that we've only done two estate plans in the last year. Most attorneys can give you a carefully phrased, honest answer that tells you how experienced they are even if they haven't drafted an estate plan in three years. If you want an honest answer that tells you a little more, ask what other types of legal issues the attorney will be able to handle for you in the future, should the need arise. No attorney can resist the chance to tell you how great they are (and to pick up future work). If the list of work he or she can do is endless, you probably haven't found an estate planning specialist; especially if it includes such diverse, unrelated areas as personal injury/automobile accidents, divorces, and drunk driving defense.

> You need to find an attorney who can look you in the eyes, ask open-ended questions, and then sit back and listen.

The point is that you should be looking for an experienced estate planning professional who listens to you and who can explain things in simple English. There is no simple test for experience. However, the person who referred you to the attorney may be able to tell you a little bit about his experience. During the interview, you may get a sense of the attorney's experience level from the ease with which he translates complex legal concepts into simple English sentences. However, you need to be cautiously skeptical when evaluating an attorney's experience. You need to be even more skeptical when it is the attorney himself touting his experience. Let me give you an extreme example.

Fifteen years ago, I got a call from a friend I used to work with when we were both young attorneys. His partner had recently begun advertising the f i rm as experts in a specific type of complex, tax-related estate planning matter in the local Bar Association Journal. In response to that ad, another local attorney had just referred an estate planning client to their firm. It turned out that my friend's partner had studied this particular estate planning technique extensively, but had never actually designed such an estate plan. He was calling to ask if I would review the work before they sent a draft to the client. Despite all the

> The guidelines that apply to selecting an attorney—ability to listen to your needs, the ability to respond in plain English, integrity, and experience in estate planning—apply equally to all members of your estate planning team.

lawyer jokes you've heard, and the fact that the credibility rating of lawyers comes in just above, or just below, used-car dealers (depending upon what year you poll the public), most lawyers won't misre p resent their expertise quite so blatantly. But I can imagine a lawyer bending the truth a little.

The guidelines that apply to selecting an attorney—ability to listen to your needs, the ability to respond in plain English, integrity, and experience in estate planning—apply equally to all members of your estate planning team. Use the same referral and interview process to make your selection. But before you go looking for the other members of your estate planning team, take a look at your estate planning needs and decide which team members you need. The more complex your situation, the more advisors you are likely to need. Some of the considerations to help you decide who to include are discussed below.

The Accountant

If you meet with your accountant once a year to give him a shoebox full of receipts and have your tax return prepared, or if you file form 1040EZ and don't have an accountant at all, odds are you don't need to involve an accountant in the estate planning process. If you own a business, or have several millions of dollars in investments, you will likely benefit from having an accountant involved in the process. If your accountant is routinely involved in your business planning or investment decisions, her input can assist in fine-tuning your estate plan. For example, as your estate increases in value, there may be planning opportunities than involve lifetime gifting of assets to family members or complex planning around charitable giving (and the resulting tax deductions). The assistance of an accountant in evaluating your options when these opportunities present themselves is invaluable.

Simply put, there is no black-and-white rule regarding when to bring an accountant into the planning process. You should, however, remain open to involving your accountant when your financial situation is more complicated, or when more complicated estate planning techniques are being considered.

The Financial Advisor

If you have an existing relationship with a financial advisor, he should become part of the estate planning team by providing information regarding your investment goals and strategy to your estate planning attorney. If you have sufficient cash to invest in something other than an interest-bearing bank account, you should have a relationship with an advisor who sees you as something more than a short-term commission.

> If you own a business, or have several millions of dollars in investments, you will likely benefit from having an accountant involved in the estate-planning process.

Selection of a financial advisor is beyond the scope of this book, but in general, you should use the same referral and interview technique discussed above. During the interview, ask questions regarding recommended investment strategy and about how the advisor will be compensated (including all fees or "load" factors that will be charged). Make sure that you understand the compete compensation package that each advisor is proposing and choose an advisor whose fee structure is designed to treat you fairly and likely to keep the advisor's personal interests in line with your investment goals.

For purposes of this book, it's enough to note that except when you have an unusually close relationship with your financial advisor, his role should be limited to providing your attorney with information regarding your current investments and your long-term investment strategy.

The Life Insurance Agent

Your estate is not complete until you have at least thought about life insurance. If you do not have an existing relationship with a trusted life insurance agent, you should employ the referral and interview technique to search for an agent who is knowledgeable regarding insurance products, and estate planning techniques utilizing insurance products. More importantly, you should look for an agent who listens to your needs and responds with carefully thought out alternatives tailored to meet your goals.

Your estate is not complete until you have at least thought about life insurance.

The most common use of life insurance is to provide security for the insured's surviving spouse and children by providing funds to pay off the mortgage on the family residence, pay the kids' way through college, and provide a steady stream of income for the family (and the surviving spouse after the kids move out). This can be done using either an inexpensive term life insurance policy, or a whole-life policy that combines life insurance and tax-deferred investment. This can be explored with your life insurance agent, with a modest amount of input from your estate planning attorney.

For estates large enough to be subject to estate tax, life insurance can provide a source of funds to pay the estate tax when it becomes due, rather than requiring the family to liquidate any assets. This is particularly beneficial when the primary asset is a valuable family business, since without life insurance proceeds it may be necessary for the family to either borrow against, or liquidate, the family business. Most often, this type of protection is accomplished through whole-life type insurance in order to avoid the large annual premium increases that are common with term policies as the insured moves closer to retirement age. To prevent the life insurance proceeds from becoming part of your taxable estate (and increasing the amount of estate tax that will be due), this insurance will usually be held in a specially designed life insurance trust that will keep the proceeds out of your taxable estate (but available to meet your family's needs).

To make sure that life insurance issues are carefully explored, and the family's needs properly met, it is important to include a qualified life insurance agent on your estate planning team.

The Trust Company

Many estate plans will involve the use of a family trust to distribute money to family members over an extended period of time. This will require appointment of a trustee to handle the money after you are gone. In many cases, the trustee will be a family member (for example, your brother, your sister-in-law, or even one of your children) or close friend. In those situations, there is no need to involve a bank or trust company. However, in larger estates, and in certain special circumstances, it may be beneficial to have the long-term involvement of an independent bank or trust company to serve as trustee. Such trust company involvement may be worth considering if assets are to be held in trust for a lengthy period of time for children who are financially irresponsible or have substance abuse problems. Similarly, using an independent trust company may be advisable in numerous other situations, such as when funds are to be held in trust for the life of your children and ultimately distributed directly to your grandchildren. In each circumstance it will be necessary to weigh the benefits of using an independent trust company against the financial costs and reduced flexibility (when compared with utilizing family members or friends).

> In larger estates, and in certain special circumstances, it may be beneficial to have the long-term involvement of an independent bank or trust company to serve as trustee.

Your estate planning attorney should advise you whenever an independent bank or trust company may be appropriate. If you decide to seriously consider a bank or trust company, you will need to go through the same referral and interview process that applies to the rest of the team. The estate planning attorney, and often other members of your estate planning team, may have experience with several banks and trust companies and be able to make a recommendation. You should meet with a trust officer from the bank or trust company (with your attorney present, if you wish) and discuss the reasons that you have set up the trust, and how you would like the trustee to treat your beneficiaries. The trust officer will be able to explain the approach that he would take as a corporate trustee for your family trust that may impact how your children are treated. Each trust company will have a slightly different approach. Your job is to find the one that is best suited to carrying out your goals. Finally, you should make the trust officer aware of the types of assets you will be putting into your trust (for example, cash, bank account, stocks, bonds, real estate, etc.), and the estimated fair market value of each asset. The officer can suggest an investment strategy for the assets and quote you a fee structure for the trust company's services. Once you have all of this information, you can assess the benefits, limitations, and financial costs of each trust company or bank and make an informed decision regarding whether to use a trust company and, if so, which one.

Defining Your Estate Planning Goals

In order to develop your estate plan, you must first understand your estate planning goals. To do this, you must honestly explore your feelings about various beneficiaries (including their strengths and weaknesses), evaluate your financial situation, and then decide how the financial resources in your estate can best be utilized to accomplish your desires with respect to each beneficiary.

An experienced estate planning professional can guide you through the exploration by asking detailed follow-up questions based on your initial answers. If you have chosen your estate planning attorney carefully, the direction of the exploration will be affected

> The "art" involved in developing your estate planning goals is getting past the answers you think you should give, and getting to your "gut-level" responses.

both by your verbal responses and your nonverbal body language. The "art" involved in developing your estate planning goals is getting past the answers you think you should give, and getting to your "gut-level" responses. No book can take the place of time spent exploring these issues with an experienced estate planning professional. This chapter, however, can lay the groundwork and get you started thinking about important issues. If you take the time to work through the questions raised here, your meeting with an estate planning attorney can be that much more productive.

Identifying Family

Start by making a list of those you care about. Include family members, friends and charitable organizations. Complete the "Your Family Documentation" form found in the Appendix. Fill in all the basic information without giving any thought as to whether or not you intend to leave anything to the person listed. This will serve as a list of *possible* beneficiaries to facilitate discussion as you continue to explore your estate planning goals. Therefore, your initial list should err in the direction of being overly inclusive. After you have completed the list, consider the issues raised below for each possible beneficiary and formulate a one sentence description of your estate planning objective for that individual. You will likely choose to leave nothing to many of the potential beneficiaries on the list. Beside those names, simply write "None."

Your Spouse

A person's spouse often—but not always—will be the primary beneficiary. This will likely depend upon such factors as whether the assets were accumulated during this marriage (as opposed to assets owned at the time of marriage or assets inherited from family before or after marriage), whether there are any children from a prior relationship, and whether the surviving spouse has sufficient assets of his or her own such that the assets are not needed to maintain his or her lifestyle.

Ask yourself how comfortable you are with the idea of leaving all of your assets outright to your spouse, especially if you have children from a prior relationship. Do you trust your spouse to fairly divide your assets between your children, her children, and possibly his or her next spouse? Alternatively, would you be more comfortable protecting some portion of your assets to go directly to your children? Your answers to these questions may be affected by the age difference between your children and your spouse, or by the nature of the relationship between your spouse and your children. Further, it may be impacted by the level of financial success that your children may or may not have achieved on their own. Although the potential stepparent-stepchild conflict over inheritance is the most common, you should also explore the same issues with respect to any other non-spouse beneficiary you are considering, such as your parents or your brother who may need financial assistance due to a physical or mental disability.

Next, consider whether or not you are comfortable with the idea of your spouse managing all of the family assets after you are gone. Will the job be overwhelming due to lack of experience, lack of financial expertise, or lack of anything else? Are there any assets that require special skills to manage, such as an active business or commodities investments? If you were to appoint someone to manage assets for you spouse, how will he or she react? If you were to appoint someone to manage the assets, or to assist your spouse in managing the assets, would it be an independent trust officer or a member of the family? What family dynamics or history exist that may cause difficulties?

Does your spouse have significant assets of his or her own? Is your estate so large that there is significantly more money available than your spouse could ever need to live the rest of his or her life in incredible comfort? If so, should the extra money stay with your spouse or go to others when you die (rather than waiting until your spouse dies)?

Keep in mind, if your spouse is not a United States citizen and your estate is large enough to be subject to estate taxes, you will need to consider a special trust called a Qualified Domestic Trust in order to avoid the money you leave to your spouse becoming subject to tax at the time of your death. This is relatively simple to do, but it must be done if your goal is to minimize taxes, and it may override some of your other goals.

After you explore the above issues, try to write a one-sentence description of your estate planning goal for your spouse. Here are some examples of common goals:

- I want to leave everything to my spouse so that she can live as comfortably as she chooses the rest of her life and I trust her to decide how to dispose of the money after she dies.

- I want to provide my husband with the lifestyle that we have become used to, but I want to make sure that my share of anything that is left when he dies goes to my children from my first marriage.

- My wife can have 70 percent of everything we own to provide well for her the rest of her life (and she can leave it to whomever she wants), and the other 30 percent of our assets should go directly to my children when I die.

- I want my husband to have everything we own available to live on and managed for him by a professional asset manager, and when he dies I would like my half to go to our children.

- I want everything to go to my spouse so that she can live in the style we are used to, except I want the house that I inherited from my parents to go to my brother and sister so that it stays in the family.

Remember, these are only samples. Your estate planning goal for your spouse may be similar or may be drastically different.

The Children

Before you delve into the specific goals for each of your children, you should decide whether you see inheritance as a "birthright," a "stick," or a "community fund."

Many parents view inheritance as a "birthright." For them, the issue is simple. Each child is entitled to an equal share of Mom and Dad's estate.

For "stick" believers, inheritance is to be wielded over their offspring's head. Disposition of assets under the will is to be adjusted frequently, as reward or punishment directly linked to behavior.

Finally, "community fund" adherents view their estate plan as the opportunity to benevolently sprinkle funds to their children where they can do the most good, irrespective of whether one child receives more or less than the other. Under this philosophy, money is directed to the child with the greatest need, irrespective of other factors. For example, the bulk of the estate may be used for the benefit of the wayward child who can't seem to hold down a job (and only calls Mom and Dad every other Christmas), while the financially successful child (who takes Mom to church every week) will receive little more than a token inheritance including a few items of sentimental value.

Each approach has its own strengths and weaknesses that you must consider both in the abstract and in the context of the personalities of your children. For example, the "birthright" approach can minimize conflict between children simply because each child is being treated equally (at least in a superficial way). However, such "equal" treatment may not be appropriate if your son has vastly greater needs arising from a physical or mental disability, or if your daughter won $100 million in the lottery last year. Meanwhile, the "stick" method may successfully mold your children's behavior, but it is equally likely to create resentment over your manipulation of their lives. Finally, the "community fund" approach can be particularly effective if your children have abilities and levels of financial success that are drastically different, but it can also drive a wedge between your children as a result of the perceived favoring of one child over the other.

You can select any one of these philosophies, or you can develop a hybrid philosophy combining some aspects of each. Remember, there is no right or wrong philosophy. The question is simply whether the philosophy you utilize fits well with your goals and desires, and your children's strengths and weaknesses. This is probably a good time to point out that all children have strengths and all children have weaknesses. No child has only strengths or only weaknesses (although I go back and forth between believing that my two daughters are perfect and believing that they'll never get anything right). You

Remember, there is no right or wrong estate-planning philosophy. The question is simply whether the philosophy you utilize fits well with your goals and desires, and your children's strengths and weaknesses.

cannot determine appropriate goals for your children if you cannot step back and take an objective view of both their strengths and weaknesses. Push yourself very hard to be honest in evaluating your children.

After you have given some thought to the various philosophies—even if you are nowhere near picking the philosophy to apply to your children—begin to think about how you will balance your desire to leave something to your children against other goals you may have (such as providing for your spouse, leaving something to other children, or providing for charitable legacies). Will your children have to wait until both you and your spouse pass away before receiving any inheritance, or will you want to leave some portion of your estate to your children even if your spouse is still living? Your answer to this question may depend on whether the children are from your relationship with your spouse or from a prior relationship.

If they are children from a prior relationship, you will need to explore the quality of their relationship with your spouse. The relationship is likely different if they were raised by your spouse than if they never lived in a house with you and your current spouse. Consider the resentment that may surface if your children have to wait until your spouse (who is not their mother or father) passes away before they see a penny, particularly if your spouse is about the same age as your children. This resentment can be even greater if there is a chance that your spouse may use up all of the assets before he or she dies. At the same time, don't forget to consider the resentment that your spouse may have if his or her lifestyle must be reduced because you leave assets to your children from a prior relationship (who he or she may view as having mistreated you, and never accepting him or her the entire 23 years you were married). Also, consider how each child will react to your other children (whether their relationship is sibling, half sibling, or stepsibling) and consider whether your estate plan may drive a wedge between the children. After you consider all of the possible resentments, decide whether or not you care. Just because your spouse or child has an opinion doesn't mean it should be part of your estate-planning goal. You may choose to make it important, but it is your decision, not theirs.

Finally, look at each child individually and assess his or her financial and emotional needs. Look objectively at each child's ability to earn money, function in a relationship, and anything else you consider important in life. Consider whether it makes sense to you to tailor your estate plan to attempt to respond to each child's individual needs. You may think it is important to respond to each child's need, or you may think it is important to let each child learn to take care of him- or herself irrespective of his or her needs or circumstances. It is your choice either way to decide what you think is right.

After exploring the issues relevant to your child, write a separate one-sentence goal for each child. Here are some examples:

- Each of my children should receive an equal share of my estate, but only after my spouse is gone and after they are old enough to be responsible with money.
- My children from my first marriage should share equally in 20 percent of my estate when I die even if my spouse is still alive (but only if there is enough left so my spouse can live comfortably). The rest should be used to take care of my spouse and be left to my children only after my spouse passes away.
- Matthew has been involved in the family business and is best equipped to run it after I am gone, so he should be given control of the business, but the income from the business and my other assets should be used to support my spouse and then left to all of my children (not just Matthew) after my spouse is gone.
- After my spouse passes away, each of my children should receive $1 million dollars from my estate (because I do not want them to become unproductive trust-fund babies) and anything left after that should go to Easter Seals Disability Services.
- Kathryn has chosen a career teaching handicapped children and will never earn the kind of money her brother the doctor makes, so I want

to leave her more assets than her brother so she can have some of the things she could not otherwise afford.

- Michael has a history of mental health problems and will not be able to earn much money or manage whatever money he has, so I want to leave his inheritance in a way that can provide him with a steady income that will pay for a clean and safe place for him to live the rest of his life.

Again, these are only examples. You need to fashion goals that you consider appropriate for your children.

Extended Family and Friends

Friends come in all varieties, especially in the context of estate planning. Some "friends" are really spouses without the formality of marriage. This can include same-sex relationships that are not entitled to the full status of marriage under state law, as well as long-term, live-in male-female relationships that simply elect not to formalize the "marriage." Others are simply friends who have been supportive of you or your family through stressful times such as divorce, illness or death, or extended unemployment.

The desire to provide assistance to extended family can arise in numerous circumstances. For example, you may wish to provide for your widowed mother who is living on a fixed income, particularly if you are her only child. In that situation, your desire to provide financial support may be on the same level as providing for your spouse and children. If, however, you are one of five siblings banding together to assist a less fortunate brother whose ability to make a living is impaired by mental or physical disabilities, or by extended illness, you may well consider your desire to assist your brother as a lower priority than assuring that your spouse and children are comfortable. As the family relationship becomes more distant, and the number of relatives able and willing to contribute toward the assistance increases, it is likely that you will feel less compelled to make assisting the distant relative a priority.

With these thoughts in mind, take a look at the people you have listed as Almost Family on the Family Documentation Form. What, if anything, would you be willing to do to assist this individual if you knew that it would place some financial stress on your spouse or children? Do you feel that you owe it to this person to help out financially (as one might, for example, in the case of a single mother who raised you as her only child), or is it something that you may wish to do only after you have provided more than enough to take care of your immediate family?

After you have determined the intensity of your desire to help out, you need to think about how much help you wish to provide. Do you want to completely provide this person's primary financial support? Alternately, is it enough for you to provide some percentage of her or his financial support, or to provide some supplemental income over and above her or his primary support? At the far end of the spectrum, is your desire simply to leave some token amount of money (for example $1,000 or $10,000), or alternatively some special piece of jewelry, artwork, or other gem of the household, to demonstrate your fondness for this individual? Ask yourself what you would like to do in the abstract, and then step back and weigh these desires against any desires that you have to provide for your spouse or your children.

If you decide to leave more than a token amount to your extended family or friend, think about what should happen if the funds you make available are not fully consumed during his or her lifetime. When your friend passes away, should the remaining funds be distributed to his or her family (or other beneficiaries that he or she chooses), or would you prefer that the unused assets be returned to your family to benefit your spouse, children, or grandchildren? Depending upon your decision, funds can either be left outright to your friend, or be held in a trust that will dictate where the funds go upon his or her death. Finally, if your goal in assisting your friend is to supplement government assistance that is providing his or her primary support, you will need to explore setting up a special-needs trust so that the availability of the funds does not terminate the ability to receive those government benefits. Keep in mind, if you are doing anything more than leaving a few token gifts to friends and distant relatives, you should consult with an experienced estate planning professional who can guide you through all of the complexities.

Once you have put these relationships in context (relative to your desire to provide for your spouse, children, or anyone else), and have determined whether you wish to help provide primary support or simply a token gift, try to write a sentence describing your goals for each family member and friend similar to the ones that follow:

- I want to provide monthly income for my mother for the rest of her life, to supplement her fixed income.
- I would like to provide my brother Jim with enough cash to pay off his mortgage since his health is deteriorating and he may not be able to continue working, but only so long as it does not require my spouse to reduce her lifestyle.
- My niece, Katlyn, should receive my good china since she is the one who has taken over most of the family get-togethers.
- I would like to set aside money to be used to supplement my sister's government benefits for the rest of her life, and when she passes away I would like whatever is left to go to my children.

Once you have figured out your goal for each potential beneficiary, you will need to determine which beneficiaries are most important and what to do if your assets at the time of your death are not sufficient to liberally provide for all those you care about. You will need to decide who will be entitled to receive what, and when. Often, your children will be required to wait until your spouse passes away before they receive their inheritance. That may or may not work for you, however, if your children are all over 40 years old and your new wife just celebrated her 32nd birthday. To help make these determinations, you will need to have a clear understanding of your financial situation. Take some time to explore the concepts in the next chapter, and then integrate what you learn there into your family planning.

Reviewing
Your Finances

Your financial review is important for determining whether or not your estate may be subject to estate tax upon your death—and that's probably the least important aspect of your financial review. You need to obtain a clear picture of your finances to make sure you have enough money for a comfortable retirement if you live a long and healthy life. At the same time, you need to know whether or not you have made adequate financial plans to care for your family if you die prematurely. If you die somewhere in between, your careful analysis of your financial situation will have enabled you to adequately provide for those you most care about (and balance the competing interests

> Your financial review is important for determining whether or not your estate may be subject to estate tax upon your death—and that's probably the least important aspect of your financial review.

between your spouse, children, and extended family and friends). By the way, while it is not the focus of this book, if you still have children living at home, this is also a good time to consider how much financial assistance you want to provide should they choose to go to college and whether or not you are making adequate progress toward funding those educational goals.

Also, your financial review can highlight assets that may require special handling, such as a family business or specialized investments, so that you can make sure any necessary special plans are in place long before the need arises. With all of the above in mind, fill out the Financial Summary Worksheet found in the Appendix. Once it is complete, look at your list of assets and liabilities, and address the issues raised below. By taking these steps, you can protect your comfortable retirement, or provide well for your family if you should suffer an untimely death.

> Your financial review can highlight assets that may require special handling, such as a family business or specialized investments, so that you can make sure any necessary special plans are in place long before the need arises.

How Much Is Enough?

Look at the completed Financial Summary Worksheet and ask yourself, "Do I have enough?" Then, ask yourself the far more important question, "Enough for what?" As long as you are taking the time to evaluate your finances, you might as well look at them from several different perspectives.

Meeting Estate Planning Goals

First, consider the interplay between your finances and your estate planning goals. In the last chapter, you identified beneficiaries you would like to provide for, set forth goals with respect to each of them, and attempted to prioritize which goals were most important. Now it's time to decide if your assets are likely to be sufficient to meet all of your stated goals, or if you will need to pick which goals will be met first and which goals may be at risk of not being met.

This may sound incredibly difficult—and it is. At the same time, there's a simple trick that can make the task manageable (and maybe even easy). Here it is: Start with a blank sheet of paper and divide it into about six columns (although there's a good chance you will only need two or three). Identify the people (or charities) that you wish to leave assets to immediately upon your death (assume, for now, that there will be more than enough money to meet all your goals). Lump together any people who are to receive equal or similar shares (such as children). List one person (or group of similar people lumped together) along the top of each column. Some people who are very important to you may not make this list. For example, Ward and June Cleaver love their kids very much, but Ward's column headings won't include Wally or the Beav. Instead, Ward will list the boys under June's name in column one. This is because Ward's primary goal is to provide fully for June. It is important to Ward that the assets go to the boys after June passes away, but there's no plan to give anything to either boy before that day arrives. The headings on Ward's Financial Summary Worksheet will look something like Figure 12-1. You may notice that columns two through six are blank. That's not a mistake. Remember, Ward and June had a 1950s lifestyle—that is, it was a lot simpler than the lives most of us lead in this new millennium.

Many contemporary families need more than one column on their Financial Summary Worksheet. When Carol Brady sits down to analyze her financial situation, she may need to use three columns. There is no doubt that she wishes to make sure Mike's life is comfortable after she's gone. At the same time, something needs to be done to protect her daughters' inheritance. After

FIGURE 12-1. **Ward's Financial Summary Worksheet**

Col. 1	Col. 2	Col. 3	Col. 4	Col. 5	Col. 6
Beneficiary 1. June 2. Wally/Theodore					

FIGURE 12-2. **Carol's Financial Summary Worksheet**

Col. 1	Col. 2	Col. 3	Col. 4	Col. 5	Col. 6
Beneficiary 1. Mike 2. The boys	1. The girls	1. Alice			

all, wonderful and caring as he is, Mike is not the father of Carol's daughters. Carol would want to be sure Mike didn't leave all of the assets to his three boys and nothing to Carol's daughters (not to mention protecting against the possibility that Mike remarried and left everything to the next Mrs. Brady). Finally, Carol always treated Alice (the housekeeper) as one of the family. Chances are Alice will need some financial assistance in her old age. When Carol Brady fills in the column heading on her Financial Summary Worksheet, it will likely look something like Figure 12-2 (above).

If you're a business owner and have a blended family, you may need to use all six columns. Remember Jock Ewing. Not only did he want to provide generously for his wife, but he knew he needed to protect Ewing Oil by placing it in the hands of either Bobby or J.R. In addition, he wanted to provide income to his son Gary (but sure didn't want Gary anywhere near the business), and also to provide something to his illegitimate son Ray (for being half a Ewing). Jock was also concerned that Gary's daughter, Lucy (who stayed on the family ranch in Texas when Gary moved to Knots Landing to get out from under Jock's control), should be well provided for since Lucy never quite seemed to get control of her life (and her father couldn't be counted on to provide the emotional or financial support that Lucy needed). Finally, although Jock was a tough businessman, he wasn't made of stone. He had his favorite charities and he remembered them in his estate plan (especially charities that understood the importance of establishing the Jock Ewing Memorial Fund). By the time Jock's secretary got done typing up his Financial Summary Worksheet, the top portion looked something like Figure 12-3 (opposite).

FIGURE 12-3. **Jock's Financial Summary Worksheet**

Col. 1	Col. 2	Col. 3	Col. 4	Col. 5	Col. 6
Beneficiary 1. Ellie	1. J.R./Bobby	1. Gary	1. Ray	1. Lucy	1. Charity

By the way, while almost everyone can complete this exercise using less than six columns, it is possible to need more than six columns. If your life is complicated enough that you need seven or more columns, go ahead and finish reading the book, but promise me you'll find the most experienced estate planning professional in the state where you live, and work closely with that attorney to complete your estate plan.

Look back at your list of potential beneficiaries from the last chapter. Determine which beneficiaries, if any, can be grouped into a single column. For example, decide whether the children in your life can be lumped into a single column or should be broken into "yours, mine, and ours" (or like the Ewings', need to be broken into those who will control the family business, those who will receive income but not control, and those who have special needs requiring different treatment). Next, decide which beneficiaries will be treated as "second in line" (like Wally and Beaver, listed as number two in June's column), and which will be given their own column.

Once you determine how many columns you need, the fun begins. Now you get to assign assets to each beneficiary's column. Keep in mind that you can place each asset in one column or freely divide it among two or more columns. If it makes sense to you, you can leave 60 percent of your house to your spouse and the other 40 percent to your children from your first marriage. (Of course, dividing your personal residence between competing beneficiaries may raise tensions that are best avoided. For example, if your spouse is living in the house rent-free, your children's 40 percent ownership interest is little more than the right to contribute 40 percent of the maintenance costs.)

Keep in mind, however, that assets such as bank accounts, stocks, bonds, and the like, are easier to divide between columns without creating tension between beneficiaries. Don't worry about getting the asset assignment "right" on the first draft. This is just a rough draft to help you analyze whether your assets are sufficient to meet all of your estate planning goals, or if you'll need to trim back your goals with respect to some of the beneficiaries.

Once you have assigned all of your assets to a column, you will need to complete some computations to assist in determining how successfully you can meet your estate planning goals. First, add up the value of the assets in each column, deduct the value of the liabilities (such as mortgages or car loans associated with the assets) in that column, and determine the net value of the assets you have assigned to each beneficiary. Then, simply look at the bottom line numbers to see if the relative proportions between the columns feel right to you. By way of example, it will rarely feel right if you have assigned 98 percent of your net worth to provide support for your elderly parents and assigned only 2 percent of your net worth to care for your surviving spouse. If, however, your surviving spouse is Bill Gates, such a division of assets may be entirely appropriate. This test is not an exact science, but you'll know by looking at the bottom line numbers whether the division of assets feels right to you or not.

The second test involves a more complicated computation, but may be the simpler to test. For each column, you'll need to compute the monthly income expected to be generated from the listed assets, and then add any other income that you anticipate will be available to that beneficiary (such as earnings from employment, pension, and/or Social Security benefits, or earnings on other assets the beneficiary may already own). Next, you'll need to list the monthly expenses associated with any of the assets you have assigned to that beneficiary, plus any other monthly living expenses you anticipate for that beneficiary. Compare the beneficiary's anticipated income with his or her anticipated expenses to determine whether the asset assignment meets your goals for that beneficiary. In the case of a surviving spouse, you may want to provide 100 percent of the necessary living expenses. For a child or grandchild, your goal may be met if the assigned assets provide any positive cash flow, even if it only covers a tiny portion of his or her living expenses. By taking the time to complete the computation, you'll be able to tell whether or not it's realistic to try to meet your goals for all of your intended beneficiaries. To assist you in completing both computations, take a look at the Asset Value and Income and Expense Tests in the Appendix.

Meeting Retirement Goals

As long as you've gone to the trouble of listing all of your assets, you may as well take a few minutes to review your pro g ress toward re ti rement. Although this book is about estate planning, there's nothing wrong with taking a brief detour to consider what's in store if you (and your spouse) live a long and healthy life. I've talked about the importance of not caring what others think of your estate plan since you won't be around to find out. It's exactly the opposite when it comes to re ti rement. You'll not only be around, but you're the one who will be eating dog food if there's not enough money to make ends meet.

Look again at the Income and Expense Test in the Appendix. This time, complete the form with all of your assets in a single column. Make adjustments to expenses as appropriate, such as deleting your house or car payment if you realistically expect either to be paid off before your retire. Don't include any income from the proceeds of life insurance since you will still be alive. If you are still actively contributing to a pension account, add in the amount that you are reasonably certain you will contribute between now and the start of your retirement. For simplicity sake, do not increase the value of your retirement accounts, or any other investments, to reflect the earnings that you anticipate between now and retirement. Although we know you will have earnings on those investments, we don't know whether or not the earnings will keep up with inflation. By not including any future earnings, and by listing your expenses at today's dollar amounts, you will have a "guestimate" of how far along you are toward saving for retirement if your investments only keep up with inflation. That may be a conservative approach, but the idea is to maximize the chances of getting to a comfortable retirement. The more conservative we are on the projections, the less likely you will be met by an unpleasant surprise when you stop working.

If your projections show that you are on track for retirement, great. If not, then do something. This is not an academic exercise. This is an important part of making your life a comfortable one. Detailed advice on what changes you should make is beyond the scope of this book. However, you should at least look into reducing your spending (as a way to increase savings so there will be more dollars invested by the time you retire), increasing your income (either by changing careers, taking on a second job, or asking for a raise), and working with an investment advisor to get better performance out of the assets you do have (being careful not to cross the line into high-risk investing). There may be plenty of other ways to improve your retirement situation. If this over-simplified test shows you are coming up short, do your homework and find solutions that fit your economic situation.

Meeting College Expenses

College tuition is tricky business. Not only can the costs of a four-year education exceed any expense in your life other than your house (one year at a private college can cost twice the price of an average car, and even tuition at a state school can reach that amount after two or three years), but if you wish to pay your child's way through college, you'll need two plans: one if you are alive, and the other if you die prematurely.

Before you tackle the difficult issues related to meeting the cost of college tuition, you need to figure out your college education philosophy. Increasingly, American parents view a college degree as a necessity ("the new high school diploma"). You may share that view, but you need to explore your philosophy deeper. Do you see college as a means to getting a particular job (for example, obtaining teaching credentials) or do you view a liberal arts education as an essential part of exploring life whether or not it makes you employable? Also, look at the factors that may influence your child's view of education. What college or graduate degrees do you and your spouse have? What degrees do your siblings have? If your child is surrounded by family members who have advanced degrees from major universities, chances are four years of college (or more) are in the cards. If few of your family members have gone to college before, expectations will be different. Think about these factors to determine how likely it is that your child will go to college (or graduate school), and decide how much financial assistance you wish to provide. Many parents believe a student who works his or her way through school will work harder, value the education more, and ultimately get more out of the experience. You need to decide if this thinking is part of your philosophy.

Once you've decided how much, if anything, you want to contribute to your child's college education, complete the Asset Value Test found in the Appendix with a single column for all your assets. Then deduct the assets that will be used to pay college expenses. Using only the assets then remaining, repeat your analysis for meeting your retirement goals. If the burden of paying college tuition causes you to fall short of your necessary retirement income, you will need to either make the adjustments suggested at the conclusion of the retirement section or reduce the amount of help you provide your children with college expenses.

In addition to determining how college expenses may impact your retirement plans, you'll need to do your homework to determine whether you will have cash available at the time your child is ready to go to college. Talk with a qualified and trusted financial advisor, or work with any one of the online planning tools provided by most of the major brokerage houses, to determine if you are saving rapidly enough to fund your goals. Finally, look into opening a "529 Savings Plan" as a means to save up the money you will need. It has two incredible benefits when compared to other methods of saving for educational expenses. First, the money can grow tax free *and* be withdrawn tax free, as long as it is used for educational expenses. More importantly, if one child doesn't go to college, or doesn't use all the money you set aside, you are allowed to move the funds to another child (or grandchild) without penalty. This is far superior to a "custodial" or "transfer to minor" account where the funds will belong to the child when he or she turns 21 (or possibly 18), even if not one penny is spent on college. Finally, if the money does not get spent on college at all, you will be able to take it back as your own (rather than letting your child spend it anyway he or she pleases) with a modest tax penalty (that will still probably leave more after-tax dollars for you than if you had never put the money in the 529 plan).

One final thought regarding college expenses: if you plan to pay college tuition for your children even if you are no longer alive by the time they finish high school, make sure you have adequate life insurance. Take a few minutes to review the insurance concepts in the next chapter.

Handling Special Assets

Put away those numbers-oriented Asset Value Tests and Income and Expense Tests and let's get back to basic principles. Remember our discussion of the family business as being the goose that laid the golden egg? You may actually have several golden-egg type assets. For example, rental real property that is actively managed by you or other members of the family may require special attention. Similarly, if rather than mutual funds or stocks managed for you through a brokerage account, you have individual stocks that you actively trade based on your personal financial investigation, those assets may require special

> Rental real property that is actively managed by you or other members of the family may require special attention.

skills. The point is simply this, you need to take a look at the financial summary you prepared earlier in this chapter, and identify any assets that require active management by the family. You then need to make sure that your division of assets places the control of any golden-egg type assets in the hands of the person or people that you believe have the skills necessary to protect the assets. Often this may require you to find creative ways to place the management or control of the asset in a single individual, while dividing the income among many members of the family. This can be accomplished through a carefully designed limited liability company (LLC), limited partnership, or corporation with special voting agreements. If your estate includes significant golden-egg type assets, work closely with a skilled estate planning attorney to make sure these assets are protected and your goals are met.

Providing for Estate Taxes

Estate taxes are important. After all, if your estate is large enough to incur estate taxes, you pay about 45 cents on every dollar that is subject to the estate tax (not on every dollar in your estate, only on the portion that exceeds the amount you can leave tax free—$2 million in 2007). Consequently, if your estate is large enough to become subject to estate taxes, you should take reasonable steps to lawfully minimize the tax you pay. For example, if you are married, you can double the amount that will be exempt from estate tax simply by properly setting up and funding a family trust (sometimes called a living trust or a revocable trust). In addition, certain types of assets can sometimes be restructured in ways that can both protect golden-egg type assets that require special handling and, at the same time, reduce estate taxes. Keep in mind that the estate tax laws are constantly changing and are extremely complex. If your estate may be large enough to become subject to estate taxes, I strongly recommend that you work with an experienced estate planning attorney to implement your estate plan (and at the same time minimize your estate taxes).

How will you know when your estate is at risk of being subject to the estate tax, and when you should consult a qualified estate planning attorney? The answer is simple, except for one problem. Under current law, the rules are set to change in 2009, 2010 and then again in 2011. Specifically, if you die in 2007 or 2008, your estate will be subject to tax only if it exceeds $2 million. In 2009, however, the first $3,500,000 will be exempt from tax. In 2010—if the law is not changed before then—there will be no estate tax (although look back at Figure 7-1 in Chapter 7 to see how the repeal of the estate tax for one year in 2010 is actually a small-business-owner tax increase for those dying that year). Finally, in 2011, the amount that is exempt from estate tax drops down to $1 million. Although the moving-target nature of the rules makes accurate planning difficult, I suggest that

> If you die in 2007 or 2008 your estate will be subject to tax only if it exceeds $2 million. In 2009, however, the first $3,500,000 will be exempt from tax. In 2010—if the law is not changed before then—there will be no estate tax. Finally, in 2011 the amount that is exempt from estate tax drops down to $1 million.

Estate Planning, Wills, and Trusts for Business Owners and Entrepreneurs

Very few estate tax professionals believe that the law reducing the exemption amount to $1 million will take effect in 2011 (or that the repeal of estate tax will take effect for 2010). Instead, most professionals expect that Congress will increase the exemption amount to somewhere between $3,500,000 and $5 million. However, until Congress takes action, there's no way to know what the rule will be in 2010 or 2011.

you consult an estate planning attorney if your assets (as set forth in the Financial Summary you filled out earlier in the chapter) are approaching $2 million in value. The attorney can review with you any changes in the law since this book was published, and help you design a plan most likely to meet your estate planning goals and minimize your estate tax obligation.

If a careful review with an estate planning attorney suggests that your estate is so large that estate tax cannot be entirely avoided, then you can explore how best to plan for the liquidity necessary to pay the estate tax. If your estate consists primarily of bank accounts, stocks and bonds, you may simply choose to let your heir(s) pay any tax by selling off sufficient assets to pay the tax. On the other hand, if the largest single asset in your estate is the family business, your heir(s) may qualify to pay any estate tax over 14 years at a very low interest rate. Finally, if you are healthy, and the premium cost is reasonable, you may buy life insurance to provide funds to pay the estate taxes. If you do buy significant life insurance, your attorney may suggest owning the policy through a life insurance trust designed to keep the policy benefits from becoming taxable to your estate (and costing you an additional 45 cents on every dollar received under the insurance policy). Once again, the rules are complex and constantly changing. Work with an experienced estate planning attorney on all of these issues.

Insurance Review

Insurance is not estate planning. It is, however, an important part of protecting yourself and your family, and can be helpful in protecting the transition of wealth to your children when your estate is large enough to be subject to estate tax. Therefore, it deserves a brief chapter outlining the issues you should consider and discuss with a qualified insurance professional.

In the right circumstance, insurance can help you accumulate and retain wealth, and minimize the cost of transitioning wealth to your children.

Generally, insurance can be utilized to accomplish the following broad objectives:

- Income replacement
- liability/asset protection
- retirement planning
- estate tax liquidity.

A brief discussion of each objective, and the available protections, follows.

Income Replacement

For those of you not born into incredible wealth, the first step in implementing your estate plan is actually earning the wealth that you will later transition to the next generation. In order to accumulate wealth, you must earn enough money to pay your routine living expenses, and have something leftover to invest. Your goal of accumulating wealth, and transitioning it efficiently to your spouse, children, and others, is at risk if your ability to earn money is cut short by illness, physical disability or death. To avoid this risk, you can obtain life insurance and disability insurance.

Life Insurance

Your estate plan—and your family life—is built upon the assumption that you will continue to be alive to provide for your family. Life insurance is a means of replacing your earning potential if that assumption is no longer true. Best as I can tell, there must be at least a hundred different approaches to calculating the amount of insurance that makes sense for your family. To determine how much life insurance is enough to meet your family's needs, you should evaluate exactly what it is that you are trying to replace with the life insurance. For many families, the income that you are trying to protect can be thought of as the future earnings necessary to

- finish paying of the mortgage on the family residence,
- put the kids through college, and
- accumulate savings in the bank (or other "safe" investments) to provide a comfortable retirement for the rest of your surviving spouse's life.

If these are your goals, you may wish to provide your family with an insurance policy that would pay benefits equal to the amount of your mortgage, plus the amount you expect to pay for each child's college education expenses, plus an amount sufficient to generate your normal monthly living expense (other than your mortgage payment) when placed in a bank account paying 5 percent interest. See the sample calculation in Figure 13-1.

Once you determine the amount of insurance you are interested in, you need to comparison shop, looking at various companies and products to determine who offers insurance in a form, and at a premium, that meets your needs.

In general, life insurance is available as either a "term" policy or a "whole/universal life" product. A standard term policy is significantly less expensive than a whole life type policy and provides one year of insurance coverage in exchange for the premium paid. At the end of the year the policy

> **Y**our estate plan—and your family life—is built upon the assumption that you will continue to be alive to provide for your family. Life insurance is a means of replacing your earning potential if that assumption is no longer true.

FIGURE 13-1. **Calculating Your Life Insurance Needs**

While there are hundreds of ways to compute your life insurance needs, this simple formula works for many families.

This example assumes a family with two children (who will attend college at a cost of $120,000 each), a mortgage balance of $350,000, existing savings totaling $135,000, and monthly living expenses of $7,000 (including a mortgage payment of $2,300).

Mortgage payoff	$ 350,000
College expenses	240,000
Monthly income fund[1]	1,128,000
Total needed	**$1,718,000**
Less existing savings	135,000
Total policy needed	**$1,583,000**

1 This is the amount necessary to generate $4,700 each month ($7,000 less the $2,300 mortgage payment), assuming it is invested at a 5% rate of return. ($4,700 x 12 = $56,400 per year. $56,400 ÷ .05 = $1,128,000.)

will lapse and be of no value unless a new premium is paid. The premium can go up each year to reflect your increasing age. A variation of the standard term policy is a ten-year-level term, or twenty-year-level term policy. As the name suggests, the premium cannot go up during the first ten (or twenty) years, but will increase each year after the level-term period. A ten-year-level term policy will be more expensive than a standard term policy for the first few years but will likely be cheaper than a standard policy in years six through ten. By using a 10- or 20-year-level term policy, you can lock in a set premium and avoid significant premium increases that may be difficult to afford. Particularly if your insurance needs will be reduced by the end of the level-term period (for example, if your mortgage is paid off or the kids complete their college education), the level-term policy can have the benefit of locking in your insurance costs at a reasonable rate.

A whole-life or universal type insurance policy combines your life insurance protection with an investment component that can build up a cash value inside the policy that is invested on a tax-deferred basis and may be available to you as a source of retirement income (usually by borrowing against the cash value of the policy and paying the insurance company a modest rate of interest so you will not have to pay the income tax on the earnings that would be due if you were simply to withdraw the cash value). The premium will be higher than the premium on a term life insurance policy carrying the same death ben-

> A whole life or universal type insurance policy combines your life insurance protection with an investment component that can build up a cash value inside the policy.

efit. If the investment portion of the policy performs well, so that the cash value increases significantly each year, the extra premium can be a good investment. Unfortunately, a significant number of people who have purchased whole-life type policies have been disappointed with the performance of the policy's investment component. If you are considering a whole-life type policy, look closely at how the cash value portion of the policy will be invested and the guaranteed minimum return on the investment component, and pay less attention to the estimated returns shown in the sales literature since these are not guaranteed. I am not a big fan of whole-life type policies to accomplish your goal of income replacement, but whole-life type policies can be useful if your goal is to build up cash value for re t i rement or to provide liquidity for payment of estate taxes.

Life insurance benefits paid to your beneficiaries upon your death are received free of income tax, but can be treated as an asset in your estate that may be subject to estate tax (at approximately 45 percent) if your total assets exceed the exemption amount for that year ($2 million in 2007 and 2008, more in 2009). If your total estate, including life insurance benefits, is likely to be subject to estate tax, you should consider creating a life insurance trust to hold the insurance policy. Properly stru c- tu red, the life insurance trust will prevent the life insurance p roceeds from being subject to estate tax (and will save your beneficiaries from paying $450,000 in estate tax on a $1 million policy).

> If your total estate, including life insurance benefits, is likely to be subject to estate tax you should consider creating a life insurance trust to hold the insurance policy.

Disability Insurance

A permanent disability, or even a temporary disability that lasts only a year or two, can wipe out your savings and knock your wealth accumulation plans off track. To replace your lost income, and minimize the financial impact of a disability, you should consider maintaining disability insurance that pays a monthly benefit to replace some portion of your income in the event you become disabled.

Disability insurance can be purchased by your employer and provided to you as a tax-free employee benefit. Alternatively, you can purchase the insurance yourself with after-tax dollars. There are serious consequences, however, to taking your disability insurance as a tax-free employee benefit. When your employer provides you with a disability policy, any benefits you receive when you become disabled are treated as ordinary income and subject to income tax in the same manner as wages paid to you by your employer (meaning that somewhere in the neighborhood of one-third of the benefit will go to the government as taxes). When you pay for your own disability policy, any benefits you receive under the policy are tax free. As a result, if you buy the policy with after-tax dollars, your disability policy can be one-third smaller than the policy provided by your employer and put the same net dollars in you bank account if you become disabled. Since the policy can be smaller, the premium will be smaller (making up for the fact that it will be paid with after-tax dollars).

Finally, when shopping for a disability policy, pay careful attention to the definition of "disability." Some policies provide benefits if you are unable to continue working in your chosen career while others will pay only if you are completely unable to be gainfully employed in any capacity. Work with a reputable insurance agent to select a policy that defines disability based upon your specific career choice.

> If you are underinsured, or uninsured, for liability that can arise from negligence related to operating your business, driving your car, or maintaining your personal residence, assets that you intend to use in your retirement, and then leave to your spouse and children when you die, could be dissipated by the costs of defending a lawsuit and paying the resulting judgment.

Liability/Asset Protection

Although often overlooked in the context of estate planning, proper liability insurance is essential to wealth preservation. If you are underinsured, or uninsured, for liability that can arise from negligence related to operating your business, driving your car, or maintaining your personal residence, assets that you intend to use in your retirement, and then leave to your spouse and children when you die, could be dissipated by the costs of defending a lawsuit and paying a resulting judgment.

As long as the estate planning process has focused your attention on protecting your assets, spend a little time with an experienced insurance agent to review your business liability policy, homeowner's liability policy, and automobile liability policy. Make sure that your policy limits are sufficient in comparison to your net worth. Look into obtaining an "umbrella" policy that extends the policy limits on your automobile and homeowner's policy to an amount that is sufficient to protect your net worth. Often, an umbrella policy can increase your policy limits to several million dollars for a premium of just a few hundred dollars per year.

Retirement Planning

Some people choose to use whole-life type insurance policies to meet their income-replacement insurance needs, while at the same time creating a "mandatory" savings plan. The higher premiums of whole-life insurance (compared to term insurance) are used to fund an investment component attached to the policy that can provide a cash value component that will increase on a tax-deferred basis. Your policy can be designed to provide substantial cash build up that can be accessed at the time of your retirement. Tax savings can often be maximized by borrowing funds against the built-up cash value of the policy (rather than outright withdrawal of the money) and paying modest interest to the insurance company.

The tax benefits of tying an investment component to a life insurance policy are real, and using a whole-life type policy as a part of your retirement investment strategy may make sense. You need to do some careful research to determine whether a particular policy fits your goals. Meet with an experienced insurance agent and ask for several options based upon your specific family and financial situation. Then, take the financial projections prepared by your insurance agent to an independent advisor such as a CPA to get a critical analysis of the projections. Make sure your decision is based upon reasonable assumptions and expectations, not unrealistically optimistic projections prepared by the insurance company's sales department.

Estate Tax Liquidity

If your estate is large enough that you anticipate it will incur estate taxes, and especially if it contains primarily assets that you would prefer not need to be liquidated—such as a family business or a family vacation compound in Hyannisport or Kennebunkport—then you should consider obtaining a whole-life type insurance policy to provide the funds to pay the anticipated estate tax. This should be a whole-life type policy so the premiums do not increase drastically in your later years, when your family needs the insurance the most. If you are married, you should consider a second-to-die policy that pays benefits only when both you and your spouse have passed away, since that's when the estate tax will be due. The premium on a second-to-die policy will be lower than a policy on either spouse's life individually since statistically it will likely be paid over a longer period of time. Finally, this insurance should be held in a separate life insurance trust so that 100 percent of the insurance benefits will be available to your family to pay the estate tax. If you do not use a life insurance trust, the policy benefits will be included in your taxable estate and 45 percent of the policy proceeds will go to pay additional estate tax that didn't need to be incurred.

The amount of insurance you will need to pay estate taxes has nothing to do with what your family needs to pay for the house, pay college tuition, or provide future income (although you can buy a little extra coverage to include those amounts, if you wish). Work with your accountant and estate planning attorney to estimate the amount of estate tax that you are likely to incur. That's the amount of insurance you may need.

Estate Planning Tools

Simple Will

N ow that you have a basic understanding of estate planning philosophies, and have carefully explored your personal estate planning goals and financial situation, it's time to learn about the basic (and not so basic) estate planning tools available to you. Should you have a will or trust—or both? Should you consider some of the more complex solutions such as life insurance trusts, qualified personal residence trusts, charitable remainder trusts, and family limited partnerships? Obviously, you can't decide what techniques are appropriate for you until you understand each of the available tools, know their strengths and weaknesses, and know when each may be appropriate. The chapters that follow explain each estate planning technique, point out its pluses and minuses, and suggest situations where each may work for you.

A word of caution. Unless you fall cleanly within the group that is well served by a simple will, I strongly suggest that you work with a qualified estate planning professional to implement your wishes. Each technique has its own set of complex rules that must be understood and analyzed to ensure that your goals are met. This book can open your mind to possibilities worth considering, and can prepare you to better express your goals and ideas to your estate planning attorney, but it is no substitute for several years of law school and a decade or more of drafting estate plans and advising clients through probate procedures and the trust administration process.

The most basic—and most widely known—estate planning technique is a simple will. Your will identifies who you want to receive your assets when you die, either by naming a specific individual to receive an assets or by identifying a class of people (such as "my children") to share an asset. It can identify specific assets (for example, "my personal residence," "my jewelry," "bank account number 121855 at Bank of Dad," or "$10,000") to go to your beneficiaries, or it can leave a specified beneficiary a designated percentage of the value of the assets in your estate. In addition, your will should contain a clause indicating who should receive any assets not specifically left to identified individuals or groups of people. A simplified example of the distribution provisions of a common will is set forth in Figure 14-1.

> Your will should expressly identify any close relative, such as spouse or a child, who you have intentionally decided should receive nothing.

In addition to leaving assets to specific individuals or groups of people, your will should expressly identify any close relative, such as spouse or a child, who you have intentionally decided should receive nothing. If you do not make clear your desire to omit a close relative from your will, most states assume that the omission was an oversight and allow your heir to take a portion of your estate anyway.

Finally, if you have minor children, your will should nominate someone to finish raising your children if something happens to you (and your spouse) before the children become

FIGURE 14-1. **Common Distribution Provisions**

I hereby leave my assets as follows:

- My jewelry and personal effects to my wife if she is alive, or alternately to my children in equal shares.

- My personal residence to my wife.

- My car to my son, Mario.

- Bank of Dad, account number 121855, to my daughter, Dakota.

- $10,000 to Easter Seals Disability Services.

- The balance of my estate to my wife if she is alive, or alternatively to my children in equal shares.

adults. If you do not nominate a guardian to take care of your children, a court will appoint someone to serve as the surrogate parent. Any of your relatives or friends are free to ask the court to appoint them, but if no one steps up (or if the court does not believe that they are fit for the job) a "public guardian" may be appointed to supervise raising your children (possibly in a foster care setting). Obviously, nominating a guardian for your children may be the most important part of your will.

Who Should Have a Will?

If you have children who are not yet adults, you should have a will. Other factors will help you decide if the will should be part of a larger estate plan (perhaps including one or more trusts), or can be your entire estate plan.

If your total assets are substantially less than the estate tax exemption amount—remember, that is $2 million in 2007 and 2008, more in 2009 and 2010, and less after 2010—you may be a candidate for a simple will. You will still need to look closely at your situation and objectives to decide whether or not a simple will can work well for you. If, for example, you have children from a prior relationship, a simple will leaving everything outright to your current spouse will not protect any portion of your assets for the benefit of your children. If this is important to you, you may elect to establish a family trust instead. If you wish to leave everything outright to your spouse, but do not want a list of your assets filed at the local courthouse after you pass away (because court documents are open to the public), you may elect to utilize a trust to protect your family's financial information from business competitors (or snoopy neighbors). Finally, if the size of your estate is modest and your family situation is uncomplicated (closely resembling the Leave it to Beaver situation) you may be able to achieve your estate planning goals using will substitutes (discussed in the next chapter) once all of your children have reached adulthood.

Good Things About a Will

A simple will is just that—simple. It is less expensive to create than other estate planning techniques; therefore, you keep more of your money available to live on. In addition, other than signing the will and having it properly witnessed by two or three witnesses, there is nothing more you have to do during your lifetime. Other estate planning techniques may require some additional administrative steps while you are alive.

Bad Things About a Will

If you use a will, rather than a trust or a will substitute, your assets will be subject to probate at the time of your death. This will result in some cost to your estate (thereby reducing the assets available to go to your beneficiaries).

> If you use a will, your assets will be subject to probate at the time of your death.

Usually the cost of probate will be greater than the upfront costs of creating a trust, but it may still be better for you since the cost is paid years later, after you are dead (rather than coming out of money you could otherwise use to live on each month). In addition, probate may result in a delay in getting assets to your family (often one or two years in duration), although probate allowances can give your family access to funds necessary to live on, and additional preliminary distributions of funds may be made along the way once it is clear that there are sufficient assets to pay any debts you owed at the time of your death. Finally, the probate process will include filing a list of your assets with the court after you die. If you do not want relatives, friends, or others to have access to this information, you should use a trust rather than a simple will to protect your privacy.

> A simple will can be a costly mistake if your estate is large enough to be subject to estate tax since a will does not lend itself to reducing estate taxes in any fashion.

If your family situation involves more than providing for a spouse who is the other parent of all of your children (or simply allocating assets between your spouse and children immediately upon your death), a simple will may not meet your needs. If you need to leave all of your assets to your spouse (to ensure that he or she will have sufficient funds to provide support for his or her remaining lifetime), and also want to ensure that some of the assets will go to your children from your first marriage when your current spouse dies, then a trust will likely work better for you than a simple will.

Finally, a simple will can be a costly mistake if your estate is large enough to be subject to estate tax since a will does not lend itself to reducing estate taxes in any fashion.

An Over-Simplified Sample

Figure 14.2 shows an over-simplified example of a simple will, with comments (*in italics*) to highlight the issues you should think about when working on your will. The language of many of the provisions has been simplified to clarify the purpose of the paragraph. Many technical provisions that are necessary to make the document work may be missing (if I did not think they were necessary to illustrate a point). Finally, the document is based upon the requirements of California law and may not comply with the technical requirements of your home state.

In short, use this sample to help you understand concepts and to think through issues. Do not use this document as a "form" to prepare your will, as it will not work.

FIGURE 14.2 **A Simplified Simple Will**

LAST WILL OF BONITA K. TOVAH

I, Bonita K. Tovah, formerly known by my maiden name, Bonita Sansei, and my prior married name, Bonita Bellfleur, a resident of Orange County, California, declare that this is my will. I hereby revoke all prior wills and codicils.

[Your will should identify all names that you have formerly used, including your maiden name, any prior married names, and any variation that you may have used. For example, if Bonita also goes by her middle name, she should include the phase: "also known as Katherine Tovah."]

ARTICLE ONE - INTRODUCTORY PROVISIONS

1.1. **Disposal of Property**. I intend that this will dispose of all of my property.

[One of the things that gives a will legal effect is a clear expression that you intend for it to function as a will and transfer your property.]

1.2. **Exercise of Power of Appointment**. I do not exercise any power of appointment that I now possess or that hereafter may be conferred on me.

[Sometimes your spouse or your parents—and on rare occasions someone else—will designate in their will or trust that you can designate who will ultimately receive assets that they have set aside (with the ultimate distribution occurring either upon their death or upon your death). This is called a "power of appointment." If you intend to designate someone (for example, your children) to receive these assets, this provision in your will should specifically refer to the document giving you the power of appointment, and indicate to whom you elect to leave the property.]

1.3. **Contract Affecting Will**. I have not made any agreement requiring me to leave assets to anyone.

[Although rare, occasionally contracts are entered into obligating a person to leave assets to a specified person or group of people. For example, a divorce settlement may obligate one spouse, or both, to leave certain assets only to the children from the marriage.]

ARTICLE TWO - IDENTITY OF SPOUSE AND CHILDREN

2.1. **Spouse**. I am married to Moses R. Tovah, and all references to "my husband" are to him.

2.2. **Children**. I have two children from a prior marriage, whose father is Sam Bellfleur, Sr., as follows:

Name	Date of Birth
Sam Bellfleur, Jr.	December 23, 1996
Sarah Bellfleur	November 18, 2001

All references in this will to my "child," "children," or "issue," refer to the above children and any children later born to or adopted by me.

2.3. **Deceased Children**. I have no deceased children.

ARTICLE THREE - SPECIFIC GIFTS

3.1. **Specific Gifts**. I give the following items of property as indicated below:

(a) I give to my daughter, Sarah Bellfleur, all of my jewelry if she survives me. If she does not survive me, I leave my jewelry to my female grandchildren, to be distributed among them as they shall agree (or if they cannot agree, as my executor determines). If my daughter is not alive and I have no female grandchildren, then this gift shall lapse and become part of the residue of my estate.

[Aside from being sexist, this provision works to get some specific property to your daughter. When leaving property to anyone, you need to think about what you want to happen to the property if your chosen beneficiary passes away before you do. This provision addresses the issue by leaving the jewelry to an entirely new group of people (as opposed to "Sarah's children") since the female grandchildren may be either Sarah's daughters or Sam's daughters.]

(b) I give to my son, Sam Bellfleur, my 2003 Mustang convertible, if he survives me. If he does not survive me, then this gift shall lapse and become part of the residue of my estate.

[This provision may or may not work, depending on what is your real intent. If you are leaving Sam the Mustang convertible because he always loved that car, then the provision works well. However, if you are leaving the car to Sam to offset leaving the jewelry to his sister, this provision will not work if you have replaced the Mustang before you die. Even if you now own a Porsche convertible, that won't benefit Sam because this provision is very specific: Sam gets the Mustang convertible. If you no longer own the Mustang, Sam does not receive anything under this provision (and the Porsche will go wherever you have left assets not specifically assigned to a named individual, sometimes referred to as the "residue of your estate").]

(c) I give to my friend, Erica D. Grate, $50,000, if she survives me. If she does not survive me, this gift shall lapse and become part of the residue of my estate.

[Be very careful when leaving cash bequests since the rule of law is that "specific" bequests will be paid first. This means if your estate has gone down drastically in value, either due to bad investments or to huge medical bills, Erica will still get the full $50,000 and your residuary beneficiaries may get less than you intended. For example, if you were worth $1 million when you wrote your will, it made sense to leave your friend, Erica, $50,000 since your spouse and children will still receive $950,000. If your medical bills for the last year of your life are $800,000, then leaving $50,000 to Erica and $150,000 split between your spouse and children probably doesn't make sense. When I draft documents leaving cash bequests, I usually use language like: "I leave Erica the lesser of $50,000 or 5 percent of the then-value of my estate." That way, if the estate is only worth $200,000 when you die, Erica will get $10,000 and your spouse and children will share $190,000.]

ARTICLE FOUR - RESIDUARY PROVISIONS

4.1. **Disposition of Residue**. I leave the residue of my estate as follows: (1) two-thirds (2/3) to my husband, if he survives me, and (2) one-third (1/3) to my children, in equal shares. If my husband does not survive me, his share should become part of the share for my children. If either child of mine does not survive me, that child's share should go to that child's issue, in equal shares. If a child of mine does not survive me and does not have any living issue at the time of my death, then that child's share should go to my other child (or, if that child is also not living, then to that child's issue). If neither child survives me, and neither child has issue living at the time of my death, then my children's share should go to my spouse.

[This provision does some things well and other things not so well. Note the detailed provisions for handling property if one or more of your beneficiaries die before you. Thinking those distribution provisions through carefully is good. On the other hand, if you have any ownership interest in the house that you and your spouse have been living in, this provision may not be good since it does nothing to make sure your spouse can continue living in the house. You need to consider whether you own any assets that should be solely in one person's control before including language that divides your assets between two or more individuals.]

ARTICLE FIVE - EXECUTOR

5.1. **Executor**. I nominate my husband as executor of this will.

5.2. **Successor Executors**. If my husband is unable (for any reason) or unwilling to serve as executor, I appoint the following as successor executor, in the order indicated,:

First, my friend, Erica D. Grate;

Second, National Trust Company.

[Selection of an executor is important. This person will be responsible for collecting all of your assets and seeing that they are distributed as you have directed in your will. During the probate process, it may be necessary for your executor to make decisions regarding investment of the assets during the year or two that probate is ongoing, to decide whether or not to challenge any claims made by people claiming to be owed money by you, or to mediate disagreements among your beneficiaries. Make sure the person you select for this job is someone who is completely trustworthy, has the common sense to make the necessary decisions (and will know when to seek the help of professional advisors), and is able and willing to deal with any stress that may arise from disputes among your beneficiaries. If you cannot think of someone who has all the characteristics needed, then consider designating a bank or trust company to serve as executor. It will cost money, but the job will be done properly.]

5.4. **Bond**. No bond or undertaking shall be required of any executor nominated in this will.

[A bond is an insurance policy that will reimburse your estate for any missing assets if your executor acts improperly. The premium for the bond, if you require one, will be paid from the assets in your estate (and reduce the amount going to your beneficiaries). Bond is not required for a bank or trust company, but should be considered if you are appointing an individual. As a general rule, do not appoint someone—friend or relative—unless you have known them a long time and observed them in a variety of situations, so that you are sure they have the integrity needed for the job. If you have any doubts regarding their integrity, I recommend that you cross them off the list rather than require a bond.]

5.5. **Independent Administration**. The executor shall have full authority to administer my estate under the California Independent Administration of Estates Act.

["Independent" or "unsupervised" administration of your estate is a simplified process that allows your executor to take most actions necessary to collect your assets, sell assets that need to be sold, and prepare to distribute your assets, with minimal court supervision. If you do not expressly permit independent administration of your estate, a good number of the actions your executor will need to take can only be accomplished after scheduling a hearing and getting express approval from the judge (unless your beneficiaries unanimously agree to waive this requirement). This can delay distribution of assets to your beneficiaries and can result in increased costs of administration. You should consider permitting independent administration unless you anticipate disagreements between your beneficiaries (in which case, the additional court supervision may help keep the disputes under control).]

5.6. **Powers of Executor**. Subject to any limitations stated elsewhere in this will, the executor shall have, in addition to all of the powers now or hereafter conferred on executors by law, and any powers enumerated elsewhere in this will, the power to perform any of the acts specified in this section:

[An exhaustive list of powers should be included here, so that your executor will be equipped to deal with everything that comes up in your probate.]

5.7. **Incapacitated Persons**. If any beneficiary is a minor, or it appears to the executor that any beneficiary is incapacitated, incompetent, or for any reason not able to receive payments or make intelligent or responsible use of the payments, then the executor may make payments to the beneficiary's conservator or guardian; to the beneficiary's custodian under the Uniform Gifts to Minors Act or Uniform Transfers to Minors Act of any state (including a custodian selected by the executor); to one or more suitable persons deemed proper by the executor (such as a relative of the beneficiary), to be used for the benefit of the beneficiary; to anyone providing services for the beneficiary's benefit; or to accounts in the beneficiary's name with financial institutions. The receipt of payments by any of the above shall satisfy the executor's obligation to distribute assets to that beneficiary.

[Make sure that a provision like this is in your will so your executor will not be faced with the expensive proposition of bringing a court proceeding to appoint a conservator if one of your beneficiaries is under 18 or is physically or mentally incapacitated at the time the assets are to be distributed.]

ARTICLE SIX - CONCLUDING PROVISIONS

6.1. Simultaneous Death. If any beneficiary under this will and I die simultaneously, or if it cannot be established by clear and convincing evidence whether that beneficiary or I died first, I shall be deemed to have survived that beneficiary, and this will shall be construed accordingly.

6.2. Period of Survivorship. For the purposes of this will, a beneficiary shall not be deemed to have survived me if that beneficiary dies within thirty (30) days after my death.

6.3. No Contest Clause. If any person (including any entity or charity), directly or indirectly, contests the validity of this will, or any codicil to this will, in whole or in part, or opposes, objects to, or seeks to invalidate any of its provisions, or seeks to succeed to any part of my estate otherwise than in the manner specified in this will, any gift or other interest given to that person under this will shall be revoked and shall be disposed of as if he or she had predeceased me without issue.

[This can be a very important part of your will. Will contests can tie up your estate for several years, and can easily cost hundreds of thousands of dollars in legal fees. A "no-contest" provision disinherits any beneficiary who challenges your will. However, if you have intentionally left nothing to one of your children, the no-contest clause has no affect since that child has nothing to lose. Unless you are so upset with that child (or spouse) that you cannot bring yourself to leave him or her anything, it is usually better to leave enough to the disfavored child so that there is something to lose by contesting the will. Also, note the last two words of the no-contest clause; "without issue." These words are important. Without them, if a child of yours successfully contests the will, the no-contest clause would prevent the child from receiving any portion of your estate, but that child's share could go to his or her children. Often, this is an acceptable outcome for your child and he or she will not be deterred from bringing the legal challenge. By adding the words "without issue," you are disinheriting any child who challenges your will and also disinheriting that child's children and grandchildren. The result is that the child cannot benefit, even indirectly, from challenging the will.]

6.4. Definition of Incapacity. For purposes of this will, a person shall be deemed "incapacitated" if and for so long as a court of competent jurisdiction has made a finding to that effect, or a guardian or conservator of that person's estate or person duly appointed by a court of competent jurisdiction is serving, or upon certification by two physicians licensed to practice under the laws of the state where the person is domiciled at the time of the certification, that the person is unable properly to care for himself or herself or for his or her property. The latter certification shall be made by each physician in a written declaration under penalty of perjury.

Executed on _____, 20_____, at _____, California.

_____

Bonita K. Tovah

[Witness Page]

On the date written above, we, the undersigned, each being present at the same time, witnessed the signing of this instrument by Bonita K. Tovah. At that time, Bonita K. Tovah appeared to us to be of sound mind and memory and, to the best of our knowledge, was not acting under fraud, duress, menace, or undue influence. Understanding this instrument, which consists of _____ pages including the pages on which the signature of Bonita K. Tovah and our signatures appear, to be the will of Bonita K. Tovah, we subscribe our names as witnesses thereto.

We declare under penalty of perjury under the laws of the State of California that the foregoing is true and correct.

Executed on _____, 20_____, at _____, California.

_____   residing at   _____
Signature   Street Address

_____   _____, California
Print Name   City

_____   residing at   _____
Signature   Street Address

_____   _____, California
Print Name   City

[This witness page is critical. Without two witnesses—three in some states—your will is not valid. The witnesses should be at least 18 years old, legally competent, and not receiving assets under the will. A neighbor, co-worker, or friend, can be an excellent witness. If you prepare your own will without the help of any estate planning attorney, make sure you comply with all the formalities required in your state. Do not, do not, DO NOT use this form as it is incomplete and may not meet the formalities required in your state. This form is only useful in illustrating the issues that you need to consider in designing your estate plan.]

Family Trusts

When you desire greater control over distribution of the assets from your estate—whether to manage assets for your children until they reach a level of financial maturity, to distribute assets in several steps to allow your children time to learn how to handle money before they receive all of your assets, or because one or more of your beneficiaries has special needs requiring greater control of his or her assets—a family trust is more likely to fit your estate planning goals than is a simple will. Your friends may have mentioned their "living trust," "revocable trust," or "A-B trust." These are just different names for a family trust.

A family trust can be used by you to manage the distribution of your assets whether you are married or single. However, if you are married, it can also be used to reduce estate taxes.

A family trust is commonly used when there is concern that distribution of your entire estate in a single lump sum will be difficult for your beneficiaries to handle, either because they are young and don't have much financial experience or because the amount of money is frighteningly large compared to the amount of money your beneficiaries are used to dealing with. In addition, if your children are young at the time of your death, the trust can keep the assets in a single, common fund to be used to finish raising the children just as you would do if you were still alive (as opposed to dividing the money into equal shares for the children and having each child pay the remaining cost of being raised—and put through college—from his or her own share). Finally, if your estate is large enough to be subject to estate taxes, the family trust is the simplest way to reduce or eliminate taxes.

Most often, a family trust will manage assets for the benefit of your children, or other beneficiaries, for a period of time (and provide them with sufficient income to maintain the lifestyle that you established for them), and then gradually transfer your assets to your children in several steps (so that they can make financial mistakes with a small portion of their inheritance and learn to avoid those mistakes before they receive the bulk of the assets). A simplified example of common distribution provisions of a family trust is set forth in Figure 15-1.

Just like a will, your trust should expressly identify any close relative, such as your spouse or a child, to whom you have intentionally decided to leave nothing. If you do not make clear your desire to omit a close relative, most states assume that the omission was an oversight and allow the omitted heir to take a portion of your estate anyway.

Important issues arising with respect to family trusts are discussed below.

Who Should Have a Family Trust?

If you have children who are not yet adults and your assets are substantial enough that you are not comfortable with your children having complete

FIGURE 15-1. **Common Trust Distribution Provisions**

- After my death, the trustee should distribute money to my children from time to time, as necessary to maintain the lifestyle each child had immediately prior to my death.

- As each child turns 27, the trustee should distribute to that child 15% of his or her share of the trust.

- As each child turns 30, the trustee should distribute to that child 30% of his or her share of the trust.

- As each child turns 33, the trustee should distribute to that child the balance of his or her share of the trust.

control of the assets on their 18th birthday, you should consider establishing a family trust. You will still need a will to nominate a guardian to finish raising your children, but the provisions governing distribution of your assets will be in your family trust rather than in your will.

If the total value of your assets is approaching the estate tax exemption amount—$2 million in 2007 and 2008, more in 2009 and 2010, and less after 2010—and you are currently married, you should look into a family trust as a means of reducing possible estate taxes.

If you have children from a prior relationship and want to keep the bulk of your assets available to your current spouse to live on, while protecting some portion of your assets for the benefit of your children, then you should consider creating a family trust.

If you do not want a list of your assets filed at the local courthouse after you pass away (because court documents are open to the public), you may elect to utilize a trust to protect your family's privacy.

> If the total value of your assets is approaching the estate tax exemption amount— $2 million in 2007 and 2008, more in 2009 and 2010, and less after 2010—and you are currently married, you should look into a family trust as a means of reducing possible estate taxes.

Good Things About a Family Trust

First and foremost, a family trust can finish raising your family—at least financially. If you live to a ripe old age, you would likely do two things to guide your children to financial maturity.

First, you would provide for their financial needs—a home to live in, food on the table, and possibly some tuition money—until they reach an age you consider appropriate for a child to declare their financial independence. For many, the age of independence is shortly after your son graduates college, for others it does not occur until your daughter graduates medical school (or earns at least some graduate degree), and for still others it happens moments after the child celebrates his or her 18th birthday. The timing of your child's financial declaration of independence is entirely up to you.

The second contribution you make toward your child's financial maturity is the advice, guidance, and a certain level of control that you provide for your child as he or she is starting out on his or her own. You watch as their income grows from "nothing" to "slightly more than nothing." You point out lessons to be learned when they make poor decisions regarding purchases or credit cards that set them back a month's wages (while quietly you are thankful that their gigantic loss is still much less than your monthly mortgage payment). With proper advice and guidance, perhaps by age 25 or 30 or 45, your child may be ready to make intelligent financial decisions on his or her own.

If you die young, who will provide this financial support and guidance? A simple will can't do it. A trust can. A trustee, who may be your children's aunt or uncle, or a close family friend, can distribute assets to your children as needed to continue providing for their day-to-day financial needs. This can continue well past their 18th birthday, until an age when you anticipate your children may have developed the necessary financial maturity to deal with the wealth that was accumulated during your lifetime. By comparison, a simple will might put the entire family fortune into the hands of your 18-year-old son. Take a moment to think about the keen financial decisions an 18-year-old boy might make. Mutual funds, real estate, and retirement accounts may not be the first things that come to your mind. I guarantee they won't be the first things that come to his mind either. I'll spare you the details, but girls, cars, drugs, etc. come to mind pretty easily. I don't know about you, but I'd be leaning pretty hard toward the concept of a trust right now.

There's another more subtle aspect of providing financially for your children that may be equally important if you have more than one child, particularly if they are more than a few years apart. Say, for example, you have two daughters, ages 20 and 15. You probably hope to get them both through college, out on their own financially, and then into solid, long-term relationships that last a lifetime (theirs, not just yours). You certainly don't plan to give them their inheritance until many years from now, and long after you've stopped spending your hard-earned money on raising them. But, sometimes life doesn't follow our plans. If an unexpected terminal illness or accident takes you out of the picture today, do you want to divide a lifetime of accumulated wealth (perhaps $1 million, $2 million, or more, counting the house, business, retirement accounts, savings, and life insurance) into two equal stacks and give one stack to each daughter? Would you tell the 20-year-old, "Here's $750,000. Use $40,000 to pay for your last year of college, then do what you wish with the remaining $710,000"? Would you be equally comfortable turning to your 15-year-old and saying, "Here's $750,000. Use $160,000 to pay for your four years of college, then do what you wish with the remaining $590,000"? If that $120,000 difference make you uncomfortable, you can set up your family trust to keep the entire $1,500,000 together to provide for both children until the "baby" is old enough to have completed college. Then, what's left can be divided equally. Your $1,500,000 will be reduced by $200,000 ($40,000 for the 20-year-old's senior year and $160,000 for the 15-year-old's college career), and the remaining $1,300,000 will then be split into two equal shares of $650,000 each.

In addition, your family trust can keep your assets out of probate, avoiding unnecessary delay and expense to the family. Probate costs vary widely from state to state, and also based upon the size of your estate. However, it is probably fair to assume the cost will be between 2 percent and 4 percent of the value of your assets. On that $1,500,000 estate, the cost would be between $30,000 and $60,000. A trust will not be entirely free of legal and accounting fees at the time of your death, but the cost is more likely to be in the ballpark of $5,000 to $15,000 in most common situations. Beyond the financial savings, avoiding probate also means keeping your family finances private. If your assets go through probate, a complete list of your accumulated assets, and their appraised value, will be filed with the court. In theory, any friend, relative, or nosy neighbor could go to the courthouse and look at the list. In most cases, nobody will go to the trouble, but if you are a particularly private person, a trust may appeal to you.

Finally, if you are married when you create a trust, it can be used to minimize (or eliminate) estate taxes. By now, you may recall that the first $2 million of your estate is exempt from estate taxes (more in 2009 and 2010, less after 2010). No doubt, you also recall that there is no estate tax between husband and wife (if the surviving spouse is a United States citizen). If you and your spouse have accumulated $4 million in assets and you die with a simple will leaving everything to your spouse, there is no estate tax on your death. However, when he or she dies a few years later and leaves everything to the kids, the first $2 million is tax free and the second $2 million will be taxed at approximately 45 percent, resulting in $900,000 of estate tax. The children will share $3,100,000, after estate taxes.

If you use a family trust, the result is drastically different. The trust creates a legal fiction that allows you to leave the kids $2 million tax free, at the same time that your spouse also leaves the kids $2 million tax free (your share—since in this example you get to die first—is held in one side of the family trust as "your money," but used to help support your spouse, and then left directly from you to the kids when your spouse dies a few years later). It's a "legal fiction" because the kids don't really inherit anything directly from you, but when your spouse subsequently dies the law treats the assets held on "your side" of the family trust as if they were inherited directly from you. The bottom-line result is your kids share $4 million (instead of $3,100,000), after taxes. By setting up the family trust, you have made a $900,000 gift to your children—a gift from their Uncle Sam.

Bad Things About a Family Trust

A family trust will cost you more to set up than a simple will, perhaps as much as $1,000 or $2,000 more. Obviously, if you can save your kids $900,000 in estate taxes that's a modest price to pay. If, however, your estate is under the

$2 million exemption amount, you need to consider more carefully whether or not the trust is worth the additional up-front cost.

If you are married when you set up your living trust, there will also be some additional costs incurred as a result of the trust after your spouse passes away. While you're both alive, the trust is essentially transparent. Any income earned in the trust is treated as belonging to you and your spouse, and you simply report it on your joint tax return just as you did before the trust. However, after your spouse dies, the same fiction that allows you to double the $2 million estate tax exemption (and save the kids $900,000 in estate taxes) will require you to file a second tax return each year (and to account for your spouse's side of the trust separately from yours). This can cost you anywhere from a few hundred dollars to several thousand dollars each year. Again, not a big expense if you are saving the kids $900,000 in estate taxes, but something to think about if you are below the $2 million estate-tax exemption amount.

Finally, having a family trust can be bad because it avoids probate. Wait! Didn't I just say a few paragraphs ago that avoiding probate was a good thing about a family trust? Yes, in most cases. But sometimes probate is a good thing. If you, or your spouse, have been engaged in a high-risk profession (from a liability point of view), such as doctor, architect, estate-planning attorney, etc., probate can greatly reduce the amount of time that former patients and clients have to file a lawsuit making a claim against you (or against the assets that the family inherits). Particularly if your profession is one where damages often don't occur for many years—architects and estate-planning attorneys are prime examples of this—the probate requirement that all claims must be filed within several months (rather than ten years or more) is a huge benefit to your family. The inheritance they receive will not be at risk due to something you did at the office ten years ago. In most states, you can achieve the same result with an optional procedure that is available to family trusts, but since it is optional many families don't think to take advantage of

> After your spouse dies, the same fiction that allows you to double the $2 million estate tax exemption (and save the kids $900,000 in estate taxes) will require you to file a second tax return each year (and to account for your spouse's side of the trust separately from yours). This can cost you anywhere from a few hundred dollars to several thousand dollars each year.

> Sometimes probate can be a good thing. If you, or your spouse, have been engaged in a high-risk profession (from a liability point of view), such as doctor, architect, estate-planning attorney, etc., probate can greatly reduce the amount of time that former patients and clients have to file a lawsuit making a claim against you.

it. If you are in a high-risk profession, think about utilizing an estate-planning technique that will require probate. You can also consider putting a clause in the family trust requiring the trustee to put your assets through the optional probate procedure to cut off liability.

An Over-Simplified Sample

Figure 15-2 is an over-simplified example of a family trust, with comments (*in italics*) to highlight the issues you should think about when working on your family trust. The language of many of the provisions has been simplified to clarify the purpose of the paragraph, and many technical provisions that are necessary to make the document work may be missing (if I did not think they were necessary to illustrate a point). Finally, the document is based upon the requirements of California law and may not comply with the technical requirements of your home state.

In short, use Figure 15-2 to help you understand concepts and to think through issues. Do not use this document as a "form" to prepare your trust, as it will not work.

FIGURE 15-2. **Sample Family Trust**

SANSEI-TOVAH FAMILY TRUST

ARTICLE ONE - CREATION OF TRUST

1.1. Declaration. Bill Tovah and Bonita Tovah, residents of Orange County, California ("settlors" or "trustees," depending on the context), hold property in trust, to be held, administered, and distributed according to the rules of this trust.

1.2. Name of Trusts. This trust shall be known as the SANSEI-TOVAH FAMILY TRUST.

[You can name your family trust anything you want. It doesn't even need to have your name in it. You can call it the "Flying Monkey Trust" if you want. Two things to keep in mind: (1) make the name unique, and (2) keep it short. After all, short names are easier to print on checks or put on the deed to your house. I have seen documents prepared by other attorneys who would name this trust the "Mr. Bill Tovah and Mrs. Bonita Tovah Revocable Family Trust of 2007." That's certainly unique. It's definitely not short. I prefer to combine the wife's maiden name with the family name. It's unique and it's short. I've never seen another attorney use this method of naming a trust, but it's possible some do.]

1.3. Definitions of Child, Children, and Issue. As used in this instrument, the terms "child" and "children" refer to both children by birth and children I have adopted, whether before or after the date of this trust, and the term "issue" refers to all children, grandchildren, and great-grandchildren, and other lineal descendants.

[This definition of child/children will apply to your children and to your children's children. If you have adopted a child, you are making a conscious decision to treat them as your own. If you only have children by birth, you may or may not be comfortable automatically including any child that your son or daughter adopts. Think this through and use a definition that you are comfortable with.]

ARTICLE TWO - TRUST ESTATE

2.1. Trust Estate. Any property put into this trust at any time shall be referred to as the "trust estate" and shall be held, administered, and distributed as provided in this instrument.

2.2. Character of Trust Assets. All community property and its proceeds shall continue to be community property under the laws of California. All separate and quasi-community property shall remain the separate or quasi-community property, respectively, of the contributing settlor.

ARTICLE THREE - RIGHTS AND POWERS OF SETTLORS

3.1. Amendment: Both Settlors Living. While both settlors are alive, this trust may be revoked or terminated by both settlors, and may be modified or amended by both settlors, acting jointly.

[You are free to change the trust in any way, even terminate it completely, so long as you and your spouse are alive and mentally competent.]

3.2. **Amendment: After Death of One Settlor.** After the death of one settlor, the surviving settlor may amend, revoke, or terminate the Survivor's Trust. All other trusts shall become irrevocable and shall not be subject to amendment.

[When your spouse dies, the rules applicable to his or her half of the trust become etched in stone. There may be some flexibility built into the rules, but the rules can't change. Make sure you understand the rules and are comfortable that you can live with them after your spouse dies.]

3.3. **Power to Direct Investments: Both Settlors Living.** While both settlors are alive, the settlors may direct trust investments, and have the power to direct the trustee to do any or all of the following:

(a) Invest trust funds in specified investments,

(b) Retain specified investments, and

(c) Sell, encumber, lease, abandon, or dispose of any asset.

3.4. **Power to Direct Investments: After Death of One Settlor.** After the death of one settlor, the surviving settlor shall have the power to direct trust investments (as defined in the previous section) of the Survivor's Trust and of the QTIP Trust, only.

ARTICLE FOUR - DISTRIBUTIONS WHILE BOTH SETTLORS LIVING

4.1. **Income: Both Settlors Living.** While both settlors are alive, the trustee shall distribute all income on the trust assets to, or for the benefit of, the settlors, in monthly or other convenient installments (but not less often than annually).

[While you and your spouse are both alive, all income of the trust comes out to the two of you. Of course, you can put it right back in. The simple point is, while you're both alive, the trust is essentially transparent. It's your money.]

4.2. **Principal: Both Settlors Living.** While both settlors are alive, the trustee shall distribute to, or for the benefit of, the settlors as much of the principal of the trust as the trustee deems necessary to provide for the settlor's comfort, welfare, and happiness.

[It's still your money. I just want to point out the phrase "comfort, welfare, and happiness." That's legalese for "whatever makes you and your spouse happy." Or, in other words, "It's still your money."]

4.3. **Principal: Request of Settlors.** While both settlors are alive, the settlors may withdraw as much of the principal of the trust as they wish.

[If that thing about "happiness" in Section 4.2 wasn't clear enough, this is here to remind you; it's still your money.]

4.4. **Incapacitated Settlor.** If either settlor is personally unable to request a withdrawal of principal due to lack of capacity, that settlor's attorney in fact may make the request pursuant to a durable power of attorney. If a settlor has not appointed an attorney in fact, then the trustee may voluntarily distribute principal to, or for the benefit of, that settlor, up to the amount that settlor could have requested if he or she were competent.

[This section is more important than it looks. A durable power of attorney appoints someone to manage your assets in the event that you become physically or mentally unable to do so for yourself (see Chapter 23 for a full discussion of durable powers of attorney). If you and your spouse have appointed each other, this section is probably no big deal. If your spouse has appointed his daughter from his first marriage, do you want her to be able to force you to spend money on a five-star care facility for your husband if you have a three-star budget? Discuss the impact of this section with your estate planning advisor.]

ARTICLE FIVE - ALLOCATION AFTER FIRST DEATH

5.1. **Death Taxes, Debts, and Expenses.** After the first death, the trustee shall pay the death taxes, debts, and expenses of the settlor's estate, as requested by the executor or other personal representative of the estate.

[This simply assures that your personal debts and burial expenses will be paid, as well as any estate taxes if your estate is large enough to incur any.]

5.2. **Division of Trust Estate After First Death.** When the first settlor dies, the trustee shall divide the trust estate, including amounts added by reason of the settlor's death (such as from the settlor's estate or life insurance) into three shares, as set forth below.

(a) The first share, referred to as the Survivor's Share, shall include the surviving settlor's one half (1/2) interest in the settlors' community property, plus all of the surviving settlor's separate property. The Survivor's Share shall be held, administered, and distributed according to the terms of the Survivor's Trust.

[This is your half of the money. After your spouse passes away, you are free to do whatever you want with your half.]

(b) The second share, referred to as the Spousal Deduction Share, shall include assets equal in value to the amount necessary, if any, to reduce the Exemption Amount Share enough to eliminate (or reduce as much as possible) federal estate tax arising from the first death. The Spousal Deduction Share shall be held, administered, and distributed according to the terms of the Qualified Terminable Interest Property (QTIP) Trust.

[This part of the trust will only be funded after the first spouse dies, and then only if the deceased spouse's half is larger than the estate-tax exemption amount—that's right, $2 million now, then more,

then less. If you are the surviving spouse, the QTIP trust gives you all the income and allows you access to the principal if you need it, but when you die, the remaining assets will go where you and your spouse agreed. You cannot change who will receive this money. This is often used to protect your spouse's children from a prior relationship. If you are a Leave-It-To-Beaver family, rather than a Brady-Bunch family, you can use something called a "Power of Appointment" trust instead of the QTIP. You would still have access to the money to live on, and you would have the power to leave the remaining assets to whomever you choose. Discuss this provision with your estate-planning advisor and customize it to fit your family.]

(c) The third share, referred to as the Exemption Amount Share, shall include all the remaining assets of the trust. The Exemption Amount Share shall be held, administered, and distributed according to the terms of the Bypass Trust.

[This is the part that doubles the estate-tax exemption amount. You will likely have access to the income, and what's left over when you die will go as agreed upon by you and your spouse.]

5.3. **Allocation and Valuation.** Assets allocated to the Spousal Deduction Share should meet all of the requirements necessary to be exempt from estate tax on the death of the first spouse.

5.4. **Intent to Meet Marital Deduction Requirements.** The settlors intend to have the Spousal Deduction Share meet the requirements for the federal estate tax marital deduction and this trust should be construed as needed to meet that objective. No power is granted to take any action that may impair the federal estate tax marital deduction.

5.5. **Disclaimer.** If the surviving settlor disclaims any property, the disclaimed property shall be held, administered, or distributed according to the terms of the Disclaimer Trust.

[Usually, the best estate tax result is to delay all estate taxes until after the second spouse dies. Delaying the estate tax is better because it leaves the surviving spouse more money to live on (and who knows, he or she may need it all), and also better because (assuming the tax will be the same amount) a five-, ten- or twenty-year delay in paying the tax gives you the benefit of holding on to the money for free. However, in a few limited circumstances, it can be better to pay a portion of the estate tax on the first death. For example, if both spouses are in their late 90s when the first one dies, you might reasonably assume that the survivor is not likely to live more than a year or two after the first death. If the law at the time has a lower a bracket for the first million dollars (as it has in the past) then paying estate tax on the first million dollars when the first spouse dies may save a few hundred thousand dollars of estate tax. This section is simply a mechanism that makes it possible for the surviving spouse to sit down with her attorney and accountant a few months after the first death and decide what will achieve the best tax result. There is nothing to do at this point. Just remember, when your spouse dies, you need to meet with your attorney and accountant.]

ARTICLE SIX - DISTRIBUTION AFTER FIRST DEATH

6.1. **Survivor's Trust.** The assets of the Survivor's Trust shall be held, administered, and distributed, as follows:

[This is your half of the money. That's why subparagraph (a), below, gives you all the income; (b) gives you as much of the principal as you need for your happiness (see the comment at Section 4.2, above); and (c) lets you take as much as you want. It's your money.]

(a) **Income.** For the rest of the surviving settlor's life, the trustee shall distribute all of the income to, or for the benefit of, the surviving settlor, in monthly or quarterly installments.

(b) **Principal.** For the rest of the settlor's life, the trustee shall distribute principal to, or apply for the benefit of, the surviving settlor, in an amount necessary to provide for the surviving settlor's comfort, welfare, and happiness. In determining the amount necessary, the trustee should consider all other income and resources then available to the surviving settlor to provide for these purposes. The trustee's decision regarding distribution under this subparagraph shall be within the trustee's sole discretion and shall be final and incontestable by anyone.

(c) **Withdrawal of Principal.** The trustee shall distribute to the surviving settlor as much of the trust principal as the surviving settlor requests from time to time.

(d) **General Power of Appointment.** When the surviving settlor dies, any property then in the trust shall be distributed to any people or entities selected by the surviving settlor, subject to any trust, terms, or conditions specified by the surviving settlor. The surviving settlor's right to select people or entities, or to impose any trust, terms, or conditions may only be exercised by a provision in the surviving settlor's will that expressly refers to, and expressly indicates an intention to exercise this power of appointment.

[When you die, you can leave your half of the money to anyone you want. You just have to do it the right way, using your power of appointment. This makes sense. It's your money.]

(e) **Payment of Death Taxes, Debts, and Expenses**. When the surviving settlor dies, the trustee may pay the death taxes, debts, and expenses arising on the death of the surviving settlor, subject to any power of appointment exercised by him or her.

(f) **Default to Bypass Trust.** If the surviving settlor does not exercise the power of appointment, or if an attempted exercise was ineffective, the remaining principal plus all net income in the trust, after any payment of taxes, debts, and expenses, shall be distributed as if it were part of the Bypass Trust. However, the property in the Survivor's Share shall not become part of the Bypass Trust unless both trusts have the same inclusion ratios for federal generation-skipping transfer tax purposes.

[If you don't leave your half of the money to someone else, it will automatically go where you and your (deceased) spouse agreed when you created the trust.]

6.2. **Qualified Terminable Interest Property Trust.** The assets of the Qualified Terminable Interest Property (QTIP) Trust shall be held, administered, and distributed as follows:

[This is part of your spouse's half of the money—the part left over after funding the estate-tax exemption amount (that's right, $2 million in 2007, etc.). This is set up to qualify for the spousal deduction so you won't pay a penny in estate taxes when your spouse dies, while still protecting the assets for your spouse's children from a prior relationship. That's what a QTIP trust is best suited to do. It has highly technical requirements that must be carefully met, and that's what these sections do.]

(a) **Administration of Trust by Trustee.** If the executor elects to qualify the trust for the federal estate tax marital deduction under Internal Revenue Code Section 2056(b)(7), the trustee shall administer the trust so as not to invalidate the election. Any provisions of this trust that could be deemed to invalidate the qualification under Internal Revenue Code Section 2056(b)(7) shall be disregarded.

(b) **Income.** For the rest of the surviving settlor's life, the trustee shall distribute all of the income to, or for the benefit of, the surviving settlor, in monthly or quarterly installments. For this purpose, "income" shall include all income that is required to qualify for the marital deduction under the federal estate tax law. Settlors intend that the surviving settlor shall have the degree of beneficial enjoyment of the trust that the principles of the law of trusts accord to a person who is unqualifiedly designated as the life beneficiary of a trust. The trustee shall not exercise discretion inconsistently with this expressed intention.

[You will receive all of the income generated on the assets in this part of the trust. This is required by federal tax law in order to defer the estate tax on this portion of the trust until after you die.]

(c) **Principal.** For the rest of the surviving settlor's life, the trustee shall distribute principal to, or apply for the benefit of, the surviving settlor, in an amount necessary to provide for the surviving settlor's health, education, support, or maintenance. In determining the amount necessary, the trustee should consider all other income and resources then available to the surviving settlor to provide for these purposes. The trustee's decision regarding distribution under this subparagraph shall be within the trustee's sole discretion and shall be final and incontestable by anyone.

[You can access the principal in this portion of the trust, if necessary, to maintain the lifestyle to which you are accustomed. This does not mean "poverty level." This means the income level that you are used to enjoying.]

(d) **Withdrawal of Principal.** The surviving settlor shall not have any right to withdraw principal from the Trust.

[You do not have the right to voluntarily take money out of this portion of the trust, since that violates the QTIP rules, and would trigger unnecessary estate tax when your spouse dies.]

(e) **Termination.** When the surviving settlor dies, the QTIP Trust will terminate and the remaining assets shall be distributed to the children of both settlors.

[This section can be used to distribute this portion of the trust to any person or group that you and your spouse select. Often, this paragraph is designed to protect assets for the future benefit of children from a prior relationship.]

(f) **Estate Taxes.** The trustee shall pay any estate tax allocable to the property of the trust by reason of Internal Revenue Code Section 2207A.

6.3. **Bypass Trust—After First Death.** While the surviving settlor is alive, the assets of the Bypass Trust shall be held, administered, and distributed, as follows:

[This is the first $2 million of the deceased spouse's half of the trust—more in 2009 and 2010, less after that. It's also the part that will go tax free to the children after the second spouse dies even if it has tripled in value, or more. That's why the surviving spouse shouldn't take more distributions from this part of the trust than he or she needs to maintain his or her lifestyle. This is probably a good time to point out the phrase "health, education, support, or maintenance" in section (a). That's legalese for maintaining the lifestyle that you are used to. It's got nothing to do with poverty level or objective standards. If you are used to traveling six weeks every year and staying in five-star hotels, just keep doing it. You can even go eight or nine weeks. It's not an exact standard; it's a ballpark sort of thing.]

(a) **Income.** For the rest of the surviving settlor's life, the trustee shall distribute income to, or for the benefit of, the surviving settlor, in an amount necessary to provide for the surviving settlor's health, education, support, or maintenance. In determining the amount necessary, the trustee should consider all other income and resources then available to the surviving settlor to provide for these purposes. The trustee's decision regarding distribution under this subparagraph shall be within the trustee's sole discretion and shall be final and incontestable by anyone.

[You can receive income as needed to maintain your lifestyle, but only to the extent needed to supplement other income you have available. This is because the growth that accumulates in this part of the trust will ultimately go to the next generation free of any estate tax.]

(b) **Principal.** For the rest of the settlor's life, the trustee shall distribute principal to, or for the benefit of, the surviving settlor, in an amount necessary to provide for the surviving settlor's health, education, support, or maintenance. In determining the amount necessary, the trustee should consider all other income and resources then available to the surviving settlor to provide for these purposes. The trustee's decision regarding distribution under this subparagraph shall be within the trustee's sole discretion and shall be final and incontestable by anyone.

[See the comments to subparagraph 6.3(a), above.]

(c) **Withdrawal of Principal.** At the request of the surviving settlor, the trustee shall distribute to the surviving settlor additional amounts from the trust principal, up to the greater of $5,000 or 5 percent of the value of the principal of the trust, determined as of the end of the calendar year. This right of withdrawal expires each year and is not cumulative. If the surviving settlor withdraws less than the full amount allowed in any calendar year, the right to withdraw any remaining amount shall lapse at the end of the calendar year.

[To give the surviving spouse a little flexibility and a financial cushion, the right to withdraw up to 5 percent of the assets held in this part of the trust is included. This can be exercised once a year, but if you don't withdraw money this year, you can't take 10 percent next year. Remember, you shouldn't use this right to withdraw money without careful thought, as it will make the money you withdraw subject to estate tax on your death, when it would be free of estate taxes if it had been left in this portion of the trust. By the way, the 5 percent limit isn't arbitrary. If the trust allowed you to withdraw more than 5 percent of this trust and you didn't, at the end of the year you might owe a gift tax because you left money in the trust that may theoretically go to someone other than you. You don't need to become an expert on this rule; I just highlight it as an example of the kind of complex and unexpected rules that are out there. Did I mention that you should work with an experienced estate-planning professional?]

(d) **Death of Surviving Settlor.** When the surviving settlor dies, the remaining assets will be held, administered, and distributed, as set forth in Section 6.4.

6.4. **Bypass Trust: After Second Death.** After the surviving settlor dies, the assets of the Bypass Trust shall be held, administered, and distributed as follows:

(a) **Sprinkling Trust: Child Under Age 22.** So long as any living child of the settlors is less than 22 years old, the property shall be held, administered, and distributed pursuant to the terms applicable to the Sprinkling Trust (section 6.6).

[This is important if you want to finish raising all the children (financially speaking) before you divide what's left into equal shares. See section 6.6 for the details. The age used here is 22. That's probably based upon the assumptions that the kids will go to a four-year college and they are likely to graduate college in four years. If that's what you and your spouse both did, that may be a good bet. If all of your siblings and your spouse's siblings went straight through college, too, then it's even a better bet. If you didn't graduate college until the third time you enrolled, and were 27 when you graduated, then think about whether you want to allow a little more time for your children to find their way. If everyone in your family is a doctor or Ph.D., that's another good reason to consider raising the age. Look at the circumstances in your family and try to adjust the age accordingly.]

(b) **Individual Trusts.** If no child is less than 22 years old, the property shall be divided into the number of equal shares necessary to create one share for each living child of settlors and one share for each deceased child of settlors who has left living issue. Each share shall be placed into an individual trust for that child (or issue of a deceased child), to be held, administered, and distributed as set forth in Section 6.4.

[In this version, each of your children will receive an equal share. If one of your children has prede- ceased you, leaving surviving grandchildren, those grandchildren will share their parent's share. Of course, you can leave your assets to anyone, not just your children. Further, you can divide the assets any way you choose. It does not have to be equal shares.]

(c) **Income.** So long as the child (or issue of a deceased child) is alive, the trustee shall distribute income to, or for the benefit of, that beneficiary, in an amount necessary to provide for his or her health, education, support, or maintenance. In determining the amount necessary, the trustee should consider all other income and resources then available to the beneficiary to provide for these purposes. The trustee's decision regarding distribution under this subparagraph shall be within the trustee's sole dis- cretion and shall be final and incontestable by anyone.

[This is the part that allows the trustee to distribute money to your children, or other beneficiaries, to maintain the lifestyle they are used to, either because you provided it for them or because they've been earning it. In some circumstances, you may elect to put restrictions on this. Some parents allow the trustee to stop distributions if a child displays an alcohol or drug problem. Others limit distribution to an amount equal to the child's earnings (unless the child is in school, disabled, or raising children). Whatever seems right to you is appropriate, but be careful when "controlling from the grave." Rules that seem appropriate in the abstract may be difficult to implement in the real world.]

(d) **Principal.** So long as the child (or issue of a deceased child) is alive, the trustee shall distribute principal to, or for the benefit of, that beneficiary, in an amount necessary to provide for his or her health, education, support, or maintenance. In determining the amount necessary, the trustee should consider all other income and resources then available to the beneficiary to provide for these purposes. The trustee's decision regarding distribution under this subparagraph shall be within the trustee's sole discretion and shall be final and incontestable by anyone.

[See comments to subparagraph 6.4(c), above.]

(e) **Early Distribution.** The trustee may give any child (or issue of a deceased child) a portion of the principal in his or her individual trust early, if the trustee determines there is a valid reason to do so. However, such early distributions (taken in the aggregate) shall not exceed 30 percent of the assets in the trust. No Distribution Beneficiary who is a trustee shall have the power to make early distributions of principal to him or herself pursuant to this subsection.

[This provision is certainly optional. By including it, you allow the trustee to make early distributions to a child for any purpose that the trustee considers worthwhile. In essence, you are appointing the trustee as surrogate parent to decide what is right for your child. The purpose here is usually to help a child buy a first house, start a business, etc. If you are more comfortable, you can spell out the specific purposes

that are acceptable to you. I prefer to give the trustee discretion and then pick the trustee very carefully, since it is difficult to predict what will be best for your children after you are gone.]

(f) **Lump Sum Distributions.** The principal of each individual trust will be distributed in lump sums, as follows:

[This is where you have to decide when to let your child have control over the assets. Sometimes the answer is "never." In that case, this provision would keep the assets in trust until the child dies, and then leave the assets directly to your grandchildren. That probably makes sense if there is substance abuse involved, or even just terrible spending habits. It's entirely up to you. If you decide that your child can handle the money, you have to decide when and how much. I follow two guiding principals: (1) a large percentage of people will blow through their first inheritance before they realize it, and (2) most children start to learn financial responsibility no earlier than about three years after they get out of school (and start working full time). To keep your child from blowing through all of his or her first inheritance (because most of us won't get a second inheritance), I suggest a three-step distribution (sections (i), (ii) and (iii), below). That allows your child two opportunities to learn how to handle an inheritance without losing everything. If they don't learn financial responsibility the first two times, then "good luck," because when you get the third inheritance it's "three strikes and you're out." If the three-step distribution makes sense to you, then you have to decide the ages of distribution and the percentages at each age. I try to pick an age about three years after the client expects the children to finish their education (whether that means high school, college, or graduate school). Then, I try to pick percentages that will make the first distribution likely to be at least $100,000 (more in larger estates), the second distribution about twice as much as the first, and still leaves more than half for the third distribution. You'll want to work with your estate-planning professional to work this out for your family.]

(i) Assets having a value equal to 10 percent of the then fair market value of the trust assets will be distributed outright to the beneficiary of that individual trust on the later of (1) the beneficiary turning age twenty-eight (28), or (2) six months after the death of the surviving settlor;

(ii) Assets having a value equal to 20 percent of the then fair market value of the trust assets will be distributed outright to the beneficiary of that individual trust on the later of (1) the beneficiary turning age thirty-two (32), or (2) two and one-half ($2^1/_2$) years after the death of the surviving settlor; and

(iii) The balance of the assets will be distributed outright to the beneficiary of that individual trust on the later of (1) the beneficiary turning age thirty-five (35), or (2) four and one-half ($4^1/_2$) years after the death of the surviving settlor.

(g) **Distribution If No Child Living.** If no child of the settlors is alive when the surviving settlor dies, but issue of the settlors are alive, the trust assets shall be distributed outright to those issue, by right of representation.

(h) **Distribution If No Issue Living.** If no issue of the settlors is alive when the surviving settlor dies, the trust assets shall be distributed one half ($^1/_2$) to the heirs of each settlor.

6.5. **Disclaimer Trust.** The assets of the Disclaimer Trust shall be held, administered, and distributed as follows:

[This portion of the trust is designed to minimize estate taxes if the health or age of the surviving settlor is such that he or she is expected to live only a year or two after the death of the first spouse. Meet with your estate planning attorney or accountant shortly after your spouse passes away to determine whether or not to take steps to fund this portion of the trust.]

(a) **Income.** For the rest of the surviving settlor's life, the trustee shall distribute all of the income to, or for the benefit of, the surviving settlor, in monthly or quarterly installments.

(b) **Principal.** For the rest of the settlor's life, the trustee shall distribute principal to, or apply for the benefit of, the surviving settlor, in an amount necessary to provide for the surviving settlor's health, education, support, or maintenance. In determining the amount necessary, the trustee should consider all other income and resources then available to the surviving settlor to provide for these purposes. The trustee's decision regarding distribution under this subparagraph shall be within the trustee's sole discretion and shall be final and incontestable by anyone.

(c) **Default to Bypass Trust.** The remaining principal plus all net income in the trust, after any payment of taxes, debts, and expenses, shall be distributed as if it were part of the Bypass Trust. However, the property in the Disclaimer Trust shall not become part of the Bypass Trust unless both trusts have the same inclusion ratios for federal generation-skipping transfer tax purposes.

6.6. **Sprinkling Trust.** The assets of the Sprinkling Trust shall be held, administered, and distributed as follows:

(a) **Discretionary Payments.** Before the Sprinkling Trust is divided into shares, the trustee shall distribute to, or apply for the benefit of, any child of settlors (or any issue of a deceased child of settlors) as much of the income or principal of the trust as the trustee deems proper to provide for that beneficiary's health, education, support, or maintenance. The trustee may distribute more income or principal to (or for the benefit of) one or more beneficiaries (and less to others). No beneficiary will be required to repay any portion of any distribution made pursuant to this subparagraph. The trustee shall consider all other income and resources that are available to each beneficiary. All decisions of the trustee regarding distributions shall be final and incontestable by anyone. Any income not distributed shall be added to principal.

[This allows you to pay all the financial costs of raising the children from a common family pot of money, before dividing what's left into equal shares for each child. You may choose to do this if the age difference between your youngest and oldest child is more than a few years, to avoid the younger

child receiving a smaller share of your estate (after paying for all the expenses of growing up, including college tuition).]

(b) **Early Distribution.** The trustee may give any child (or issue of a deceased child) a portion of the principal in the trust early, if the trustee determines there is a valid reason to do so, and it appears to the trustee that the assets remaining in the trust will be sufficient to provide for the health, education, support, and maintenance of all of the beneficiaries. Such early distributions (taken in the aggregate) shall not exceed 30 percent of the value of the assets that would be in that beneficiary's individual trust if the assets were divided pursuant to subparagraph 6.6(c) at the time of the distribution. No Distribution Beneficiary who is a trustee shall have the power to make early distributions of principal to him or herself pursuant to this subsection.

(c) **Division of Trust: No Child Under Age 22.** When no then-living child of settlors is less than 22 years old, the property shall be divided into the number of equal shares necessary to create one share for each living child of settlors and one share for each deceased child of settlors who has left living issue. Each share shall be placed into an individual trust for that child (or issue of a deceased child), to be held, administered, and distributed as set forth in Section 6.4.

6.7. **Spendthrift Clause.** No beneficiary can sell his or her interest in this trust, nor assign it to his or her creditors, nor borrow against future distributions from this trust. If a beneficiary attempts to sell, assign, or borrow against, his or her interest in the trust, or a creditor of the beneficiary attempts to attach his or her interest in the trust, the trustee may suspend distributions to that beneficiary. If distributions to a beneficiary are suspended, the trustee may still make distributions directly to third parties for the beneficiary's education or support.

6.8. **Generation-Skipping Trusts.**

[Detailed provisions relating to Generation-Skipping Trusts need to be in the trust if the Generation Skipping Tax could be triggered, intentionally or otherwise. They are omitted here since they are both voluminous and highly technical. Seek the advice of an experienced estate planning attorney if you are leaving assets to anyone besides your spouse and children.]

ARTICLE SEVEN - TRUSTEE

7.1. **Settlors' Power re: Successor Trustees.** So long as both settlors are alive, the settlors, acting jointly, may select a person or entity to serve as a successor trustee or cotrustee. If either settlor is legally incapacitated, the other settlor may exercise this power alone.

7.2. **Surviving Settlor as Sole Trustee.** If a settlor dies or becomes incapacitated, the other settlor shall become the sole trustee, unless a cotrustee has been designated pursuant to paragraph 7.1.

7.3. **Successor Trustees.** If neither settlor is able to serve as trustee, the following shall serve as successor trustee, in the order named:

[Selecting a trustee is important. Select the wrong trustee and this will all be a very unpleasant experience for your family. Take a look at Chapter 24 regarding selecting trustees.]

(a) First, _____, who resides at _____, _____, _____;

(b) Second, _____, who resides at _____, _____, _____;
and

(c) Third, _____, who resides at _____, _____, _____.

7.4. **Surviving Settlor's Appointment of Successor Trustee.** The surviving settlor may appoint any persons or entities to serve as trustee, either before or after the successor trustees named in paragraph 7.3.

7.5. **Removal of Trustee.** The settlors can, at any time and for any reason, or for no reason, with or without cause, remove any trustee.

7.6. **Waiver of Bond.** No bond or undertaking shall be required of any individual who serves as a trustee under this instrument.

[A bond is an insurance policy that can replace money for your family if the trustee improperly handles, or simply steals, assets. The insurance premium will be paid by the trust (and reduce the money for your family). The key here is to select a trustee that you trust, trust, trust. You then have to decide whether or not you need to incur the expense of a bond.]

7.7. **Compensation of Individual Trustees.** Any individual serving as trustee shall be entitled to reasonable compensation for services rendered, without court order.

[Most family members or friends that serve as trustee will do so at no charge; at least at first. If things go smoothly, they are likely to continue serving for free. If your family is fighting, or otherwise making things difficult, serving for free will be less attractive. If you do not permit a reasonable fee, your relative or friend will need to keep serving for free or resign. If you don't want your trustee resigning when things get a little heated, then include a provision allowing reasonable compensation.]

7.8. **Trustee's Powers.** The trustee shall have all the powers necessary to carry out the purposes of this trust, including but not limited to those set forth below.

[A broad list of possible trustee powers should be set forth in the trust. A few of the potential powers are set forth, and commented upon, below.]

(a) **Hire Agents.** The trustee may employ or terminate agents, such as attorneys, accountants, investment advisers, custodians of assets, property managers, real estate agents and brokers, appraisers, and others, to advise and assist the trustee, and may compensate them from the trust property.

[Of course, the trustee can hire agents. But what if your trustee is also an attorney or accountant who has expertise in estate planning? Consider expressly permitting the trustee to hire members of his or her firm. If you don't expressly permit it, it may be a prohibited conflict of interest.]

(b) **Retain Property.** The trustee may retain property that is already in the trust, whether or not income producing, if the trustee believes it to be in the best interests of the trust or in furtherance of the settlor's goals, subject to the standards of the prudent investor rule.

[If you own property that should stay in the family, but is not income producing—for example, the cabin on the lake that your grandfather built—make sure the trust has a provision allowing the trustee to retain that specific property (or non-income-producing property, generally). Otherwise, your trustee will be obligated to sell the non-income-producing property so that your family can earn a fair return on the trust assets.]

(c) **Self-Dealing.** The trustee, acting individually or for any entity or another trust, may do any of the following: purchase property from, or sell property to, the trust at fair market value; exchange property for trust property of equal value; lease property from, or to, the trust at fair rental value; borrow funds from, or lend funds to, the trust at prevailing interest rates; and receive a reasonable salary from any business owned by the trust (in whole or in part).

[Assuming you have chosen a trustee that you trust, trust, trust, you may wish to allow the trustee to enter into deals with the trust. Sometimes he or she will give the trust a better deal than a third party will. Decide if you want your trustee to have this power.]

(d) **Retain Family Residence.** The trustee may retain any interest in the settlors' principal residence ("the family residence"), subject to the following terms and conditions:

[This is the same issue as raised in section (b), above (with respect to the family cabin). However, with respect to the family residence, you'll also need to deal with who can live in it and what portion of the mortgage, upkeep, etc. will be paid by the trust.]

(i) The surviving settlor may occupy the family residence (or any substitute residence) free of any rent.

(ii) The trustee shall pay the mortgage payments, property taxes, insurance, maintenance, and ordinary repairs on the family residence (or any substitute residence) in proportion to the trust's proportionate interest in the family residence.

(iii) The surviving settlor may direct the trustee to sell the family residence. In the event the family residence is sold, the surviving settlor may direct the trustee to use the proceeds of the sale to purchase a substitute residence selected by the surviving settlor.

ARTICLE EIGHT - CONCLUDING PROVISIONS

8.1. **Perpetuities Savings Clause.** This trust must terminate no later than twenty-one (21) years after the death of the last to die of the settlors or their issue who were alive at the creation of the trust.

8.2. **Simultaneous Death.** If both settlors die simultaneously, or in a way that the order of their deaths cannot be established, each settlor shall be deemed to have survived the other. If any beneficiary and either settlor die in a way that the order of their deaths cannot be established, settlor shall be deemed to have survived the beneficiary.

8.3. **Survivorship Requirement.** A beneficiary shall be treated as not surviving a settlor if that beneficiary dies within three (3) months after the settlor's death.

8.4. **No Contest Clause.** If any beneficiary, alone or acting with others, directly or indirectly contests this instrument, any amendment to this instrument, or the wills of the settlors, in whole or in part, or opposes, objects to, or seeks to invalidate any of the provisions of this trust (or amendments), or the wills (or codicils) of the settlors, or seeks to take any part of the estate of the settlors other than as specified in this trust (or amendments), or in the wills (or codicils) of the settlors, then the right of that person to take any interest given to him or her by this trust or any amendment to this trust shall be void, and any gift or other interest in the trust property to which the beneficiary would otherwise have been entitled shall pass as if he or she had predeceased the settlors without issue.

[This is big. Make sure you have a strong no-contest clause (unless you are okay with your family members fighting it out in court). Also, you should leave enough to everyone, even those to whom you would rather leave nothing, so that everyone has something to lose if they challenge your wishes. If you leave absolutely nothing to one of your children, that child's attitude may be "Why not challenge it in court, after all, is there is anything to lose?"]

8.5. **Definition of Education.** "Education" shall mean the following:

[If you have a broad view of what is education (that you are willing to pay for) then make sure your definition is included here. If traveling to remote parts of Africa is an educational experience that you are willing to pay for, then include that here.]

(a) Formal education at public or private elementary, junior high, middle, or high schools, including boarding schools;

(b) Formal undergraduate, graduate, and postgraduate study in any field, whether or not of a professional character, in accredited colleges, universities, or other institutions of higher learning;

(c) Formal or informal training in music, theater, handicrafts, or the arts, including by individual private instruction; and

(d) Formal or informal vocational or technical training, whether through programs or institutions devoted solely to vocational or technical training, or otherwise.

ARTICLE NINE - SIGNATURE AND EXECUTION

9.1. **Execution.** We certify that we have read this trust document and that it correctly sets forth the terms and conditions under which the trust estate is to be held, administered, and distributed. As trustees of the trust, we approve this declaration of trust, and agree to be bound by its terms and conditions. As settlors of the trust, we approve this declaration of trust in all particulars, and agree to be bound by its terms and conditions.

Executed on _____, 20_____, at _____, California.

SETTLORS

_____

Bill Tovah

_____

Bonita Tovah

TRUSTEES

_____

Bill Tovah

_____

Bonita Tovah

Life Insurance Trust

A simple will or a family trust can dispose of all of your assets. As long as you have one or the other, all of your wishes can be carried out. Why then should you consider any of the other estate planning tools discussed in this book? I can think of a few reasons:

- If your estate is large enough to be subject to estate taxes (you remember, $2 million now, more in 2009, less after 2010), and you would like to reduce or eliminate the tax, you should consider tax saving techniques such as a life insurance trusts, a qualified personal residence trust, or one of the various charitable trusts.

- If one or more of your beneficiaries has a mental or physical disability, or susceptibility to drug or alcohol abuse, you may need to implement a "special needs" trust to gradually disburse funds in a carefully designed fashion that will not cause loss of government benefits that are essential to providing properly for your loved one.
- If you own a business—either outright or as one of several partners—you need to explore methods of smoothly transitioning ownership and preserving the value of your "golden goose" so that your family is assured of a steady steam of income after you are gone. You will need to know more about family limited partnerships, use of limited liability companies, and proper use of buy-sell agreements, to protect your interests when you have a business partner.
- If you are curious about what "tricks" successful people (and sometimes, the incredibly rich) are using to maximize their incomes and provide well for their families—and hoping to steal some of the ideas to use for yourself—you may want to spend a little time reviewing the chapter on charitable remainder trusts, charitable lead trusts, and pooled charitable trusts.

In addition, you'll want to review the chapters on advance health care directives and durable powers of attorney. Most of what's in this book is of great benefit to the family you leave behind, but doesn't even become effective until you die. The chapters on advance health care directives and durable powers are for your benefit. These two documents actually take care of you during your lifetime. At least read about them.

With all of this in mind, this chapter is about life insurance trusts (reading about "trusts" wasn't boring enough, so I thought I'd throw in "life insurance" to spice it up a bit). Enjoy the read.

A life insurance trust looks a lot like a family trust but is drastically different in two significant ways. First, unlike a family trust, your life insurance trust will be irrevocable—that is, the rules that you create when you sign the trust document will be etched in stone. You may remember from the family trust, however, that the "rules" often give the trustee discretion to make decisions, such as how much money to provide your children to "maintain their lifestyle," or whether or not to distribute funds early to help a child buy his or her first house or start a business. This same flexibility in the rules can exist in your life insurance trust, but once you decide on the rules, and sign the trust document, you can't go back and change the rules.

The second, and equally significant, difference is that you cannot serve as the trustee of your life insurance trust. That is probably acceptable to you since the life insurance benefits won't be available until you're dead anyway. In any event, it's the way it has to be for tax reasons. The main purpose of a life insurance trust is to prevent the life insurance benefits from being added to your taxable estate, and avoid unnecessary estate taxes on the insurance proceeds. If you serve as the trustee of the life insurance trusts until your death, the tax law would treat the insurance proceeds as part of your taxable estate, and (assuming your estate is already large enough to incur estate taxes) your family would end up giving 45 percent of the life insurance proceeds to the government as estate taxes. That's why you'll need to let someone else serve as trustee. Most often, the trustee will either be a close friend, a distant relative, or a bank or trust company.

> The main purpose of a life insurance trust is to prevent the life insurance benefits from being added to your taxable estate, and avoid unnecessary estate taxes on the insurance proceeds.

Aside from these important differences, however, your life insurance trust will function much like your family trust. You can design the distribution provisions to provide support for your surviving spouse, and you can set the rules to liberally provide for his or her "comfort, welfare, and happiness" or the somewhat more limited "health, education, support, and maintenance" standard. In fact, you are free to fashion a specific set of rules to govern distribution to your surviving spouse. In addition, you can set forth a detailed, three-step distribution regimen for your children, just as you did in your family trust, so that the money will ultimately be distributed to them over time and free of estate tax.

Who Should Have a Life Insurance Trust?

Your family can benefit from a life insurance trust if your estate is large enough to incur estate taxes—$2 million in 2007 and 2008, $3,500,000 in 2009, or only $1 million in 2011. Of course, if you are married and have a properly structured family trust, your estate can be twice as large without incurring estate taxes. When calculating the value of your estate to decide whether or not to set up a life insurance trust, remember to include the amount of the life insurance proceeds payable under your policy.

You may find it especially beneficial to provide a significant life insurance policy held in a life insurance trust if you own a successful family business. The life insurance proceeds can be used to pay any estate taxes due on the family business without triggering any additional estate taxes on the life insurance proceeds. This will make it possible for the family to continue operating the business without having to borrow the money necessary to pay the estate tax due, or worse yet, having to sell the business to pay the estate tax.

> Using a life insurance trust life insurance proceeds can be used to pay any estate taxes due on the family business without triggering any additional estate taxes due to the receipt of the life insurance proceeds.

On the other hand, you may not desire to set up a life insurance trust if you have no children (or other close relatives other than your spouse) since there is no estate tax when you leave assets to your spouse. If your estate plan leaves a significant part of your estate to charity after your spouse passes away, there may not be significant estate tax due (since the portion left to charity is not subject to the tax). Alternatively, if you will be leaving the bulk of your assets to friends and distant relatives after your spouse passes away, you may find it acceptable for them to pay whatever estate tax is due, rather than you paying premiums on a life insurance policy to cover the tax.

Good Things About Life Insurance Trusts

Tax savings. Huge tax savings. A $1 million life insurance policy owned by you directly is worth $550,000 to your children when you die (assuming your estate is large enough to incur estate taxes). The same policy held in a life insurance trust is worth $1 million to your children. That's $450,000 in cash just for setting up a life insurance trust.

In addition, all the good things about a family trust apply to life insurance trusts as well. Your life insurance trust can finish raising your family by providing the necessary income, and by spreading out distributions over time while your children (hopefully) develop financial maturity. Further, your life insurance trust can sprinkle income among your children until each has been given the opportunity to complete a college education.

Bad Things About Life Insurance Trusts

At the risk of repeating myself, let me remind you that life insurance trusts are irrevocable and unamendable. Once you sign the document, the rules are etched in stone. That makes the process slightly scarier, and slightly more expensive. Knowing the trust cannot be changed once it is signed, even if your attitude about your children or your estate plan changes, you will need to take more time to understand the provisions and make sure you will be comfortable with them over the long haul. You will need to work with your attorney to make sure the trust perfectly reflects your desires. That takes more time. Time is money, especially when an attorney is involved.

Further, beginning the day you establish your insurance trust, you will incur maintenance costs. Each year when the insurance premium is due, you will give the trustee the money to pay the premium. In addition to sending a check to the insurance company, the trustee will also need to prepare a couple documents to avoid unnecessary gift tax consequences. There will not be any gift tax to be paid, but the trustee (or the attorney) will need to spend a little time preparing and delivering forms. Depending on who does the work, and whether or not they are a close friend, that could cost you a few hundred dollars a year, or more.

Finally, if you have chosen to purchase a whole-life type insurance policy in hopes that you live long enough to use some of the cash value for your retirement, it may be difficult to meet your needs using a life insurance trust. You can't borrow against the cash value of your life insurance policy without making the insurance proceeds taxable in your estate, but you can probably give your spouse the ability to borrow against the cash value as a beneficiary of the life insurance trust. If you are still married to each other when you retire, that can work. If, however, you are divorced by the time you retire, you won't like the result since your ex-spouse will have the money and you won't. It may be possible to achieve your goals, but it will take careful planning with an experienced estate planning professional. But let's be honest, if you are considering a life insurance trust, you should be working with a qualified estate-planning attorney anyway.

Special Considerations

Life insurance trusts, like most specialized estate planning techniques, are subject to numerous complex rules. Miss one of the requirements and the result may not be what you expect. Here's an example: If you own a life insurance policy and transfer it into a life insurance trust, the policy proceeds will be free of estate tax only if you live at least three more years. There's a rule in the estate tax law that requires you to add back to your estate anything that you have given away in the three years immediately before you pass away. On the other hand, if you buy a brand new life insurance policy in the name of the trust, you are free to die tomorrow and the proceeds won't be subject to estate tax. An estate-planning attorney will point this out to you, and you might decide to buy a brand new insurance policy, even if you don't like taking the blood test that the insurance company requires for a new policy.

Similarly, if the trustee doesn't fill out the necessary notices each year when you contribute money to the trust to pay the premium, it can actually increase your ultimate estate tax by a few thousand dollars (nothing compared to the $450,000 your family may save on a $1 million policy, but a waste of money nonetheless). In simple terms, here's how it works. If the notices are completed each year, the $5,000 premium you pay will be treated as a gift to your children that is exempt from gift tax because it is less than $12,000 per child during the calendar year. If the trustee doesn't send the notices, the $5,000 premium will be deducted from the amount you can leave to your children free of estate tax ($2 million in 2007, etc.) at the time you die. If you pay the premium for ten years, when you die you can only leave $1,950,000 to your children free of estate tax ($2 million less $50,000). Consequently, your children will receive $22,500 less from your estate. Don't feel you need to learn all these rules. You do need to work with an experienced estate-planning attorney so you don't fall into any traps. After all, you might as well save your kids $450,000 in taxes on your $1 million life insurance policy.

Will
Substitutes

I f your assets are well below the estate tax exemption amount ($2 million in 2007 and 2008, more in 2009 and 2010, and then only $1 million after 2010), and your relationships are simple, you may be able to transfer all of your assets where you want without a will or a trust. Instead you may be able to use "will substitutes." Will substitutes include various forms of owning property that allow you to designate who will inherit your assets. Common examples include owning real property in "joint tenancy," opening a bank account that designates a "payable on death" beneficiary, or annuities and life insurance policies that are payable directly to your designated beneficiary on

Will substitutes include owning real property in "joint tenancy," opening a bank account that designates a "payable on death" beneficiary, or annuities and life insurance policies that are payable directly to your designated beneficiary on your death.

your death. Will substitutes will not work, however, if you have any significant assets that cannot be transferred using some form of will substitute, since you would need a will or trust to deal with these remaining assets.

Who Should Use Will Substitutes?

Will substitutes make sense only when:
- the value of your estate (including life insurance) is well below the estate tax exemption amount,
- all of your assets can be transferred using some type of will substitute, and
- you want to leave your assets outright to one or more individuals (rather than, for example, distribute assets gradually over time, or keep assets available to your spouse to live on and then leave what's left to your children from your first marriage).

Modest-Size Estate

If you are considering using will substitutes, add up your assets using the financial worksheet in Chapter 12. If they are well below $1 million and you do not anticipate significant growth in their value, then will substitutes may do the job for you. Remember, your estate will include all the assets you have today, plus the value of any 401(k) or other retirement account you have, plus the life insurance benefits that are payable on your death.

Assets Transferable by Will Substitutes

If your estate is below the estate tax exemption amount, then you should look at each asset you own to determine if it can be transferred using a will substitute. Common will substitutes, and the assets they can transfer, include:
- *Joint tenancy*. You can own real estate, bank or brokerage accounts, and stocks as joint tenants with any other individual. This can work very well for a husband and wife (or similar relationship), but has potential

drawbacks in other situations. See the comments under Bad Things About Will Substitutes below.

- *Payable on Death.* Most bank or brokerage accounts, and sometime stocks, can be held under your name with a payable on death (POD) designation. You retain full ownership of the property until you die (including the right to change the designated beneficiary), and then the assets will be paid directly to your designated beneficiary.

- *Beneficiary Designation.* Certain types of assets allow you to designate a beneficiary to receive your asset upon your death. Like a POD account, you retain the full ownership rights (including the right to change the beneficiary) while you are alive, and the beneficiary becomes entitled to receive the asset only upon your death. Common examples of assets requiring beneficiary designation include life insurance policies and retirement accounts (such as 401(k)s, IRAs, etc.). In addition, assets that may allow you to designate a beneficiary include bank and brokerage accounts and stocks.

- *Life Estate.* You can transfer real estate to your beneficiary and retain a life estate for yourself. A life estate is a right to continue to live in the property and have all rights of ownership for as long as you live. When you die, your life estate ends and the property will be automatically owned by the person you have selected. Life estates are complicated and can cause serious problems relating to maintenance of the property during your lifetime (for example, should the cost of replacing a roof that may last 20 years be paid completely by you or split between you and your beneficiary who may be likely to become the owner in just a few years?). In addition, a life estate can make it difficult to refinance your property. Furthermore, life estates can trigger complex income tax, property tax, and gift tax issues. Do not create a life estate without consulting with an experienced estate-planning advisor.

- *Beneficiary Deeds.* Some states permit owners of "registered" property (such as cars, airplanes, boats, etc.) to record beneficiary deeds that transfer ownership of the registered property at the time of your death.

- *Annuities.* An annuity is a contract (usually with an insurance company or financial institution) under which you receive a stream of monthly payments for a specific period of time or for the rest of your life. Often, annuities will continue paying benefits (either in monthly payments or as a single, lump sum) to your designated beneficiary after you die.

Good Things About Will Substitutes

The expense and delay of probate can be avoided if you are able to transfer *all* of your assets using will substitutes. Transferring only some of your assets using will substitutes may avoid probate if the remaining assets are modest in value and fall below the amount necessary to qualify for transfer by declaration in lieu of probate under the laws of your home state.

> The expense and delay of probate can be avoided if you are able to transfer all of your assets using will substitutes.

Many will substitutes are inexpensive to create and do not require the assistance of an attorney or other estate planning advisor. Examples of such will substitutes include POD accounts, joint tenancy bank accounts, annuities, retirement accounts, and life insurance.

Bad Things About Will Substitutes

Will substitutes must be used cautiously. Unless you have carefully inventoried all of your assets and made sure that everything is properly transferred using a will substitute, you may not achieve your desired goals.

If you are splitting your estate between two or more beneficiaries using will substitutes (for example, leaving a house worth $350,000 plus $150,000 cash in the bank to your spouse, and retirement accounts worth $200,000 to your children), you may not achieve your desired result if either assets goes drastically up or down in value. A will or a trust can easily leave each beneficiary a specified percentage of your estate. This kind of self-adjusting distribution is more difficult to achieve with will substitutes.

Life estates have their own set of problems. While a life estate may allow you (or your spouse) to live in the family residence, and ultimately transfer ownership to your children (or other beneficiary) after you die, it may create complexities that interfere with the ongoing maintenance of the home. If you wish to significantly remodel the home, you will not be able to do so without the agreement of your beneficiaries. Disputes often arise regarding payment for major repairs to the home, such as replacing a roof, which may benefit the beneficiaries who will own the home after your death. Finally, the existence of a life estate may make it difficult to refinance your home if you need to tap the equity in your home to supplement your retirement income or pay large medical bills. Do not establish a life estate without consulting an attorney regarding the long-term ramifications.

> The existence of a life estate may make it difficult to refinance your home if you need to tap the equity in your home to supplement your retirement income or pay large medical bills. Do not establish a life estate without consulting an attorney regarding the long-term ramifications.

Finally, placing your property into joint tenancy with your intended beneficiary will trigger immediate ownership rights that are dangerous. Joint tenancy can work very well if your intended beneficiary is your spouse. However, by listing your son as a joint tenant on your house or bank account you are giving him the rights of an owner. In the case of a joint bank account, he can withdraw funds from your account without asking your permission. Worse, if he is in financial difficulty, his creditors may be able to take your bank account or house to pay his debts.

Even when the ownership and creditor issues are not a problem, joint tenancy may result in your beneficiaries paying increased taxes in the long run. Let's assume you bought your $650,000 house years ago for $100,000. If you die owning the house, your heirs can sell the house for $650,000 and pay no income tax (since they receive a "stepped-up basis" in the house for income tax purposes, as if they had bought the house for $650,000—its value on the date of your death). If you transfer the house into joint tenancy, your heirs will be treated as if they received one-half the house during your lifetime as a gift and one-half the house as inheritance at the time of your death. Inherited property receives a step-up in basis, gifted property does not. Therefore, when your heirs receive your house by use of joint tenancy, they will have a basis of $375,000 (the one-half of the house gifted when you created the joint tenancy will have a "carry-over" basis of $50,000—one-half of the $100,000 you paid for the house—and the other one-half of the house will have a stepped-up basis of $325,000—one-half of the value on the date of your death). When your heirs sell the house for $650,000, they will be taxed on $275,000 (the difference between the $650,000 sale price and their $375,000 tax basis). This will mean at least $41,250 in federal taxes (if capital gains rates stay at 15 percent), plus any taxes imposed in your home state. Simply put, do not transfer property into joint tenancy without discussing the possible consequences with an experienced estate planning professional.

Special Considerations

Will substitutes can work in certain, limited circumstances. But remember, many ownership, creditor, and tax issues are not readily apparent. It is not safe to simply use will substitutes without consulting an experienced estate planning professional. I suggest that you meet with an estate planning attorney, and during the meeting ask if joint tenancy, POD accounts, or other will substitutes may be appropriate under your circumstances. Ask the attorney to explain why or why not.

Gifts During Your Lifetime

Lifetime gifting is a type of will substitute. While most will substitutes are useful only if your estate is well below the estate tax exemption amount, lifetime gifting is most useful when your estate is significantly above the estate tax exemption amount. That's why I've broken gifting out in a separate chapter.

Gifts fall into two broad categories: annual gifts and lifetime gifts. Each year, you may make gifts totaling up to $12,000 to any individual. If you are married, you can gift up to $24,000 (even if the gift comes entirely out of your assets, and not from your spouse). This amount can be given to any number of people. For example, if you are married and have three children, all of whom are married, and each of your children has two children, then you can gift $288,000 to the extended family each calendar year using your $12,000 annual exclusion amount ($24,000 to each child, $24,000 to the spouse of each child, and $24,000 to each grandchild). In addition, you can make gifts to more distant relatives, friends, or even strangers. There is no limit on the number of people to whom you can make gifts. Gifts made using your annual exclusion are not subject to gift tax and do not use up any of your estate tax exemption amount.

> Each year, you may make gifts totaling up to $12,000 to any individual. If you are married, you can gift up to $24,000.

A slight variation on the annual gift is possible when gifts are made to a "529 Plan" to pay college expenses for a child or grandchild (or anyone else). When you establish a 529 account, the law allows you to contribute up to five years worth of annual exclusion amount up front. Consequently, you can contribute up to $60,000 to a 529 account and stay within the annual exclusion amount. Of course, you will not be able to make additional annual exclusion gifts to that beneficiary for the next four years. If you are interested in paying for your child's (or grandchild's) college education (including graduate school), a 529 Plan gift has additional benefits. Not only will the gift be out of your estate (and reduce the estate tax your family pays), but also the future growth in the 529 Plan investments will be tax free as long as the funds are spent on education. In addition, if your intended beneficiary does not need the money for college, you are able to shift the money to someone else's education account and still retain the tax benefit. Finally, if the money is not needed for anyone's education, you can take the money back and pay the income tax (and a 10 percent penalty). If that happens, you may actually end up with more after-tax dollars than if you had never put the money in the 529 Plan (due to the compounding benefits from the income tax being deferred for many years).

Lifetime gifts are gifts that exceed the annual exclusion amount during any calendar year. If you give $12,001 ($24,001 if you are married) to any one person during a single calendar year, then the entire $12,001 is treated as a lifetime gift. Lifetime gifts are subject to gift tax, and will result in a gift tax being imposed once your total cumulative lifetime gifts (including all gifts made to anyone, not just gifts made to one individual) exceed the gift tax exemption amount (currently $1 million; not to be confused with the estate tax exemption amount that is increasing through 2010 and then may come down to $1 million). The first $1 million of lifetime gifts will not incur any immediate tax, but is not entirely free of tax cost, since each dollar of lifetime gifting will be subtracted from your estate tax exemption amount (that's the $2 million, going up in 2009, and back down to $1 million in 2011). A portion of the lifetime-gift tax savings will be made up by a slight increase in the estate tax due at the time of your death. The net result, however, is a reduction in overall tax paid in transferring your estate to your beneficiaries. Figure 18-1 demonstrates the tax savings.

In addition to the direct tax savings resulting from lifetime gifts, a secondary savings occurs when the gifted assets go up in value after you give them away. For example, if you give your daughter $1 million in stocks using your lifetime gifting exemption (it could be $2 million if your spouse joins in the gift), and the stocks go up to $2,800,000 before you die, the $1,800,000

FIGURE 18-1. **Tax Impact of Gifting**

If you are single and have $5,000,000 in assets, your potential estate tax is calculated as follows:

Taxable Estate	$5,000,000
Total Gross Tax	2,130,800
Less Exemption Credit	780,800
Net Tax Due	**$1,350,000**

If you give away $1,000,000 at least three years before your die, the gift will use up your estate tax exemption amount and your estate tax is calculated as follows:

Taxable Estate	$4,000,000
Total Gross Tax	1,680,800
Less Exemption Credit	435,000
Net Tax Due	**$1,245,800**

Your beneficiaries save $104,200 in estate tax.

If you give your daughter $1 million in stocks using your lifetime gifting exemption, and the stocks go up to $2,800,000 before you die, the $1,800,000 increase is not included in your estate. Your daughter will have saved $810,000 in estate taxes.

increase is not included in your estate (since it belongs to your daughter). In addition to the savings demonstrated in Figure 18-1, your daughter will have saved $810,000 more in estate taxes ($1,800,000 increase in value times 45 percent tax rate).

If you make lifetime gifts, you will be required to file a gift tax return for the year you make the gift, even if the total gifts have not yet exceeded your lifetime gift tax exemption amount. When making lifetime gifts, you should consult with your accountant and estate-planning advisor.

Who Should Make Gifts?

Generally, you should make gifts—lifetime or annual—only if you have more money than you could possibly need to live comfortably the rest of your life. Look at what assets you have and how much income they produce. Include any pension funds or annuities in your calculation. Determine your normal living expenses, including reasonable allowance for medical or long-term care needs. Naturally, if you have sufficient insurance for medical needs or long-term care, you won't need to reserve as much money for those contingencies. Err on the side of caution. Once you gift away your money, it's gone. Even if your children are willing to use the money to take care of you if circumstances change, you can't count on it being there when you need it. After you gift it away, your money may end up paying off your son's bad business deal, or the unfortunate victim of his auto accident. Worse yet, if your son is not careful, one-half of your assets may end up owned by his ex-wife.

In limited circumstances, gifts make sense even if it is not 100 percent clear that you will have more than enough money to live as you wish the rest of your days. When you own property that is not income producing, and you will not sell the property no matter what, gifting may be appropriate. For example, if you own a cottage on the lake that has been in your family for three generations, you may be willing to gift it to your children now. After all, it's not providing income to you (more likely, it's costing you something to maintain it properly). You can consider getting it out of your estate and reducing the amount of estate taxes your family will ultimately pay. This can be particularly effective if the vacation home is likely to increase in value during your lifetime.

Good Things About Gifting

Gifting reduces the amount of estate tax that your beneficiaries will pay at the time of your death.

If the assets you give away generate significant income each year, and if your beneficiaries are in a lower income tax bracket than you, gifting can reduce the income tax paid on the annual income.

Many people who make gifts during their lifetime enjoy seeing their children (or other beneficiaries) enjoy the use of the property that has been gifted. A gift can provide the joy of seeing a grandchild go to college without the worries of student loans, or allow you to experience your children enjoying family vacations at a vacation home that has been passed down from generation to generation.

Bad Things About Gifting

Gifting means giving up control. If you gift away too much, you don't have a right to take some back. Just as importantly, if you give assets to your children, you don't have the right to control how they use them. Don't give away assets unless you are prepared to live without them, and you are prepared to watch the recipient make choices you may not agree with.

In extreme cases, gifting can trigger gift taxes. If you are thinking about making gifts in excess of the $12,000 annual gift tax exclusion, consult with your accountant regarding potential gift tax liability.

Finally, gifting should be an integrated part of your overall estate plan. Consult with your estate-planning advisor to make sure any gifting fits in well with the other aspects of your estate plan.

Qualified Personal Residence Trust

The qualified personal residence trust (QPRT) is the Toyota Prius of estate planning. Like the Prius, a QPRT is a hybrid that allows lifetime gifting of your personal residence (or a vacation home) and allows you to continue living in the home. And, much like the gasoline-electric motor of the Prius, the mechanics of the QPRT increase mileage—in the form of increased tax savings. Finally, while a QPRT can provide immense benefits, just like the Prius, it is not for everyone.

In very simple terms, a QPRT allows you to gift your residence (or vacation home) to your children (or other beneficiaries) through a trust while retaining for yourself the right to live in the house rent free for a specified number of years. In essence, you are making a gift to your children, but delaying the gift for the specified number of years. Because the ownership of the house does not pass to your children until your right to live in the house lapses, the gift you are making to your children is discounted to its present value using IRS tables. Properly utilized, the QPRT will allow you to keep living in your house while removing its value (including any future appreciation after you set up the trust) from your taxable estate, and reducing the tax cost of gifting the house to your children.

> A QPRT allows you to gift your residence to your children, while retaining for yourself the right to live in the house rent free for a specified number of years. Properly utilized, the QPRT will allow you to keep living in your house while removing its value from your taxable estate, and reducing the tax cost of gifting the house to your children.

Consider the tax consequences if you die in 2007, leaving a total estate with miscellaneous assets worth $5 million, plus your personal residence valued at $1,500,000. Your taxable estate would total $6,500,000. The first $2 million is tax free due to the estate tax exemption amount, and the remaining $4,500,000 will be subject to tax at approximately 45 percent. The total tax due will be $2,025,000.

If you had established a qualified personal residence trust in 1998 and retained the right to live in the house for eight years (until 2006), your taxable estate would be $5 million, since it would not include the house you gave away. However, your $2 million estate tax exemption amount would be reduced by the value of the gift you made in 1998 when you created the trust. If the house was worth $1 million in 1998, the present value of the gift to your children may have been approximately $600,000 under the IRS tables. Therefore, your remaining estate tax exemption amount would be only $1,400,000 ($2 million less the $600,000 gift), and the first $1,400,000 of your $5 million estate is tax free while the remaining $3,600,000 is subject to tax at approximately 45 percent. The total tax due will be $1,620,000; a tax savings to your family of $405,000.

Of course, you could have saved estate taxes without the QPRT by simply giving the house to your children in 1998. But not as much. If you gave the house worth $1 million to your children outright, the value of the gift would have been $1 million. Therefore, your estate tax exemption amount would have been reduced by $1 million (instead of $600,000). The first $1 million ($2 million less the gift of $1 million) would be tax free and the remaining $4 million would be subject to estate tax at approximately 45 percent. The total tax due would be $1,800,000; $180,000 more than when you use the QPRT. On top of saving your family $180,000 in taxes, you were able to use the house for eight years after you gave it to your children!

Two other issues are important to understand. First, if you die before expiration of the specified term during which you retained the right to live in the house, your family will pay the same estate tax as if you never set up the QPRT. There is no penalty for having tried, but if you don't live long enough, there is no benefit either. Second, after the specified term expires, you can continue living in the house but you will be required to pay your children fair market rent for the use of the house. This makes the QPRT unattractive for many individuals, but if your estate is large enough to provide sufficient income to comfortably pay rent, it may further reduce estate taxes because the money you pay as rent will no longer be in your estate. Do not establish a QPRT without carefully analyzing your cash flow needs and the income tax and estate tax consequences of creating the trust. I strongly recommend that you work with a qualified accountant and experienced estate-planning attorney to make this decision.

Who Should Use a Qualified Personal Residence Trust?

QPRTs are just like other forms of gifting. Generally, a QPRT makes sense only if you have more money than you need to live comfortably the rest of your life, including paying your children fair market rent after the specified term expires. Review your assets and income, and compare your anticipated income with your normal living expenses, including reasonable allowance for medical or long-term care needs. Take into account any insurance coverage you have that may contribute toward the costs of medical needs or long-term care. Be cautious. Once you give away your house, it's gone (and may go toward payment of your children's debts or become part of their divorce proceedings).

If you are considering a QPRT funded with a vacation home (particularly one that you want to stay in the family for future generations), it is not as important that you have more than enough money to live as you wish the rest of your days. Because the property is not income producing and you do not need to live in it, a QPRT may be appropriate.

Good Things About a Qualified Personal Residence Trust

QPRTs can drastically reduce estate taxes by allowing you to gift your family residence (or vacation home) to your children (or other beneficiaries) at a greatly reduced value for gift tax purposes.

If you live beyond the term of years that you have retained the right to live in the house rent free, the full value of the home (including any appreciation after you placed it in the trust) is excluded from your taxable estate, thereby saving your family 45 percent of the value of the home.

You can continue to live in the house during the specified term of years, and can rent the house from your children at fair market rent after that.

Until the initial term of years expires, you can continue to receive all tax benefits associated with the home, including mortgage interest and property tax deductions, and you can exclude up to $250,000 ($500,000 if you are married) of gain from being taxable if the house is sold.

Bad Things About a Qualified Personal Residence Trust

A QPRT is irrevocable. Once you set up the trust, you cannot take the house back if you change your mind or your financial circumstances change.

If you outlive the initial term for which you retain the right to live in the house, you are required to pay fair market rent to your children (or move out). This may be an unacceptable burden if your other assets are not sufficient to maintain your customary lifestyle and pay your children rent. However, if you have a large estate and substantially more income that you are capable of spending, then paying your children rent can benefit the family. Your children may pay current income tax on some portion of the rent (but only after taking a deduction for property taxes paid, mortgage interest paid, and depreciation). Most likely, the income tax paid will be significantly less that the estate tax saved. Keep in mind, not only is the house out of your estate, but every dollar you pay in rent is out of your estate, too.

If you die before expiration of the term that you retained the right to use the house, there will be no tax savings. Your family will owe the same taxes as if you died owning the house. However, there is no additional tax that results from dying prematurely. You can win or you can break even. You can't lose.

In exchange for saving estate taxes, your children will not get a stepped-up basis on the house when you die. In the example above, your children will own a $1,500,000 house with a tax basis of only $600,000. If they sell it immediately, they will owe capital gains tax on the $900,000 difference. At the federal rate of 15 percent, the capital gains tax due will be $135,000. There may also be state income tax due, depending upon where you live. Even in states like California, where the income tax could be nearly 10 percent, the total tax due would be $225,000 ($135,000 federal tax plus $90,000 California tax). Even in a high income tax state like California, the total capital gains tax is $180,000 less than the $405,000 savings on your estate tax return.

Finally, QPRTs are complex and expensive to create. You will require the help of an estate-planning attorney to prepare the trust, an accountant to analyze your finances and prepare a gift tax return, and a qualified appraiser to value the property for gift tax purposes. Ask your accountant or estate-planning attorney to estimate the costs for all of these services before you proceed.

Special Needs Trusts

If you have a child, sibling, other relative, or friend, who is not able to manage assets you may leave for their benefit, or who may need the assistance of government benefits to get by—remember Jim Ignatowski of "Taxi"—a special needs trust may be appropriate to accomplish your goals. A wide variety of "special needs" may be met by a special needs trust. The specific special needs of your beneficiary will dictate the details of the special needs trust you create.

Most commonly, when estate-planning professionals refer to "special needs," they mean physical or mental disabilities that make the beneficiary eligible for government assistance (or are likely to trigger a need for government assistance in the foreseeable future). As Jim Ignatowski's parents understood, leaving assets directly to a beneficiary with serious mental or physical disabilities may make him ineligible for government benefits until after the assets you provided have been fully spent. If, instead, you establish a special needs trust, the same assets can be available to your beneficiary to supplement—instead of terminate—government benefits. To work successfully, the terms of the special needs trust must take into account federal and state regulations regarding eligibility for various government benefits, and structure distributions to your beneficiary in a form that will not (as much as possible) reduce medical and other assistance available through government programs. Since laws vary by state, and both state and federal regulations change often, you should work with an experienced estate planning professional who understands such regulations. Carefully designed, a special needs trust can provide your beneficiary with sufficient indirect support to allow him to live a comfortable (rather than a government subsistence) lifestyle.

> Leaving assets directly to a beneficiary with serious mental or physical disabilities may make him ineligible for government benefits until after the assets you provided have been fully spent. If instead you establish a special needs trust, the same assets can be available to your beneficiary to supplement—instead of terminate—government benefits.

If your beneficiary's special needs are less directly tied to government benefits (for example, inability to control spending, difficulty managing money, or drug or alcohol abuse that has not yet impaired the beneficiary's ability to function), then a simpler form of trust can be used to limit spending, provide asset management, or limit distributions when the beneficiary shows signs of departing from sobriety. Occasionally, parents who are concerned that their child seems unable to hold down a full-time job may use similar restrictions to limit distributions when he or she is not employed (unless a valid medical excuse exists or the child is staying home full time to raise minor children). These restricted trusts typically operate like a family trust with a few added provisions tailored to meet the needs of the beneficiary. They do not have the same detailed provisions related to government benefits that are found in traditional special needs trusts, and most commonly these types of trusts are not referred to as "special needs." However, the concept of tailoring a trust to restrict distributions to meet the special needs of the beneficiary (and make sure distributions benefit, rather than harm, the beneficiary) is the same.

Who Should Use a Special Needs Trust?

If anyone you wish to provide for suffers from a mental or physical disability, you should consider establishing a special needs trust. If your intended beneficiary has few assets of his or her own and is reliant upon government benefits such a Supplemental Security Income (SSI) or Medicaid (known by different names in each state, for example, Medi-Cal in California), or is likely to need such benefits in the future, then a special needs trust can provide supplemental income in excess of the nominal amount that may be permitted by SSI or Medicaid, without terminating or reducing the government benefits necessary to maintain your beneficiary's base level of support.

Similarly, if your goals include providing support for a parent or other older person who does not have substantial assets of his or her own, a special needs trust can be used to make the greatest amount of supplemental support available.

Finally, if you desire to leave assets to a beneficiary who cannot seem to control spending, or who lacks even an ounce of common sense when it comes to investing, then a trust with special restrictions on distribution may be appropriate. Such restrictions may also be appropriate for beneficiaries who are susceptible to drug or alcohol abuse, or who seem to lack the motivation to hold down a full-time job whenever extra money is available to meet this month's rent obligation. Special distribution provisions can be tailored to meet your specific concerns regarding one of your beneficiaries.

> Special distribution provisions can be tailored to meet your specific concerns regarding one of your beneficiaries.

Good Things About Special Needs Trusts

A properly drafted special needs trust can make it possible for your money to supplement the needs of your 89-year-old father, or your disabled brother, and improve their living situations. Without a special needs trust, your funds may simply replace government SSI or Medicaid benefits

Without a special needs trust, your funds may simply replace government SSI or Medicaid benefits that would otherwise provide your family member with basic support needs.

that would otherwise provide your family member with basic support needs.

Distribution restrictions in a basic trust can prevent a beneficiary from engaging in self-destructive behavior as a result of the increased discretionary income provided by your estate. If your child has a history of drug or alcohol abuse, or simply is more likely to die in an auto accident if your money makes it possible to buy a 200-mile-per-hour sports car, then a restricted-distribution trust may make sense.

Finally, a restricted-distribution trust may be appropriate where you are concerned that the inheritance received from you will enable your child to live in a manner inconsistent with your goals, such as quitting his or her job (and no longer being a productive member of society), or spending the entire inheritance on trendy clothes and wild parties.

Bad Things About Special Needs Trusts

Circumstances change, or at least they can. Special needs trusts don't, and can't. They are irrevocable. Once you create your special needs trust (sometimes at the time of your death), you can no longer change the rules. If you have guessed right about the future, that's fine. If circumstances change that you did not (or could not) anticipate, then the special needs trust may not work as you had hoped.

In addition, the burden on the trustee to enforce distribution restrictions can be substantial. If you appoint one son to be the trustee of your other son's special needs trust, you run the risk of driving a wedge between them that may never be bridged. If no other option exists, you may take that risk, but remember—your estate plan should not blow your family apart, at least not inadvertently.

Finally, special needs trusts can be complex and expensive to create. If they are not carefully drafted, you will spend money creating a trust that does nothing to protect your beneficiary. If you need the protections that a special needs trust can provide, work with an experienced estate-planning professional to achieve your goals.

CHAPTER 21

Family Limited Partnerships

and Other Business Protection Tools

B ecause your estate includes ownership of an
ongoing business—whether it's a traditional
business offering goods or services, or a holding company managing investments such as rental real estate
that require active management—you need to protect
the viable operation of the business for the benefit of
your family. This is true whether you are the 100 percent owner of the business, or you own some portion
of a partnership, corporation, limited liability company, or other type of business entity. To be of value
to your family, the business must survive and continue
to provide the family with a stream of income, or the
business must be sold to your partner, or a third party,

> To be of value to your family, the business must survive and continue to provide the family with a stream of income, or the business must be sold to your partner, or a third party, for its reasonable value (and the proceeds of the sale invested for the benefit of your family). Unless you plan ahead, this may not happen.

for its reasonable value (and the proceeds of the sale invested for the benefit of your family). Unless you plan ahead, this may not happen.

If your family will be continuing to manage the business or actively manage your investments, you may need to impose a structure on the business that centralizes control in those family members best suited to operate the business, while allowing income to be shared with others in the family who may not be involved in the business. Although you may desire that the business' income be distributed broadly among members of the family, you may wish to make sure that those not involved in the operation of the business cannot out vote those who are active in the business and best situated to make decisions regarding the business' future. In addition, the structure you choose should not interfere with the company's banking or other business relationships. These goals can best be accomplished by placing the business or investment property into a limited partnership or limited liability company. These entities allow you to designate some ownership interests as having the management rights in the company, while other ownership interests can share in profits (but not management) of the business.

If you have partners who will likely continue to operate the business after you are gone, you should have a buy-sell agreement between you and the other partners. The buy-sell agreement will obligate your partners to buy your share of the business from your estate (so that your family will have cash to invest, and your partners will control the business without interference from your family members who have not previously been involved in the business). The buy-sell agreement should set the price your estate will be paid (by formula, appraisal procedure, or other acceptable method), and provide payments terms and security that provide your family reasonable cash flow and protection without putting undue strain on the cash flow of the business. If your partners are required to pay off your family too quickly, the financial strain may hurt the business so much that your partners are unable to complete the payout to your family. Therefore, it is in your interest, and your partners' interest, to structure a payout that is fair to both sides.

You should work with an experienced attorney to negotiate and draft your buy-sell agreement. You and your partners will need to agree on the following issues:

> If you have partners who will likely continue to operate the business after you are gone, you should have a buy-sell agreement between you and the other partners.

- What events will trigger the right to buy or sell under the agreement?
- For each triggering event, will the buying partner be required to buy, or simply have an option to buy if he or she chooses?
- For each triggering event, will the selling partner be required to sell, or simply have an option to sell if he or she chooses?
- When an interest in the business is bought or sold, how will the price be determined?
- Over what period of time will the price be paid, and will the buyer provide security for the unpaid portion of the purchase price?
- What portion of the purchase price, if any, will be covered by purchasing life or disability insurance?

In the context of estate planning, it is most important that your buy-sell agreement obligate your partners (or the company) to buy your interest in the business upon your death. The buy-sell agreement should set the purchase price either by some agreed formula applied to the company's most recent several years of financial performance, by an agreed appraisal procedure or valuation method, or by annual agreement of the partners. Each method has its strengths and weaknesses, and the costs of certain methods can be significant. Consult with your accountant and business attorney to select a pricing mechanism that fits your business situation.

> In the context of estate planning, it is most important that your buy-sell agreement obligate your partners (or the company) to buy your interest in the business upon your death.

In addition to triggering an obligation to purchase your interest in the business upon your death, your buy-sell agreement should address what will be done in the event of disability, retirement, termination of employment, personal bankruptcy, purchase offers from third parties, and possibly divorce. For each event, you will need to decide whether the purchase or sale should be mandatory or optional, and what pricing mechanism and payment terms will apply. Each event may be treated differently as to each issue.

A detailed buy-sell agreement is important in order to make sure that your business will survive changes in your life, and in your partners' lives. If you don't have a buy-sell agreement governing your business partnership, contact an experienced business attorney and begin negotiating one now. Keeping your golden goose alive for the benefit of your family may depend on it.

CHAPTER 22

Charitable Trusts for Personal Gain

or How to Use Tax Laws to Save Taxes and Increase Income

Charitable giving feels good. It helps cure diseases, feed and clothe the homeless, assist those with disabilities, fund college educations, and so much more. Let's be honest though, part of what feels good about charitable giving is the tax savings we get when we take the deduction at the end of the year. That's probably why so much of our charitable giving occurs during December.

There is a way that charitable giving could feel even better, and it's not illegal or socially unacceptable. In fact, it's expressly permitted by the tax code and it allows you to leave large sums to charity, save taxes, and increase your annual income, all at the

> Charitable trusts allow you to leave large sums to charity, save taxes, and increase your annual income, all at the same time.

same time. It called a charitable trust. There are two basic types of charitable trusts (and some variations). This chapter explains the basic concept.

Compared to charitable trusts, every one of the estate planning techniques discussed in the previous chapters is simple. Charitable trusts have more moving parts than the 1966 Mustang my brother and I bought when I was 17. Just like the old Mustang, charitable remainder trusts perform reliably, provide many tangible and intangible benefits, and simply make you feel good when you stop and think about how lucky you are to have one. Let's compare.

Your charitable trust can increase the amount of cash in your pocket the very first year you have one by permitting you to take an immediate income tax deduction (even though you will retain the right to all the income from the assets in the trust for a substantial period of time—possibly the rest of your life). It can also help you completely avoid paying capital gains taxes on stocks, real estate, or other highly appreciated assets that you wish to sell and replace with assets better suited to providing you with a steady stream of income. If that weren't enough, it can also improve your financial status by improving your income stream (due in part to the avoidance of capital gains taxes, and in part to possible tax-free compounding of income earned in your trust that is not immediately distributed to you). Your charitable trust can also save your family estate taxes by reducing the size of your taxable estate. Finally, your charitable trust can generate the satisfaction that comes from knowing that you have provided substantial support to a charitable cause that you care about.

Now that I think about it, my 1966 Mustang pales in comparison to a charitable remainder trust, except for one thing. The '66 Mustang used to drive me, and four teenage girls, to the beach. I'm still married to one of those girls more than 30 years later. I don't know if a charitable remainder trust has ever triggered the same kind of relationship, but it may be the next best thing.

Now that I've exhausted my charitable trust/'66 Mustang analogies, let's take a careful look at each type of charitable trust, how each works, and how one can help you.

Charitable Remainder Trusts

When you create a charitable remainder trust, you are promising to give an asset that you own to charity at some time in the future. It can be when you die, or it can be after a specified number of years that you designate when you first set up the trust. In exchange, you may be able to increase your income stream from the asset by utilizing the charity's tax-exempt status.

First, you get an immediate tax deduction that will reduce your personal income taxes due in year one. The deduction will be an amount determined using IRS tables and formulas based upon the number of years you will receive income from the trust (or, if you choose to take income for the rest of your life, the number of years you are deemed to receive income based upon your life expectancy) and the market interest rate at the time you set up the trust. If you are 89 years old and the trust will provide you income for life before leaving the assets to charity, the deduction could be 50 percent or more of the value of the assets you put in the trust. If you are 52 years old and you create the trust to provide income to you for your lifetime, and then provide income to your children for the rest of their lives, the deduction will be small, very small. Your estate-planning advisor can help you determine the amount of the deduction before you make the final decision whether or not to set up the trust.

Second, you avoid capital gains tax when you sell the assets that are contributed to the trust. You can contribute an asset that you have owned for many years, that has increased tenfold in value, and then sell it from the trust without paying capital gains taxes. That leaves you 100 percent of the cash to invest in new assets to generate income for your benefit (instead of the 75 percent or 80 percent that would be left after paying federal and state taxes in most jurisdictions).

Finally, assets in the trust can grow more quickly than if you owned them directly, because any amount earned that is not distributed to you will accumulate tax free. Each year that a portion of the earnings goes untaxed, a few extra dollars remain in the trust to be invested for the following year. Just like your tax-deferred retirement account, the balance grows more quickly because the untaxed earnings compound more quickly. After 10 or

20 years you will have significantly more money in the trust working for your benefit.

Let's look at a specific example to illustrate these points. Assume that you own stocks that you bought 30 years ago for a total purchase price of $50,000 that are now worth $800,000. Since you are approaching retirement age, you want to sell them and invest in high-grade bonds to reduce the risk of your principal going down in value. If you simply sell the stocks, you will pay capital gains tax on the increase in value. At current tax rates, you would pay federal tax of approximately $112,500 (15 percent of the $750,000 gain), and if you live in a state like California, you could pay as much as $75,000 more in state income tax. Instead of having $800,000 to invest in bonds, you will have only $612,500 after paying $187,500 in taxes. If the bonds earn 6 percent, your income on the $612,500 will be $36,750 per year. If you could invest the whole $800,000 instead, you could earn $48,000 per year. Your income just increased by almost $1,000 per month, from about $3,000 a month to $4,000 a month, for the rest of your life.

Instead of selling the stocks directly, you can contribute the stocks to a charitable remainder trust that will provide you income for the rest of your life (or even continue on for the life of your children, and possibly your grandchildren). You will receive an immediate income tax deduction for the value of the $800,000 in assets, reduced by the value of the stream of income that you are keeping for the rest of your life. The computation is based upon your life expectancy (according to an IRS table) and the market interest rates existing at the time you set up the trust. If you are 40 years old and design the trust to pay you 10 percent of the value of the assets each year, the immediate income tax deduction will be modest, perhaps only $10,000 or $20,000, and will result in a tax saving of only a few thousand dollars. If you are 85 years old and take distributions equal to 5 percent of the assets, the tax deduction may be $300,000 or $400,000, and your immediate income tax savings could be $150,000 or more (assuming your taxable income for the year is large enough to allow you to take the full deduction). Whatever the income tax savings, that's extra cash in your pocket (outside of the trust) because you reduced the amount that you would otherwise have been required to pay in taxes.

Because you have chosen to contribute your stocks to a charitable remainder trust before they are sold, you also avoid paying the $187,500 in capital gains taxes. You still retain the right to receive income for the rest of your life (or for a specific number of years, if you prefer). When you first set up the trust, you have to decide if the income that you receive will be a set amount for the entire term (with no adjustment, even to keep up with inflation), or a set percentage of the value of the assets in the trust each year (not less than 5 percent, and subject to a maximum limit discussed below). The example in the above paragraph can literally become reality and your income can increase by $1,000 (or more) per month.

There's another potential tax benefit that is somewhat more difficult to quantify. If you select the percentage-of-value option to determine your distribution amount (rather than the set-dollar-amount annuity payment), any amount earned inside the trust in excess of your distribution for the year will accumulate tax free—and increase the amount of your distribution for next year at a quicker pace than if you were required to pay tax on the full amount earned inside the trust. Let's go back to our $800,000 stock portfolio example. Assume that you invested in more growth-oriented stocks and earned an annual return of 8 percent, instead of 6 percent. The extra 2 percent will stay in the charitable trust, free of income tax. On $800,000, that's $16,000 not subject to income tax in the first year alone. Between federal and state income tax that's a savings of $5,000 to $6,000 in taxes. The full $16,000 (not just the $10,000 you would have had left if you had to pay income tax immediately) stays in the trust and continues to earn 8 percent. And you get 6 percent of that increased amount. Each year, the untaxed portion grows tax free, and you benefit from the quicker compounding of earnings (just as you do in a tax-deferred retirement account). After 10 or 20 years, or more, the compounding allows you to accumulate a much larger investment pot—and each year you receive 6 percent of that ever-larger fund.

Simply by contributing your stocks to a charitable remainder trust, you have:

- Put between $5,000 and $150,000 in your pocket outside the trust as a result of the income tax deduction for your charitable contribution.

- Preserved an extra $187,500 to invest in assets inside the trust that will generate additional income each year, some of which will be paid to you.
- Deferred income tax on a portion of the assets inside the trust so that the trust value will increase more rapidly, and the trust will distribute more income to you each year.

The charitable remainder trust discussed in this example is called a charitable remainder *unitrust* ("CRUT"). A CRUT distributes to you a set percentage of the value of the trust's assets each year. If the assets in the trust are bonds and publicly traded stocks and other securities, determining the value each year is easy. If the CRUT includes other types of assets, it will be necessary to hire an appraiser each year to determine the value of the assets in the trust. The benefit of the CRUT is that your distributions go up as the value of the assets in the trust goes up. Your distributions increase more rapidly due to the tax-free accumulation inside the trust. A CRUT will maximize the tax benefits of the charitable remainder trust and allow your distributions to increase over time.

The second type of charitable remainder trust is called a charitable remainder annuity trust ("CRAT"). When this trust is created, you set a specific dollar amount to be distributed to you each year. The amount will never increase no matter how large the trust becomes. On the other hand, if the trust assets go down in value, your distribution will not go down (as it would with a CRUT). Over time, the value of your annual distribution can be eroded by inflation. Unless your annual distribution is so large (or the CRAT is such a small part of your overall income) that increasing it to keep up with inflation is not a concern, a CRAT that lasts more than a few years can put you at risk of having insufficient income to maintain your lifestyle.

Finally, when the amount of money you are willing to commit to a charitable trust is not large enough to warrant the expense of creating and maintaining a CRUT or CRAT, you can still get the benefits of a charitable remainder trust by participating in a pooled income trust. A pooled income trust is similar to a CRUT. Your funds are combined with assets contributed by many other donors, and you are distributed your share of the income actually earned by the trust each year. Therefore, the amount of your distribution can go up and down, based on the value of the assets in the trust and the rate of return on the investment.

If you create a CRUT or CRAT, you can serve as trustee of the trust, or you can appoint someone else to serve as trustee, including the charity. If you participate in a pooled income trust, the charity will serve as trustee. Whoever serves as the trustee, including you, will have a fiduciary duty to manage the assets in a manner that is fair to you and also fair to the charity.

Whichever type of charitable remainder trust you select, at the end of the term that you are to receive distributions (either your entire life, or your entire life and then your children for their entire lives, or a specified number of years that you selected at the time you set up the trust), all of the assets that remain in the trust will go to the charity or charities that you selected. If you are healthy at the time you create the trust, you may be able to purchase life insurance to "replace" the asset for the benefit of your children. You can utilize a life insurance trust to keep the life insurance proceeds out of your taxable estate (so that life insurance equal to one half of the anticipated value of the asset can be nearly comparable to the amount that would otherwise go to your children after estate taxes).

The rules governing charitable remainder trusts are complex, and change from time to time. Work with a qualified estate-planning advisor to establish a trust, or work with a reputable charity if you wish to participate in a pooled income trust.

Charitable Lead Trust

The various forms of charitable *remainder* trusts allow you to keep the stream of income from your assets for a period of time (up to your entire life) and receive tax benefits because you have irrevocably agreed to leave the assets to charity at a later date. A charitable *lead* trust does exactly the opposite.

When you create a charitable lead trust, you are agreeing to allow a charity to receive income from your assets for a period of years, and when the specified term is over, the assets will come back to your heirs (or possibly you, if you create the trust during your lifetime). You get the same tax benefits of taking an immediate tax deduction for the value of the stream of income that is being promised to the charity, and also are able to avoid capital gains on greatly appreciated assets that are sold through the trust.

In addition, for particularly large estates, charitable lead trusts can be used to pass significant assets to your children at a greatly reduced estate tax cost. An experienced estate planning advisor can guide you through the complex IRS valuation tables to determine if a charitable lead trust can divert income to a charity for a number of years (perhaps as long as ten years or more) and then direct the (hopefully, greatly appreciated) assets back to your family with little estate tax cost. Properly structured, and so long as your family has substantial other assets (either of their own or from another part of your estate), this can be a highly effective method of reducing estate taxes.

Like charitable remainder trusts, the rules are complex and changing. Work with an experienced advisor to analyze and implement a charitable lead trust.

Who Should Consider a Charitable Trust?

Charitable trusts make sense, first and foremost, if you wish to provide a charitable legacy. While there are tax benefits associated with charitable gifting, it is still gifting. The best reason to make a gift to charity is because you care about what the charity is doing. You can use a charitable trust to benefit your church or temple, a favorite educational institution, or public charities like Easter Seals Disability Services or the American Red Cross.

Charitable trusts deserve consideration if you own highly appreciated assets that you would like to sell (either to reduce investment risk, or to increase cash flow from the investment) and reinvest in other assets better suited to your current investment needs, since the most immediate tax benefit is the avoidance of capital gains taxes upon the sale of the investment.

Good Things About Charitable Trusts

Charitable trusts provide substantial tax benefits, including allowing you to adjust your investment portfolio to provide steady income for your retirement, while avoiding the capital gains tax usually incurred by such adjustment. You can realize greater income during your lifetime than you may be able to achieve otherwise.

You get the intangible benefit of supporting a charity that you care about in a meaningful way, and of creating a charitable legacy and setting an example for your family.

Bad Things About Charitable Trusts

Charitable trusts are irrevocable. The minute you create and fund the trust, you have given away some portion of your assets and you cannot change your mind.

Although you retain a (possibly increased) stream of income, you no longer have the right to sell your asset and spend the proceeds as you wish. The income stream is yours to do with as you wish, but the asset itself is being held for charity.

Unless you replace the assets that go into the charitable trust with life insurance, your beneficiaries may receive less assets than if you left the property outright to them.

In short, charitable trusts are not for everyone, but deserve consideration in larger estates or when you have strong charitable desires.

Taking Charge of Your Estate Planning

PART FOUR

Directing Medical and Financial Decisions

While You Are Alive

M ost estate planning techniques take effect upon
your death and benefit your family by simplify-
ing the process of transferring assets to family members (or other beneficiaries) and possibly by reducing
estate taxes. With the exception of the charitable trusts
discussed in Chapter 22, the benefit to you is limited
to knowing that your wishes will be carried out in a
manner that will provide well for your family.

No estate plan is complete, however, without two
components that take care of you during your lifetime. A living will/medical durable power of attorney
(known in many states as an advance health care
directive) is necessary to make sure that your medical

desires are carried out even if you become unable to make or communicate decisions for yourself. A similar document, called a durable power of attorney for property management, provides you with the same protection with respect to control of your financial assets. These medical and financial documents are discussed in this chapter.

> A living will/medical durable power of attorney is necessary to make sure that your medical desires are carried out even if you become unable to make or communicate decisions for yourself. A durable power of attorney for property management provides you with the same protection with respect to control of your financial assets.

Importance of Avoiding Conservatorships

Earlier chapters have discussed the probate process that may come into play upon your death, and the advantage of avoiding an unnecessary probate proceeding. While there is some benefit to avoiding probate, in my experience the process is not as burdensome as some estate planning professionals suggest, and it is not always worth the up front cost needed to avoid probate.

A process similar to probate, called conservatorship or guardianship, is available to your relatives or friends if it becomes necessary for someone else to make your medical decisions or manage your finances should you become incapable of taking care of yourself. You can become legally incapacitated if you are incapable of understanding the nature of the medical or financial decisions that need to be made or the consequences of your decisions. This can result from progressive medical conditions such as Alzheimer's disease, from a serious automobile accident, or if you are physically unable to communicate your desires in any manner.

Although I believe that probate may or may not be worth avoiding, I suggest that you avoid conservatorship proceedings in all but the most unusual situations. The financial cost of a conservatorship can be far more substantial that the cost of probate, and it will be incurred while you are still alive. Therefore, the conservatorship proceeding will reduce the amount of money that is available for you to live on (rather than simply reducing your family's inheritance by 2 or 3 percent). Perhaps more importantly, if you become subject to a conservatorship proceeding, all major decisions regarding your life—

where you live, the course of your medical treatment, and how to invest your money—will be under the direct control of a judge who will likely know nothing about you or your desires. In its most extreme case, battles can erupt among family members regarding life-sustaining medical treatment with little or no regard for your personal views. What further explanation is necessary than the extreme case of Terri Schiavo, whose journey through the courts lasted years and ultimately involved the national media, the Governor of Florida, and the United States Congress?

> If you become subject to a conservatorship proceeding, all major decisions regarding your life—where you live, the course of your medical treatment, and how to invest your money—will be under the direct control of a judge who will likely know nothing about you or your desires.

What You Can Accomplish with an Advance Health Care Directive

Using an Advance Health Care Directive—a document that combines a living will with a medical durable power of attorney—you can:

- set forth your medical wishes in as much, or as little, detail as you wish,
- appoint an individual, and successor, to make medical decisions for you if you become incapacitated, and
- greatly reduce the chance of becoming the subject of a conservatorship proceeding.

Medical Wishes

In its most generic form, a living will, or the living will portion of an Advance Health Care Directive, will set forth your most basic medical wishes. For example, you can express your belief that "life is sacred" and that you should be maintained on life support systems as long as humanly possible; or, alternatively, your belief that artificial life support should be utilized only if a meaningful recovery is possible to a reasonable degree of medical certainty. If you choose, your living will can also set forth your wishes regarding organ donation, burial versus cremation, or detailed directions regarding pain medication, nutrition, hydration, or other medical situations that are of importance to you.

If you have a long-term relationship with your primary treating physician you can list him or her as the doctor who should be directly responsible for supervising your medical care.

Though not exactly "medical wishes," your Advance Health Care Directive can also authorize your agent to determine where you will live. It is probably best to expressly refer to this power in your directive, and you should consider expressly setting forth your wishes regarding staying in your family residence and receiving in-home nursing care, if necessary, as opposed to living in an assisted-living facility.

Appointing an Agent

The durable power of attorney for medical care, or the equivalent section of an Advance Health Care Directive, appoints a person to make your medical decisions for you. Most commonly, it is designed to take effect only when you become legally incapacitated, but if you prefer, it can take effect immediately when you sign it. In either event, you can appoint anyone who is at least 18 years old to act as your agent for making medical decisions, and can appoint one or more successor agents to serve in the event that the earlier-designated agent is unable or unwilling to serve when the need arises. Your designated agent may be unable to serve due to his or her own death or disability, or may be unwilling to serve because your relationship with them has changed over the years since you prepared your Advance Health Care Directive, or simply due to a bad experience he or she had (or heard about regarding) serving as the agent for someone else. To be safe, you should designate at least one successor agent, and if either of the first two choices are substantially older than you (increasing the odds that they may be unable to serve when the need arises), consider designating a second successor as well.

Some people designate co-agents to serve at the same time and jointly make their medical decisions (often, two or more of their children). This can cause problems if the co-agents do not agree. Medical treatment by vote—especially tie vote—simply does not work well. Instead, consider listing the agents in order of succession, and spell out your desire that the first agent in line consult with the successor agents (or other members of your family) before making final decisions (assuming that time permits). This can promote group decision making, while still giving one person the legal authority to make timely medical decisions for you.

In selecting your agent, keep in mind that the person should be someone who knows your medical desires and philosophies and will put your wishes first—even before their own desires. He or she must be strong enough to stand up to family pressure and to make the hard medical decisions that you want made. If you are married, you are very likely to put your spouse in the number one position, but that is not always the case. If, for example, you have adult children from a prior relationship, you may wish to select one of them first. If you have such competing relationships, you will need to carefully weigh who will best carry out your desires, and how each possible appointment may affect your relationships with the two (or more) individuals, and their relationship with each other. After all, unlike the other estate planning decisions that take effect only upon your death, this will come into play while you are alive. Family tensions may directly affect you.

What You Cannot Accomplish with an Advance Health Care Directive

Although your Advance Health Care Directive will allow your agent to make most of your medical and living decisions for you if the need arises, in most states it will not permit your agent to:

- place you in a mental or Alzheimer's facility,
- authorize extreme psychiatric treatment such as electroshock therapy, or
- authorize an abortion or sterilization procedure.

If any of these alternatives become necessary to care for you, a conservatorship proceeding, and the resulting court order, will usually be required.

In addition, mercy killing—not currently legal in the vast majority of states—is not something that your agent will be permitted to authorize without obtaining a court order. Your agent can withhold artificial life sustaining medical treatment even if it indirectly results in your death, but cannot take affirmative medical steps to hasten your demise.

Consider a Do-Not-Resuscitate Order

You may wish to consider signing and delivering a do-not-resuscitate order instructing emergency medical personnel (such as paramedics) or hospital personnel (if you are having an operation) not to use CPR, electroshock, or any similar procedure to revive you if your heart stops. These types of orders are most commonly utilized by people who have been diagnosed with a terminal illness, but are sometimes chosen by individuals simply because they have strong personal or religious beliefs that preclude such treatment.

If you wish to avoid resuscitation efforts under all circumstances, then in addition to signing a do-not-resuscitate order, you should purchase and wear a bracelet or medallion specifying your wishes. You can obtain a bracelet or medallion from any number of non-profit or for-profit organizations that sell them over the internet. One such non-profit organization is the MedicAlert Foundation (www.medicalert.com).

When to Update Your Advance Health Care Directive

Like your other estate planning documents, you should consider updating your Advance Health Care Directive whenever circumstance change, such as:

- when you move from one state to another,
- when you get married or divorced, or
- when your relationships change, either because you have become closer to someone you would like to designate as your agent, or you have become less close to someone previously designated as your agent.

What You Can Accomplish with a Durable Power of Attorney for Property Management

Using your durable power of attorney for property management, you can:

- appoint an individual, and successor, to make financial decisions and manage your assets for you if you become incapacitated, and
- greatly reduce the chance of becoming the subject of a conservatorship proceeding.

You can grant your agent complete authority to fully manage all of your financial affairs, or you can grant authority to manage only those specific areas you identify. Generally speaking, the individual areas that you may identify include managing real estate (including your personal residence or investment property), personal property, stocks and bonds, banking, managing a business you own, insurance and annuities, litigation, personal/family maintenance, retirement plans, tax matters, or government benefits. If one of your goals is to avoid a conservatorship proceeding, then the full power is more likely to accomplish your goal.

Your agent will be obligated to follow general fiduciary rules applicable to durable powers of attorney, such as placing your interests first and foremost (and certainly ahead of his or her own interests), the prudent investor rule (requiring investments to be "safe," meaning designed primarily to avoid losing money), and avoiding commingling of your assets with his or her own assets. Where appropriate, you may wish to modify one or more of these rules by express language in your durable power of attorney. For example, if your first choice to serve as your agent is your spouse, then you may wish to waive the commingling rule (and possibly the prudent investor rule, as well). It is possible for you to waive the rule if your spouse is serving as your agent but not waive the rule if an alternate agent is serving. Think through each rule carefully with the help of any experienced estate-planning advisor before waiving any protection.

As with the Advance Health Care Directive, you should only appoint an agent whom you trust completely. Except in the rarest of situations, select an individual who will act alone, rather than two or more individuals who must act jointly. As with medical powers, difficulties can arise if jointly acting agents do not agree. To complicate things further, with a financial power of attorney, you can require co-agents to act by unanimous agreement, or permit each agent to act separately. The unanimity requirement can result in deadlock, while the individual authority option can result in mismanaged assets and poor record keeping if the two agents fail to coordinate their decision-making.

Finally, while you can grant your agent the power to appoint a successor agent if you have not appointed one, this option should be used cautiously.

Remember, granting this authority means that your carefully-selected agent is free to pick the next person that will manage your assets while you are still alive. Giving your agent the authority to select a successor can avoid a conservatorship proceeding if your selected agent can no longer serve; only time will tell if you are more comfortable with the unknown successor agent or a court-appointed conservator. Unless you have a personal relationship with the successor agent that makes you comfortable trusting him or her, you may be better off with the court supervision that comes with a conservatorship.

What You Cannot Accomplish with a Durable Power of Attorney for Property Management

You cannot grant authority to your agent to draw up a will or other estate-planning document for you. This is a highly personal matter and can be done only by you, or under court supervision in a conservatorship proceeding. Also, while not purely financial, it is worth pointing out that your durable power of attorney cannot grant authority to vote on your behalf, adopt a child, or enter into marriage.

> Your Advance Health Care Directive or durable power of attorney for property management will do no good unless it is available when your medical needs arise. Never store your directive in a safe deposit box or other location that cannot be accessed both day and night.

Some Practical Considerations

Your Advance Health Care Directive or durable power of attorney for property management will do no good unless it is available when your medical needs arise. Never store your directive in a safe deposit box or other location that cannot be accessed both day and night. Keep the original in your home where it can be accessed at any time. Consider leaving a copy with each of your designated agents, so they will have it available whenever needed. Presenting a copy is just as good as having the original. Further, if you have a relationship with your family doctor, consider keeping a copy on file at his or her office. Finally, if you are going into the hospital for any procedure, provide the hospital with a copy in advance so that it will be in your medical chart if the need arises.

CHAPTER 24

Selecting Trustees and Guardians

You've determined your estate planning goals and carefully designed a plan to implement those goals. Now all you have to do is select a trustee (and successor trustees) who will carry out your wishes after you are gone, and a guardian to finish raising your minor children. A client of mine—an experienced litigation attorney who routinely handles complex, multimillion-dollar litigation—recently told me that selecting a trustee to handle his family trust is one of the toughest decisions he has ever had to make. Although the individual issues that go into selecting your trustee are simple, he was finding the decision difficult because resolving numerous issues that often conflict with each other and point toward different solutions is far more difficult.

The process of selecting the right trustee or guardian is a little like training to become a Jedi Knight. There is so much to learn and understand, but you cannot truly master everything you need to know until you allow the Force to be with you. Toward the end of the first Star Wars movie (Episode IV), Luke Skywalker shuts down the computers onboard his jet fighter and guides his vessel deep into the trenches of the Death Star by relying on the Force. The future of the Rebel Alliance and the Jedi Knights is riding on Luke's shoulders, and the task cannot be properly accomplished by relying on state-of-the-art computers to analyze material and guide Luke to the solution. Only reliance on the Force—some outside spiritual guide or good old-fashioned intuition—can lead Luke where he needs to go. Your search for a trustee is much like Luke's mission to destroy the Death Star, and I am your Yoda (only slightly taller and marginally better looking). Were I not concerned with violating copyright, I would start your journey to find a trustee with a solemn "May the Force…[you know the rest]"

> The process of selecting the right trustee or guardian is a little like training to become a Jedi Knight.

Qualities to Seek in a Trustee

The qualities that make a good trustee vary depending upon your goals and values, and upon the assets contained in your trust. There is no such thing as a comprehensive list of the qualities to seek in a trustee, but there are numerous qualities that are desirable in virtually all situations. Listed in this section are many of the qualities that are important in a trustee.

Trust and Integrity

The five most important qualities in a trustee are 1) trust, 2) integrity, 3) trust, 4) integrity, and 5) trust. Before you designate someone to manage every asset that you have ever earned, and everything you are leaving for your family to live on, ask yourself if he or she can be absolutely trusted. If your answer starts with "I think" or "probably," then cross that name off the list and move on to the next name. Although you can require a trustee to post a bond that can provide a form of insurance to reimburse your family for the financial loss caused by an untrustworthy trustee, recovery of the lost funds can take a long time and your family may experience difficult financial and emotional times during the process. Trustee selection is not the time to take up gambling.

> Before you designate someone to manage every asset that you have ever earned, and everything you are leaving for your family to live on, ask yourself if he or she can be absolutely trusted.

You should select your trustee based upon his or her character, not reputation. Coach John Wooden—a man known for his great success in understanding life as well as his winning college basketball teams—cautions individuals to be more concerned with character than with reputation. "Character," he points out, "is what you really are. Reputation is what people say you are." In the context of selecting a trustee, this means you should base your decision upon years of observing an individual in all kinds of situations. The best trustee is one that you have observed placing the interests of others before his or her own, even when no one else is watching. Most of us have been lucky enough to know a few people like this. Think about close friends or family whose integrity you admire, and put them on your short list of possible trustees.

> When selecting a trustee, you should base your decision upon years of observing an individual in all kinds of situations. The best trustee is one that you have observed placing the interests of others before his or her own, even when no one else is watching.

Financial Responsibility

Your trustee should be financially responsible. That is not the same as being financially sophisticated. You are not looking for an investment advisor. You are looking for a trustee who understands the need to invest prudently, and who knows his or her limitations (or, as I like to say, "Someone who knows what they know, and knows what they don't know.") Your trustee can hire a financial advisor to assist in making investment decisions. You are looking for a trustee who will understand when to hire an advisor, and will exercise care in selecting the advisor.

> You should select a trustee who understands the need to invest prudently, and who knows his or her limitations. A good trustee will understand when to hire an advisor, and will exercise care in selecting the advisor.

At the same time, your trustee should be financially secure. That is not the same as independently wealthy. It does mean that you are looking for a trustee with a steady source of income who always lives within his or her means. A trustee who cannot live within his or her means will likely have trouble managing money for your family. And, of course, a trustee who is dealing with financial stress in his or her own life may be tempted to "borrow" from the trust, just for a short time. Unfortunately, what starts as a short-term loan can quickly become a deep financial hole from which the trustee will find it difficult to emerge. By selecting a financially responsible trustee, you decrease the odds that your trustee will be tempted by a quick financial fix, and also increase the odds that your family will retain the financial benefit of your life's work.

Family Awareness

Often, your trustee will be handling investments and controlling distributions to your family for many years into the future. If you become physically or mental incapacitated, your trustee may step in and determine how to spend your money (for your benefit) while you are alive. Whether decisions are made for your benefit, or the benefit of your children and grandchildren, you will want a trustee who is aware of your values and concerns. Your trustee should understand whether you believe each of your children should work hard and save money to buy a $5,000 used car, or should receive a new Mercedes as a 16th birthday gift. If you die prematurely, many of your primary parenting duties will be assumed by the person you select as guardian of your children (discussed later in this chapter), but many parenting decisions are financial decisions as well. Those financial decisions will be made by your trustee, and will better achieve your goals if your trustee is aware of your values and parenting philosophy. This can be even more of an issue if one or more of your beneficiaries needs additional financial help and guidance due to physical or mental limitations. A trustee who knows your family well, and who has seen how you balance the needs of each family member against the others, will be better equipped to make those decisions in a manner that is consistent with your desires.

Family Unity

Perhaps even more important than balancing the financial needs of the various members of your family is the need to consider the emotional needs of each of your family members. Notice that I said "consider" not "meet." If your family is anything like mine, you pick and choose which emotional "needs" of your children you will attempt to meet and which are ignored (in hopes of teaching lessons and building character). Ideally, your trustee will know your family well enough to understand the dynamics that existed while you were alive, or at least be aware enough of family dynamics generally, and your view of life specifically, to make choices similar to those you might have made if you were still alive.

> Ideally, your trustee will know your family well enough to understand the dynamics that existed while you were alive to make choices similar to those you might have made if you were still alive.

Most likely, you will want your trustee to consider both the individual needs of each child, and the possible resentments between your children, when deciding to make early distributions to one child but not the other. Your trustee must have an awareness of each child's strengths and weaknesses, and decide when it is appropriate to allow early distributions to a particular child (for example, to use as a down payment on a house). If you were alive, you might loan (or gift) money to one child to help buy a house, but that does not mean you would do the same for another child. While you love them both, their needs, strengths, and weaknesses, are different. A loan that might help one child buy a starter home and begin to sink roots into a community, might cause another child to quit his or her job and live a life of leisure (at least until the loan money ran out). Your trustee should have the skills and knowledge to make these kinds of judgments, just as you would if you were still alive. At the same time, you may want your trustee to consider the potential impact on the relationship between your children if early distributions are made to one child and not the other. Rather than allow an early distribution to "blow your family apart," it may be more prudent to minimize the frequency and size of any early distributions. Select a trustee who is equipped to weigh these factors and make decisions in place of you.

Time and Commitment

By now, you probably realize that serving as your trustee is a serious commitment. It is an emotional commitment to your family, and it is a time commitment to your family. Select a trustee who is willing and able to commit the time necessary to manage your investments, keep detailed records regarding the trust, communicate frequently with your family, and carefully weigh the decisions that need to be made.

Ideally, your trustee will take the time necessary to explain decisions to your family. This can minimize misunderstandings and resentment over distribution decisions. Minimizing misunderstandings and resentment increases the odds of maximizing family unity.

> Select a trustee who is willing and able to commit the time necessary to manage your investments, keep detailed records regarding the trust, communicate frequently with your family, and carefully weigh the decisions that need to be made.

Team Player

In addition to understanding and communicating with your family members, your trustee may need to coordinate actions with others involved in your care or the care of your family members. For example, if you are mentally or physically incapacitated, your trustee will need to work with your agents under your Advance Health Care Directive and your durable power of attorney for property management to make sure that your trust assets are invested and paid out in a manner that supports the actions that your agents are taking to provide for your care. Similarly, if your children are living with a guardian that you appointed in your will, your trustee will need to coordinate with that guardian to make sure the children's financial needs are met.

Simply put, view your trustee and the other people you appoint to fill various other roles (agent under an Advance Health Care Directive or durable power of attorney, guardian, etc.) as members of a team. Make sure they are all team players.

Other Considerations in Selecting a Trustee

Of course, there is more to selecting a trustee that simply identifying the best individual to carry out your wishes and look after your family. In fact, sometimes an individual isn't the best choice to serve as trustee. In some situations, you will be better served by an institutional trustee (a bank or trust company). In other situations, you may wish to use two or more trustees simultaneously. However you decide, you will need to think about how to compensate your trustee.

Individual or Institutional Trustee

Family members and friends will most likely provide the greatest degree of flexibility in administering your trust. A concerned family member may take a liberal view of trust provisions in order to provide additional financial support for your family. This can be a good thing. It can also be a bad thing. When one or more family members display difficult or self-destructive behavior, such as drug or alcohol abuse, a more by-the-books approach may be appropriate. A trust officer employed by a bank or trust company will have an easier time saying "no" to your family when it needs to be said. In addition, letting an unrelated trust officer be the bad guy allows restrictions to be enforced without driving a wedge between the difficult family member and a family member-trustee. That wedge can quickly expand to include the entire family when each member of the family weighs in on one side or the other of the disagreement. In this type of situation, using an institutional trustee provides the best protection against blowing up the family. Remember, you should never allow your estate plan to blow your family apart, at least not unintentionally.

You may consider an institutional trustee if your estate is sufficiently large or complex to require sophisticated financial management. Banks and trust companies provide trustee services, but they are also well positioned to provide expert financial advice and services. If your estate will be overwhelming to your friends or family members, then an institutional trustee may be the answer.

Finally, institutional trustees can be the simple answer when your trust is likely to last longer than the reasonable life expectancy of those individuals you may consider as possible trustees. A trust for your children may be in place for 20 or 30 years, or more. Your pool of individual trustees may not include people likely to be active for that period of time. Unlike human trustees, a bank or trust company can be around virtually forever.

When to Use Co-Trustees

Appointing co-trustees makes sense in certain limited circumstances. Most often, co-trustees create added burden and expense or, at least, risk of stalemate when the co-trustees are unable to agree on how to invest funds or when to make distributions. Consequently, use of co-trustees should be limited to those circumstances that warrant additional cost or risk of stalemate.

When you wish to blend the professional management expertise of an institutional trustee with the flexibility of an individual trustee, you may be able to achieve your goals using co-trustees or special trustees. Co-trustees share equal power, while a special trustee exercises power over some specially designated aspect of the trust (for example, deciding when to make early distributions) and s e rves in conjunction with another trustee who exercises all other powers over the trust. If you have circumstances that do not lend themselves cleanly to either an individual trustee or an institutional trustee, work with an experienced estate planning professional to design blended management of your trust. Explore carefully the division of duties between the individual and the institutional trustee. Then, discuss your proposed division of duties with local trust companies that you are considering appointing. Professional trust officers have experience (both good and bad) with split-trustee arrangements. Each trust company will have its own policies regarding such arrangements. By seeking the trust company's input, you can fashion a division of duties that is likely to best accomplish your goals.

Occasionally, it may be beneficial to appoint two or more individual trustees to serve together. This is sometimes done when trust assets are intended to benefit two separate branches of a blended family, for example, when you and your spouse each have children from a prior marriage. If it is not practical to create two entirely separate trusts, you may consider appointing co-trustees from each branch of the family (for example, one adult child from your prior relationship and one adult child from your spouse's prior relationship). This can avoid the negative feelings (and potential abuse) that might arise if a sole trustee with loyalty to only one branch of the family were appointed. If you appoint co-trustees, you will need to decide whether the co-trustees must act unanimously or whether each can act independently. Again, before appointing co-trustees, discuss your goals with an experienced estate planning professional.

Appropriate Trustee's Fees

One of the nice things about working with an institutional trustee is that fees are clear. The institution will have a listed schedule of fees based upon the size of the estate and the type of assets under management. The fee is typically a percentage of the value of the assets held in the trust each year. The fee is often 1 percent of the value of the trust assets (more on smaller estates and less on larger estates). You should shop around to compare fees and services. Don't be afraid to discuss fees and negotiate a fair fee in light of the assets in your estate.

When you appoint a family member or friend, the issue of fees is more difficult. Often the trustee is willing to serve without a fee ... at least until family disputes erupt and the trust administration becomes far more time consuming than the trustee anticipated. Your trust agreement should address the issue of fees. You can simply permit the trustee to receive "reasonable fees," or you can be more specific by establishing an hourly or annual fee, or by specifying that the fees should be comparable to institutional fees. There is no right answer, but out of fairness to your trustee, the issue should be dealt with.

Qualities to Seek in a Guardian

> Selecting a guardian for your children is far more difficult than selecting a trustee. The guardian you choose must share your parenting philosophies and be a comfortable fit for your children.

Selecting a guardian for your children is far more difficult than selecting a trustee. Financial decisions—both investing your assets and controlling distributions to your children until they are mature enough to deal with a lifetime of accumulated wealth—are easy when compared to parenting decisions. Your guardian must share your parenting philosophies and be a comfortable fit for your children. To complicate the selection process, the feelings of various relatives (and your children's relationship with all the relatives after you are gone) may be a factor. Realize that choosing a guardian may be a difficult, emotional journey. Keep in mind that your spouse's desire to have the children raised by his or her side of the family is entirely natural (and needs to be fairly considered and discussed calmly to avoid marital problems), and explore the issues raised below. Good luck.

Parenting Philosophy

Your children's guardian should have a parenting philosophy and style that is comfortable for you. Are you a militaristic disciplinarian or a free-spirited flower child? Should children learn respect or learn to speak their mind? Do you "explain and guide" even in the face of the most unruly behavior or do you prefer to bring out the belt and "nip things in the bud?" Do you emphasize education or work ethic, or both? Is college about education for the sake of education or is it intended to prepare your child for a career? Explore as many issues as you can think of and understand your philosophies and goals. Realize that your attitudes may change as your children get older.

Once you understand who you are as a parent, make a list of potential guardians. Include everyone you may be willing to consider. For now, it's okay to list couples but, as discussed below, ultimately you should choose an individual (and possibly include the individual's spouse as an alternate choice). Most people start with family. If your parents (or your spouse's parents) are young enough to be up to the job (through your youngest child's 18th birthday), they can be on the list. Brothers and sisters (yours or your spouse's) deserve consideration. If you have older children who are already adults and well-established in life, they may make the list as well. Often, cousins make the list. Finally, close friends may also deserve consideration.

Take your list and compare parenting (and general lifestyle) philosophies. This will be easier if people on the list have kids of their own, particularly if the children are junior high age or older, so that child-rearing philosophies have had a chance to crystallize. Remember, if you select your parents, they will not be the same parents they were when you were raised. Not only are they 30 years older, but your children are not you. To begin with, your parents are used to relating to your children as grandparents. That means your children are used to a lot more leniency that your parents demonstrated when you were growing up. Second, you watched "Leave It To Beaver" and thought Virginia Slims ads were racy. Your children watch South Park and think Guess Jeans ads (featuring female models wearing only jeans) are tame. If you are considering your parents to raise your children, try to envision how they will parent today. Be objective about each person on the list and rank them in order of compatibility with your parenting philosophy.

Emotional Comfort (for Your Children)

Keep in mind that the guardian you select will only be needed if you (and your spouse) die prematurely. The day that your children move in with your chosen guardian they will be grieving the recent loss of one or both of their parents. At that moment in time, providing comfort and security is important. Obviously, a family member or close friend who has been an active participant in your children's lives can meet this objective well. Your business partner who is a wonderful parent and cares about your children because of your close relationship, but who sees your children once a year at the company Christmas party, does not provide the same level of comfort. Beyond emotional closeness—your child's relationship with the proposed guardian—you should factor in geographic location. If you have two equally good candidates, one who live two miles away and one who lives across the country, it is usually better to make it possible for your children to remain in the same community. Continuity is a good thing when your parents have just died.

At the same time, broader family issues can impact your decision. A potential guardian who is already raising six children of her own may not be in a position to take on your two children. Your sister-in-law who is a wonderful parent and lives two blocks away may not be a good choice if she looks down on your side of the family and is likely to cut off all contact between your children and their grandparents and aunts and uncles.

Other Considerations in Selecting a Guardian

In addition to finding the best fit for your children's needs, there are practical considerations that go into designating a guardian. Your children have already experienced the loss of both parents before their 18th birthday. Good planning will avoid the possibility of them becoming embroiled in a custody battle, or other unnecessary stresses. Therefore, you should think about the following issues.

Appoint Individual Guardians, Not Couples

There is an excellent chance that the guardian you select is married. You may even think of this person as part of a couple. There is nothing wrong with selecting your sister-in-law as your first choice to raise your children and her husband as the first alternate. However, if you designate them as a couple, your children may become part of their custody battle if they divorce. By selecting each person individually, you avoid that possibility. Divorce battles are difficult enough when it's your own parents. No need to drag your children into someone else's divorce after they've already buried you and your spouse.

Financial Considerations

Low on the list, but still a factor, is the financial ability of the proposed guardian to raise your children, particularly if adding your children to the family may require the purchase of a larger house or larger car to accommodate the expanded family. In evaluating this situation, keep in mind that income from your trust may be available to provide for these costs. If this is necessary (or helpful), make sure that your trust allows for distributions to the guardian to pay specified costs of housing or transporting your children.

Timing Distributions to Beneficiaries

In some instances, you will decide to leave your assets outright to your beneficiaries, either because the amount is modest or because the beneficiaries you have chosen are sufficiently mature to handle a sudden influx of wealth. Often, however, you will elect to distribute the assets in your estate gradually after your death. A trust is the simplest way to achieve this result.

Gradual, or multi-step, distribution is desirable whenever you are concerned that your beneficiaries may not be ready to properly manage a large sum of money. Inherent in this belief is an assumption that a high percentage of people who inherit money will spend the bulk of their inheritance before they realize

> Gradual, or multi-step, distribution is desirable whenever you are concerned that your beneficiaries may not be ready to properly manage a large sum of money.

what they are doing. I have seen this happen many times—even when the "children" are already over 50, 60, or even 70 years old. Some people will elect to distribute their entire inheritance shortly after their death, even if the distribution will be several million dollars. Their philosophy is that the kids (or other beneficiaries) should lead their own life and make their own mistakes, no matter how financially costly. Others prefer to establish a trust that can hold and invest the inheritance, provide income as needed to the beneficiary, and then make several lump-sum distributions to the beneficiaries over several years.

This chapter discusses some of the issues to consider when distributing your estate over time.

Gradual Distribution

If you have achieved the American dream—that is, your children have been given more opportunities than you were and they have achieved greater financial success than you—you may be comfortable leaving them your assets outright upon your death. They will have already invested their own earnings and made their own mistakes. The additional money is likely to be handled in a responsible manner and enhance your children's life.

If, however, you die before your children are old enough to be well established or they continue to struggle financially despite the opportunities that you have worked hard to provide, you may prefer a gradual distribution process that allows your trustee to distribute income as necessary or helpful each month, but transfers complete control of your assets gradually to allow your children to develop financial responsibility (and, if necessary, learn from their own mistakes with only a portion of your assets). Most often, this will take the form of a three-step distribution process at designated ages or stages in your children's lives. Factors that should be considered in developing a gradual or multi-step distribution plan are discussed below.

Providing Supplemental Income

If you elect to defer distribution to your children (or other beneficiaries), you will need to determine rules for distributing supplemental income to each child during the period after you die and before he or she will receive complete control of your assets. You must first decide what you wish to accomplish by delaying distribution. If you are delaying distribution so that your children will be forced to earn their own way, then your trust should allow distributions during the interim period only for necessities or emergencies, such as income during times of disability or expenses of medical treatment. You may, or may not, choose to modify this to allow distribution to pay educational expenses (or even living expenses while your beneficiary is enrolled in a full-time educational program), depending upon your views regarding the value of your child earning his or her way through college or graduate school.

Alternatively, you may elect to provide income to each of your beneficiaries to maintain a lifestyle that you consider appropriate. This will require you to define the lifestyle that you are willing to support so that your trustee can implement your wishes. This can be difficult to define, and can create tension between your beneficiaries and the trustee, but you are free to define a lifestyle with reference to the standards of a particular geographic community, or with respect to your lifestyle or the lifestyle that has been achieved by most of your children. If you choose to distribute income in a restrictive manner, you may consider working with a bank or trust company as trustee to minimize the personal side of the potential tension between beneficiary and trustee.

Two common standards for distribution of support to beneficiaries are providing for "health, education, support, and maintenance," and providing for "comfort, welfare, and happiness." Both standards have evolved from federal tax law principals. The first, "health, education, support, and maintenance," is considered by the tax law to be an objective standard that requires the trustee to distribute income as needed to maintain the beneficiary's accustomed lifestyle. It is not an objective, poverty level standard, or even an objective, community standard. It is a ballpark approximation of the beneficiary's normal lifestyle. This is easy to determine for your surviving spouse, since it should approximate the lifestyle that you and your spouse have been enjoying. It is a little more difficult to pinpoint when applied to your children or other beneficiaries since it may still be a moving target (for example, if your child is still in college at the time of your death, his or her lifestyle may be modest, although you and the trustee likely expect it to become more substantial after college). Most trustees are comfortable with the guidance provided by referring to "health, education, support, and maintenance," but if you wish to tailor a more specific standard (and can carefully define your wishes), you are free to do so.

The second standard, "comfort, welfare, and happiness," is a more subjective standard and is largely in the hands of the beneficiary to define. After all, comfort—and even more so, happiness—are highly dependent upon the state of mind of the beneficiary. This subjective standard is often used for a surviving spouse, but should be used sparingly for other beneficiaries.

Make sure that your trust provides as much income as you desire for your beneficiaries during the period that the trust assets are managed for their benefit—and not more than you desire.

Matching Distributions to Financial Maturity

The primary goal of a multi-step distribution process is to match the ultimate distribution of assets—that is, the turning over of complete control of your assets—to the coming of age (financially) of your beneficiaries. When you are controlling assets for the benefit of your children, you may wish to defer the transition of control until a point in time when your child is likely to understand the value of money. You need to explore when that may occur given your family history and the social environment in which you are raising your children. With rare exception, most people do not begin to understand the value of money until they have been self sufficient, and employed full time, for at least a few years. Some take much longer than that. Guessing the precise age that any child reaches financial maturity is impossible. You can, however, make a reasonable guess by looking at family and neighborhood influences, and factoring in what you have observed about your children's personalities (you've likely noticed that some children spend their allowance within hours, while others save for larger objectives).

If you are planning to assist your children financially through college (or graduate school), you may want to delay the first lump-sum distribution until a few years after you anticipate they will graduate from college. Again, look at your family history and social environment to help you guess whether your children are likely to graduate college in four years, six years, or more. If you, and most of your siblings, attended college and graduated in four years, it is probably reasonable to assume your children will do the same (unless you are aware of other factors that make it unlikely). If that is the case, you may wish to permit the first of three lump-sum

> The primary goal of a multi-step distribution process is to match the ultimate distribution of assets—that is, the turning over of complete control of your assets—to the coming of age (financially) of your beneficiaries.

distributions at age 24 (about three years after anticipated college graduation). However, if children in your family are not fully grown until completing graduate school (at age 25 or 27), then you may wish to set the first distribution at age 29 or 30. Of course, if you are still alive, no distributions will be made to anyone (except you). In case you die prematurely, try to pick an age when you expect your children to be financially mature enough to manage the assets you leave behind.

Once you determine the age for the first distribution, you will need to decide how far apart to space out subsequent distributions. The purpose of spacing out the distributions is to allow your children time to learn from their mistakes. If your son receives a lump-sum distribution of $150,000 when he turns 28, he will likely feel quite rich. Even if he is several years out of college and is making $150,000 per year, he is not used to receiving a single check for $150,000. If he is paid twice a month, his gross paycheck is $6,250 per pay period. After taxes, his check is perhaps $4,000. When he receives the initial $150,000 check, he will undoubtedly think he is rich. There is a reasonable possibility that six months later, he will be looking around wondering what happened to all the money. If that happens, it's not the end of the world (or his inheritance). By utilizing a three-step distribution, we have been able to keep the bulk of his inheritance preserved and protected for his benefit. After he has learned his lesson (by blowing through his first inheritance)—perhaps two to five years after the first distribution—your trust can make a second distribution. Make sure the second distribution is sufficiently large so that your son will feel rich again (twice as large as the first distribution is probably sufficient). This will give your son a second chance to learn how to hold on to, and manage, money. Then, schedule the final distribution for two to five years after the second distribution. Unless you are of a mind to control the money for your child's entire life—and you can if you wish—the third chance will be the end of the line. If he hasn't learned from the first two opportunities, he just might never learn to manage money.

After you select the appropriate ages for distribution, you will need to decide what percentage of your estate to distribute at each age. Try to make each distribution large enough so that your child feels wealthy when he or she receives it. While we hope your child is financially mature before the first distribution, the real purpose of the multi-step distribution plan is to allow your children to learn from their mistakes. The impression that the mistake makes on your child is directly proportional to how rich he or she feels receiving the first distribution. If the distribution is only $10,000, the fact that it is gone in just a few months is no surprise (and does not teach your child anything). At the same time, do not make the initial distribution too large. An initial distribution of 10 to 20 percent of each child's total share of the estate is ideal. If your son "blows through" the first distribution without even noticing, there is still 80 to 90 percent of the value remaining after the first opportunity to learn the lesson. The second distribution can be 20 to 35 percent of the remaining balance and still be significantly larger than the first distribution (to increase the chance that your son will learn the second time if he didn't quite get the message the first time around). Even if your son is a slow learner (financially speaking), he'll still have 50 to 70 percent of his inheritance left after the first two mistakes. If he has matured financially by the third distribution, the inheritance you left him can still make his life substantially easier.

By the way, if you are not comfortable pegging distributions to age, rather than to achievement or actual maturity, it is theoretically possible to condition distribution on the occurrence of specified events, or on the trustee's subjective analysis of your children's financial maturity. However, each of these concepts has difficult issues. If your son does not graduate college, either because he joins the military or because he starts a successful computer-based business, would you defer his inheritance indefinitely? What distribution, if any, would you make if your son marries young and works 60 hours a week to provide for his family (but fails to meet the benchmarks you have set for distribution)? If you give the trustee discretion to decide when your children are financially mature enough to receive their inheritance, will you set standards for the trustee to follow in making the determination? Whether or not you set objective standards for the trustee to follow, imagine the tension between the trustee and each of your children over whether or not he or she has achieved financial maturity. Performance-based (rather than age-based) criteria should be used carefully, and only when you believe that the age-based rules will not achieve your objective. If you choose performance-based criteria, work with an experienced estate planning professional to explore the consequences carefully. Take the time to make sure that your distribution criteria doesn't cause unintended consequences.

Special Protection Situations

The three-step distribution works well for many families. It does not, however, work well in every situation. When your beneficiaries display a greater need for protection from themselves—for example, due to mental or physical limitations, financial irresponsibility that persists well into middle age, or alcohol or drug abuse—you should consider tailoring your trust to meet these special needs.

> When your beneficiaries display a greater need for protection from themselves—for example, due to mental or physical limitations, financial irresponsibility that persists well into middle age, or alcohol or drug abuse—you should consider tailoring your trust to meet these special needs.

Financial Irresponsibility

Some children never grow up. When I was a young attorney, my very first "brother-sister" dispute over Mom and Dad's estate involved a brother and two sisters who were all over the age of 70. Some 70-year-olds are still spending every penny the minute they touch it, or sooner. If one or more of your children (or other beneficiaries) spends like there's no tomorrow—particularly if you do not approve of the spending decisions he or she makes—then you may not want to distribute assets directly to that child, even in three steps over several years.

Your trust can be structured to provide lifetime income to the financially irresponsible beneficiary without allowing access to the assets in the trust. A sibling of the irresponsible beneficiary, a close family friend, or an institutional trustee (bank or trust company) can invest the trust assets and make distributions to the beneficiary only as needed to provide monthly support to the beneficiary. The assets that remain after the beneficiary passes on can be left to his or her children (or anyone else you select). You will, of course, need to define how and when to distribute income to the beneficiary, just as would be necessary for supplemental income distributions under the three-step distribution plan. Mandating distribution as necessary for the beneficiary's health, education, support, and maintenance can provide reasonable support without permitting the beneficiary to waste the entire estate. Keep in mind, however, that the "comfort, welfare, and happiness" standard—that allows the beneficiary substantial say over the distributions—is not consistent with the purpose of restricting the distributions.

Substance Abuse Problems

As in the case of financial irresponsibility, outright distribution of assets to a beneficiary who is battling substance abuse is not desirable. But where substance abuse is a problem, even monthly distribution to provide basic living expenses can be undesirable.

If you are concerned that the inheritance you leave your children may enable one or more of them to finance self-destructive behavior—for example, drug or alcohol abuse—you should consider giving your trustee the authority to withhold distributions when appropriate. You can empower your trustee to limit distribution when outward signs of drug or alcohol abuse appear, or you can vest your trustee with the right to insist on periodic (and/or random) drug testing. In either case, the trustee's job will be difficult and the tension between the trustee and the beneficiary will likely be substantial (not unlike the difficult "tough love" decisions that a parent can be faced with when a child experiences substance abuse problems during the parent's lifetime).

Be objective about your children (or other beneficiaries) and when they display self-destructive behavior, discuss appropriate restrictions with your estate-planning advisor.

Physical and Mental Disability

You should consider substantial limitations on distributions to a beneficiary who is receiving, or is likely to need at some time during his or her lifetime, government benefits such as medical care or disability payments that are based upon financial need. As discussed in detail in Chapter 20, a properly structured trust can supplement government benefits, while outright distributions may reduce government benefits (so that the inheritance you leave your child does nothing to improve his or her situation). If you are in this situation, use a special needs trust designed to meet your particular needs. By doing so, your child's inheritance can enhance his or her living situation, rather than merely replace funds previously provided by government programs.

After providing your beneficiary with a lifetime of supplemental income, the assets remaining in the special needs trust can be left to your beneficiary's children, or to anyone else that you choose.

Reducing Blended-Family Tension

Family dynamics are difficult enough if you are a Leave-It-To-Beaver family. Today's extended Brady-Bunch families present land mines for day-to-day life that loom even larger in the estate-planning context. Providing assets for your surviving spouse to live on—such as a paid-off house, ownership in the family business, a retirement account, and some savings—is a challenge. Structuring those same assets to provide for your surviving spouse, your children from your first marriage, the children from your spouse's prior marriage, and the child you have with this spouse, is a nightmare. Competing claims on your assets from step-relatives (especially when they have

Structuring your assets to provide for your surviving spouse, your children from your first marriage, the children from your spouse's prior marriage, and the child you have with this spouse, can be a nightmare.

never lived in the same home) raise financial and emotional issues that require careful exploration. Some common situations are discussed in this chapter.

Providing for the Stepparent/Spouse

Stepparents come in all varieties. If you remarry when your child is in preschool, your new spouse may be thought of simply as a "parent" without the normal baggage associated with a "step" relationship, particularly if your child lives with you and your spouse full time. On the other extreme, a 30-year-old bride of a 70-year-old father is barely even considered a stepparent. How the existence of "step" relationships will affect your estate plan will depend upon where you fall along the continuum. Decide whether your spouse is accepted as a parent, or merely tolerated as a stepparent. Take off your rose-colored glasses and be objective.

In order to protect and provide for both your spouse and your children, you need to understand their relationship with each other. Start by examining the objective factors. Was your spouse in the picture when your children were growing up, or did he or she come into the picture later? Did your children ever live with you and your spouse, or were you the weekend parent? Does your spouse have children from a prior relationship and, if so, how do your children get along with your spouse's children? Do you and your spouse have children together? If so, how do your children relate to their half brother or sister? If your children grew up living in a home with you and your spouse, and your spouse does not have children of his or her own (who may be favored over your children), then there is a greater likelihood of family harmony. If your spouse entered the picture after your children were grown, and you spend most family holidays with your spouse's grown children (rather than your own), there is a good chance that the relationship between your spouse and children is remote.

Once you understand the relationship between your spouse and your children, you need to decide on your goals. You may wish to leave all of your assets to your spouse (who has been a wonderful companion through good and bad times), knowing full well that everything you own may someday belong entirely to your spouse's children. This is fine if it makes sense to you. Understand, however, that leaving everything to your spouse is an expression of your estate planning philosophy. You will be saying to your children, "Inheritance is not a right." This philosophy may feel right to you, especially if you provided your children with the things you considered import during your lifetime (for example, by providing a college education that helped them get a good start on life). It may be even more appropriate if your relationship with your child is strained. On the other hand, you may wish to ensure that your children receive some portion of your assets either simultaneously with your spouse or after your spouse no longer needs the assets to live on. Once you figure out your personal goal, your trust can be designed accordingly.

If you elect to provide fully for your spouse so long as he or she lives, irrespective of how that impacts your children's inheritance, you can create a trust that keeps all of your assets available to maintain his or her lifestyle for life and then leaves some or all of the remaining assets, if any, to your children. If your primary goal is to provide for your spouse, you will need to decide whether money should be liberally provided to support any lifestyle he or she chooses, or the distributions should be limited to maintaining a lifestyle comparable to the one that you shared with your spouse when you were alive. Then, you will need to decide who will serve as trustee (and be responsible for making the initial determination regarding the appropriate amount of the distribution). Will it be your spouse or one of your children? Either choice allows the person serving as trustee to push the rules slightly in their own favor. More importantly, unless your spouse and children have a particularly close relationship, there is a significant chance that the tension between them will be magnified by the monetary issues. For that reason, some people elect to use an institutional trustee (bank or trust company) to determine the appropriate amount of the distribution. No answer is right or wrong. You simply need to decide which goal is most important to you and design your trust to favor the desired outcome. If you are the sole provider for your spouse and the relationship has been strong, then risking that your children receive little or no inheritance (because your spouse needs everything to maintain an affluent lifestyle) may make sense. If your spouse has significant assets of his or her own, or the marriage was relatively short in duration, you may choose to take greater steps to protect your children's future inheritance.

If your wealth is great enough so that your spouse can survive nicely on less than all of the assets (or you simply want to provide some immediate inheritance to your children), you can divide the assets upon your death and leave some portion available to your spouse while leaving the rest directly to your children. The portion left to your spouse can be left completely within his or her control (such that it can then be left to your spouse's children, or to someone that your spouse marries after you are gone), or can be kept available to him or her for life and then be distributed to your children. Once again, you must decide what feels right for you and implement a plan that achieves your goals. A good estate planning attorney can guide you through these issues and make sure your trust works in a manner consistent with your desires.

Allocating Among Children and Stepchildren

Other issues arise for a married couple providing for children from prior relationships. Consider a slightly different Brady Bunch—for example, if Marcia, Jan, and Cindy didn't get along with Greg, Peter, and Bobby. Then, imagine how much more complicated it would be if Mike and Carol added a seventh child to the family by having a child together (let's call him Benny). How would Mike and Carol divide the money between the Brady Girls, the Brady Boys, and Benny, if none of them got along with each other? If Carol died first, could she count on Mike to provide fairly for Marcia and the girls? How would Greg and the boys fare if Mike died first? Let's consider some options.

Option 1: If You Can't Trust Your Spouse, Who Can You Trust?

Mike and Carol are fair people. More importantly, they both love all the kids equally. They can trust each other to treat all the kids fairly and do what's right. So keep things simple. Why not give the survivor control over everything? For example, if Mike dies first, let Carol use all the assets to live on. To maximize estate tax benefits, we'll designate one-half of the assets as Carol's (the Survivor's Trust) and one-half the assets as Mike's (the Bypass Trust). Carol can draw on both halves equally to maintain her lifestyle. When she passes away, divide what's left into seven equal shares (one for each of the three Brady girls, one for each of the three Brady boys, and one for baby Benny), but give Carol discretion to increase or decrease a child's share. The flexibility will allow her to leave more to a child with greater financial needs (for example, if Cindy's husband dies in an auto accident leaving her with two small children to raise on her own), or less to a child who has enjoyed great financial success (for example, if Greg hits it big as a computer nerd in the first dot-com boom). But remember, this isn't the Brady Bunch you knew on TV. Marcia, Jan, and Cindy don't trust Greg, Peter, and Bobby, and the feeling is mutual. All of the original Brady kids dislike Benny, because he is clearly Mike and Carol's favorite (after all, he's the only one that is a product of their love). Imagine the jockeying for position after Mike passes away. Even if Carol wants to be fair to everyone, how can she when every decision she makes will be met with suspicion? And, what if she actually does leave everything to the Brady girls (or the girls and Benny)? Is that what Mike expected or wanted? Not likely. More importantly, instead of reducing tension in the family, this plan seems to pit stepchild against stepchild and increase tension and distrust. In most situations, leaving complete discretion to the surviving spouse is not the best way to reduce tension among stepchildren.

Option 2: To Each His Own

This time, let's not put Carol if the middle of everything. When Mike dies, let's take his half of the assets and keep it available to Carol if she needs it to supplement her own half of the assets. If she doesn't need to use Mike's half of the assets, it will be divided into equal shares for his four children (the three Brady boys and baby Benny). When Carol dies, she can leave her share to the three Brady girls (and can include baby Benny if she wishes). Under this plan, the Brady boys no longer have to worry that their stepsisters are lobbying Carol (that is to say, their "real" mom) to leave nothing to the boys (or vice versa if Carol dies before Mike). The tension is reduced between the two groups, and the pressure on Carol drops accordingly. Of course, the tension won't be completely gone if Carol's share is too small. Carol may resent that her lifestyle is limited by the boys' future claim on Mike's half of the money. In addition, if Carol's half shrinks every year because her living expenses exceed the income earned on her half, while Mike's half grows each year, Carol's daughters will ultimately receive far less than the boys. There is no simple answer. You need to explore the possible tensions in light of the size of your estate (and the nature of the assets) and find a resolution that works best for you. An experienced estate planning professional can help you find your way through these potential conflicts.

Yours, Mine, and Ours

You may have noticed that many of the ideas for reducing stepfamily tensions also result in disproportionate distributions to each child. Two issues arose when we divided the money into Mike's half and Carol's half. If Mike dies first and Carol is required to live primarily on her half of the assets, the boys will likely receive larger shares than the girls since Mike's half is safely invested to grow larger each year while Carol is using her share to live on. For example, if the total estate is $2,400,000, each half (consisting of $1,200,000 of assets) could generate $72,000 per year (assuming a 6 percent return on investment). Carol would use the $72,000 generated by her half to live on, while Mike's half grew at the rate of $72,000 per year. If Carol lives for 10 years, her half will still be worth $1,200,000, while Mike's half has increased to $1,920,000 (ignoring the effects of compounding the growth). When Carol dies, each of the girls will receive $400,000, while each of the boys will get $640,000. This result may be acceptable to you, or it may not. That's entirely up to you. But understand that the restrictions intended to lessen stepfamily tension will also have unintended consequences.

But remember, we added baby Benny to the equation. How does he fare under this example? Let's assume that Carol divides her half into four equal shares; one for each girl and one for Benny. What if Mike does the same with his share (for Benny and the boys)? Each of the girls will receive $300,000

($1,200,000 ÷ 4), each of the boys will receive $480,000 ($1,920,000 ÷ 4), and Benny will receive $780,000 ($300,000 + $480,000). This doesn't seem fair, at least not on the surface. Some parents (and stepparents) are not satisfied with the disproportionate result. Others find the result acceptable. Why? Some parents reason that Benny will inherit money only from them, while the stepchildren may inherit something from "the other side of the family." Let's look at the Brady Bunch, again. We know that Mike was widowed. I don't recall whether Mike's first wife's parents were still alive, but if they are, it's possible they will leave some inheritance to the boys. Add what the boys receive from their maternal grandparents to their $480,000 and it may seem fair when compared to Benny's $780,000. The same may be true of the girls. I don't know if Carol was widowed or divorced, but each of the girls may stand to inherit from their father (if Carol was divorced) or their paternal grandparents (if Carol was widowed). If you want to equalize for possible "outside inheritance" you need to do two things:

1. carefully evaluate the potential for inheritance from other sources (such as your former spouse or former spouse's family); and
2. make sure you really know what the outside source is (or is not) going to do.

The second part of the equation is important. Just because your former spouse has money doesn't mean he or she intends to leave any of it to one of your children. He or she may be leaving everything to a new spouse, or even to charity. If it is important to you to leave each child a mathematically equal amount, then make sure you have all the facts that go into the mathematical equation (although it may be impossible to find out your former spouse's net worth or estate plan). Do the best you can, but understand that there is no perfect solution.

Communication Is the Only Solution

You may have gathered by now that you won't achieve perfect mathematical equality and that you won't completely avoid tension between members of the stepfamily. In fact, you won't even avoid all tension if you are a 1950s Leave It

To Beaver family. Money—and inheritance is money—often brings out the worst in people (and your family is made up of people).

There is, however, one way to reduce tension and achieve some level of equality (even if it is not mathematical equality). That is communication. If you are comfortable, talk to your children (and other beneficiaries) about your personal estate planning goals. If you are not comfortable discussing such things during your lifetime, at least incorporate some explanation of your goals into your estate planning documents. You can incorporate language into a will or trust, or you can write a separate letter that can be kept with your estate planning documents to be read after your death.

Whether you choose discussion during your lifetime, or a letter to be read at a later date, you should explain what you have chosen to accomplish in your estate plan. If you are leaving more to one child because of physical or mental limitations that reduce his or her ability to earn an income, tell the other children that this is why they are getting a smaller share. If you are leaving less for your daughter from your first marriage because you think she will inherit millions from your first spouse, make sure she knows that. Explain why money is being distributed to your children slowly over time. The more you can explain the reasoning that went into designing your estate plan, the lower the tension may be. Like everything else about estate planning, this is not a perfect solution, but it usually can reduce tension and result in a smoother transition upon your death.

Avoiding Costly Estate Disputes

T wo of the most common goals in estate planning are:

1. providing for a smooth, efficient transition of your assets to your family (or other chosen beneficiaries), and

2. minimizing the cost of the transition (by avoiding or reducing probate expense and by minimizing estate taxes).

If your family members or beneficiaries end up in a dispute over your will or trust, neither goal will be met. A disputed will or trust is neither smooth nor efficient, and certainly does not reduce costs. A dispute can literally involve years of litigation in the local probate court with each side (and there can be more than two sides) incurring attorney's fees quickly mounting into the tens or hundreds of thousands of dollars.

What causes disputes over your will or trust, and what can you do to reduce the risk for your family?

How Do Disputes Arise?

Disputes arise either from problems related to documentation or problems related to implementation.

Documentation Problems

A documentation problem arises when one or more of your family members or other beneficiaries believes that your estate planning documents leave them less than you intended (or less than they would receive by law if you had no will or trust). Although you are free to leave your assets where you see fit, others can challenge your documents after you die *if they have a legally proper reason*. Some of the common reasons for disputing a will or trust are as follows:

- The will or trust was procured by fraud—someone who is benefiting under the will or trust literally tricked you into signing it by telling you it was some other (less important) document.

- The will or trust was procured by undue influence—someone who is benefiting under the will or trust used improper influence to force you to sign the document. Holding a gun to your head would be an extreme case of this, withholding medical care or living assistance is a more common situation. In many states, caretakers and estate planning advisors are presumed to have exercised undue influence if the will or trust leaves anything to them (unless they are also close relatives).

- The will or trust was signed at a time that you were mentally incapacitated—you signed the document even though you were not able to understand that it had the legal effect of disposing of your assets upon your death.

- The will or trust inadvertently omits an heir that you would likely have intended to include.
- The will or trust is a forgery—someone signed your name without your knowledge or consent.

Implementation Problems

Implementation problems occur when the person legally responsible for implementing your estate plan fails to carry out his or her duties (see Chapter 29, Administering Trusts Post-Death), or the rules that you established are unclear and a dispute arises regarding the proper interpretation of the rules. I call this a brother-sister dispute, since it commonly occurs in moderate-sized trust situations where one sibling has been appointed to manage the trust assets for a period of time and then distribute the assets among the siblings or the siblings' children. Whether the situation arises from an innocent misunderstanding, or from the trustee-sibling intentionally attempting to take more than his or her share of the assets, the result can be lengthy litigation costing tens or hundreds of thousands of dollars in legal fees.

Your estate plan should be designed to minimize the risk of disputes, whether from documentation or implementation.

Reducing the Risk of Documentation Disputes

Two simple drafting "tricks" can reduce the chance of a documentation dispute. The risk of most potential documentation disputes can be reduced by including a carefully drafted "no-contest" clause in your will and trust, so that anyone who challenges your documents will be disinherited. In addition, proper reference to intentionally excluding any potential heir that you do not want to receive a share of your assets will reduce the chance of a successful challenge on the basis that the heir was inadvertently omitted from your estate plan.

> The risk of most potential documentation disputes can be reduced by including a carefully drafted "no-contest" clause in your will and trust, so that anyone who challenges your documents will be disinherited.

In addition, clear communication of your desires—either verbally during your lifetime or in writing to be opened upon your death—can reduce the risk of a dispute. Many disputes arise because different beneficiaries have distinctly different views of what you really wanted to achieve through your estate plan. The more clearly you explain your goals, the less room for disagreement.

The No-Contest Clause

The most common technique to reduce the risk of a documentation dispute is inclusion of a "no-contest" clause in your estate planning documents. The clause should be included in your will and your trust, and should make clear that it will apply to all future amendments to either document. A typical no-contest clause in a trust document reads something like this:

"No-Contest Clause. If any beneficiary, alone or acting with others, directly or indirectly contests this instrument, any amendment to this instrument, or the wills of the settlors, in whole or in part, or opposes, objects to, or seeks to invalidate any of the provisions of this trust (or amendments), or the wills (or codicils) of the settlors, or seeks to take any part of the estate of the settlors other than as specified in this trust (or amendments), or in the wills (or codicils) of the settlors, then the right of that person to take any interest given to him or her by this trust or any amendment to this trust shall be void, and any gift or other interest in the trust property to which the beneficiary would otherwise have been entitled shall pass as if he or she had predeceased the settlors without issue."

The no-contest clause does not prohibit anyone from challenging your estate plan. It only acts as a deterrent. The deterrent effect will only be significant if the heir who wishes to challenge the trust has something to lose. You may wish to leave something significant to an heir you believe may challenge the will so that he or she will be faced with losing something of value as a result of the challenge. If you leave little or nothing to the potentially disgruntled heir, he or she sees little risk in challenging the document. Instead, with no inheritance at risk, he or she may chose to contest the document since a successful challenge may invalidate the entire document, including the no-contest clause.

Consider this example. A father who has not spoken to his son for 15 years has accumulated a multi-million dollar estate. Since he has no relationship with his son, and has no other relatives, he has decided to leave his entire estate to charity. He expressly intends to exclude his son from the will and includes language making that clear. He does not want to leave even $100,000 to his son (for its deterrent effect), even though that is less than 1 percent of his estate. By leaving his son nothing, he is making it less risky for his son to challenge the will. If the son contests the will unsuccessfully, he will receive nothing; the same amount he will receive if he does nothing. If dad had been willing to leave his son $100,000, the cost of challenging the will would be $100,000, since the no-contest clause would take away the inheritance. Giving up $100,000 might be more than the son is willing to do.

The point is simple. Consider leaving something to an heir who may be disgruntled as a way to increase his or her cost of challenging your estate plan. Most estate disputes are the result of greed. Making sure that it costs real money to challenge your will or trust is the best way to reduce the chances of a contest.

Excluding Heirs Intentionally

If you have a spouse, child, or other close relative, who you do not want to receive anything from your estate, make clear that you have intentionally excluded him or her from participating. Do not simply leave his or her name off the list of people you want to share in your estate. Use language something like this: "I have not seen my son, Joe, in 15 years and I have intentionally left him nothing." That simple statement—that you are leaving nothing to Joe, and why—will protect your estate from Joe's claim that you inadvertently omitted him from your will or trust.

Communicate Your Wishes and Your Reasons

The best way to reduce the chance of a documentation dispute is to clearly express your wishes, and reasons, to your family and other intended beneficiaries. Many disputes erupt because one or more of your beneficiaries is surprised by your estate plan. If you make your wishes known while you are alive, your beneficiaries are more likely to go along with your plan after you pass away. Also, clear statements of your reasons, set forth in your will or trust or in a separate letter kept with your estate documents, may reduce the chance of a dispute.

Finally, if you're leaving your assets in a manner that you anticipate may provoke a dispute by one or more beneficiaries, then make sure you have carefully documented your desires and reasons. Work with an experienced estate planning professional to make sure that your desires are well documented in a manner that will best support your goals. This may not reduce the chance of a dispute erupting, but at least it will increase the odds that your estate plan will be upheld and your desires are carried out.

Avoiding Implementation Disputes

Implementation disputes arise when the trustee or executor who you selected does not live up to your expectations. Either something has changed since you selected your trustee using the criteria discussed in Chapter 24 (trust and integrity, financial responsibility, etc.), or you were not objective in evaluating the issues. I have two daughters and I know they are both perfect in most every way (not to mention, beautiful and funny). However, unless I can remain objective about their strengths and weaknesses (assuming, hypothetically, that they have weaknesses) I cannot determine whether either of them would make a good trustee for my estate plan. When you are selecting your trustee, be objective, and try to overcome your belief that your children are nearly as perfect as mine. Magnify every warning sign you see that could affect your decision. Look objectively at your child's spending habits as well as his or her level of integrity. Most importantly, look for signs of conflict between your children. After all, the implementation disputes will be the result of differences of opinion between your children. If their lifestyles and spending habits are drastically different, putting one child in charge of the trust that is intended to benefit all of your children may be a problem. Explore this carefully with an experienced estate planning professional to make sure you are making an informed and comfortable selection of a trustee.

In making your analysis, be mindful of the assets that are in the trust. If the largest single asset is your family home and one of your adult children still lives with you, making that child the trustee of a trust that is supposed to sell the house and divide the money may not work well. Your live-at-home trustee will have a built-in conflict of interest. Selling the family home so that his or her siblings can have their share of the assets you left for their benefit means that the trustee will no longer have a place to live. Appointing your live-at-home adult child as trustee is simply inviting an implementation dispute when two years go by and the house has not been sold. At the same time, making one of the other children the trustee, and putting him or her in the position of having to evict a sibling who continually finds an excuse to delay moving out of the family home, may not be any better. If your assets are such that each child is likely to have a different interest to protect, you may wish to consider a corporate trustee or a close family friend who is strong enough to rise above the potential conflict. Again, explore these issues with an experienced estate-planning attorney and fashion a solution that fits your circumstances.

CHAPTER 28

Administering Trusts During Your Lifetime

If you establish a trust, you may also need to take certain steps during your lifetime in order to achieve all of your estate planning goals. If the trust you create is a revocable family trust, then the steps will be modest. If you create an irrevocable trust (such as a life insurance trust), then you will need to take several more steps during your lifetime. This chapter outlines some the basic steps that will need to be taken during your lifetime.

Revocable Family Trusts

When you create a revocable family trust, it is generally "transparent." There is not a lot that needs to be

A revocable family trust is generally "transparent." There is not a lot that needs to be done to maintain the trust, and the way you handle your money will not change in any significant manner.

done, and the way you handle your money will not change in any significant manner. However, you do need to take a couple basic steps to fully implement your revocable trust.

First, you should execute a "pour over" will that provides that any assets that you have not put into the trust will be put in the trust upon your death. This will acts as a safety net that will make sure all of your assets are subject to the rules you created for your trust (and protected for the benefit of your family and beneficiaries).

Next, you will need to "fund" your trust. This simply means putting your real estate, bank and brokerage accounts, and other assets, into the name of the trust. If you do not take the steps necessary to fund the trust, your pour over will still brings the assets under the trust rules after you die, but your family will be put through the effort and expense of probating your assets. This cost is avoided if you take the time to fund the trust.

Funding the trust involves preparing and recording deeds for each piece of real estate that you own, transferring ownership from you as an individual to you as trustee of your family trust. Change title on the property from "John Trustor and Mary Trustor, joint tenants" to "John Trustor and Mary Trustor, co-trustees of the Trustor Family Trust udt [*under declaration of trust*] dated Jan. 1, 2001." There will be modest recording fees involved, but they will likely be minimal. Work with a qualified professional to make sure that you do not trigger any unexpected tax consequences. For example, in California transferring real estate can trigger an increase in property tax unless proper forms are filled out indicating that the transfer is exempt from reassessment for property tax purposes. The form is simple to complete, but failure to complete it can result in a significant increase in your annual property tax bill. Make sure you work with someone familiar with the rules in each state where you own real estate so that no unintended consequences occur.

Funding the trust also involves changing the name on your bank and brokerage accounts, and other assets held in your name. You can start the process by writing to your bank or brokerage and requesting that they change the name on the account from your name individually to your name as trustee of the trust. You do not need to open new accounts. It is enough to change the name on your existing accounts. In addition, you should change title to any car, boat, or airplanes that you own by contacting the motor vehicle department, Coast Guard, or other agency where the vehicle is registered. Once again, you are simply moving title from your name individually to your name as trustee of the trust.

Once the property and accounts have been transferred into your name as trustee of the trust, you can continue to handle everything just as you did before. Any income that is earned in the trust is still reported on your personal income tax return each year. The money (and everything else in the trust) is still yours to do with as you wish since the trust is revocable. Essentially, the trust is transparent while you are still alive.

If you are single, or you are married but you created your trust separately from your spouse, then there is nothing more to do during your lifetime. However, if you have a trust jointly with your spouse, one of you will have to perform an additional function during your lifetime. Whichever one of you outlives the other will need to meet with your estate planning attorney or accountant within a few months after the death of the first spouse to die. Your estate planning advisor will help you allocate the assets in the trust into two or three subtrusts (remember the Survivor's Trust, Bypass Trust, and QTIP Trust, from Chapter 15?). You will decide which assets should be allocated to which subtrust by looking at the estate tax consequences and your desire to have certain assets more subject or less subject to your complete control. Assets you allocate to the Survivor's Trust will be fully within your control and handled exactly as if you owned the asset directly. Depending on the terms you created for your trust, assets in the Bypass Trust and the QTIP Trust may be subject to limitations on your ability to use the income, leave the asset to someone on your death, or ability to sell the assets. After reviewing all of the factors, you will decide which assets should be allocated to which subtrust.

After you allocate assets to each subtrust, you will continue to exercise full control over everything in the Survivor's Trust, and any income generated by those assets will be reported on your personal income tax return each year. The Survivor's Trust is essentially transparent.

Beginning in the year that your spouse passes away, you will start filing separate income tax returns for the Bypass Trust and the QTIP Trust. However, if the income generated by the trust is distributed to you during the calendar year, the subtrust will not pay any tax. Instead, you will report the income on your tax return and pay the tax (so that the tax will be exactly the same as if you owned the assets in your own name). You will have to pay your accountant to prepare an extra tax return each year. If the terms of the subtrust do not require (or permit) you to take the income each year, then any income that is generated in the Bypass Trust or QTIP Trust will be taxable in the trust (rather than on your personal tax return). Because trusts are generally taxed at the highest rate applicable to individuals, the tax due may be slightly greater than if the income was taxable on your personal return. You and your estate planning advisors will take this into account in allocating assets to the various subtrusts, so that you are not surprised by unexpected tax consequences. Generally, the potential estate tax saving from using the various subtrusts will far exceed the slight increase, if any, in income tax.

Irrevocable Trusts

Like revocable trusts, irrevocable trusts must be funded. In addition, whenever you are dealing with an irrevocable trust, you must consider possible gift tax requirements, and you must begin filing annual income tax returns immediately. Like the Bypass Trust and the QTIP Trust (that became irrevocable after your spouse passed away), any income that is distributed to you will be added to your personal income tax return and subject to tax at your rates. Similarly, any income that is distributed to another beneficiary (such as your children) will be included on their personal income tax return and taxable at his or her income tax rate. If your child who receives a distribution of income is under 18 years old, the income tax rules will require the income to be taxed at your rate rather than your child's. Any income that is kept in the trust and not distributed during the year will be included on the trust's income tax return and tax will be paid at the trust's income tax rate (equal to the highest personal income tax rates on all but the first few thousand dollars of income).

Whenever you put money into an irrevocable trust, you will need to determine whether or not a gift tax return needs to be filed. Certain gifts to individuals that do not add up to more than $12,000 during the calendar year do not require a gift tax return. However, gifts into an irrevocable trust will require a gift tax return to be filed even if the total for the year is less than $12,000 unless special provisions within the trust exist that give the individual beneficiary-recipient the right to withdraw the money within a certain period of time after you make the gift. If your estate planning advisors have helped you establish this type of trust, you will need to send notices to the beneficiary-recipient any time that funds are contributed into the trust. Work with your estate-planning advisor to make sure these notices are prepared in a timely fashion.

If you contribute more than $12,000 to an irrevocable trust, or you contribute less than that to a trust that does not allow the beneficiary-recipient the right to withdraw the contribution, you will be required to file a gift tax return. This does not mean you will owe gift tax. Remember, you can make gifts totaling $1 million over the course of your lifetime without triggering a penny of gift tax. The gift tax return merely notifies the government how much of your $1 million lifetime exemption you have used. If you exceed the $1 million of gifting during your lifetime, you will pay gift tax on every dollar you give away over the $1 million. Whether or not you owe any gift tax, the amount of the taxable gifts reported over your lifetime will reduce the amount that you can leave tax free upon your death. If you were to die in 2007, you could leave $2 million tax free. However, if you made $800,000 in reportable gifts during your lifetime, you could only leave $1,200,000 tax free.

Whenever you put money into an irrevocable trust, check with your estate planning professional to determine whether or not you need to file a gift tax return.

Administering Trusts Post-Death

After you pass away, your successor trustee will need to take appropriate action to administer your trust and wind up your estate. The best way to accomplish this is to work with an experienced estate planning attorney and accountant. Rules will vary somewhat by state and change over time. In general, however, your successor trustee will need to take the following steps:

- Inventory and collect your assets.
- Consider whether notice should be given to creditors in order to shorten the statute of limitations for assertion of claims against your estate.
- Prepare an estate tax return, if required.

- Arrange for payment of burial expenses, debts of the estate, etc.
- Prepare annual income tax returns for the trust each year until termination of the trust (for example, final distribution of the trust assets to children or other beneficiaries).
- Provide an accounting of trust assets, income, and expenses, on an annual basis.
- Distribute assets to your spouse, children, or other beneficiaries in the manner required or permitted by the trust.

Each of these post-death duties is discussed in more detail below.

Inventory and Collection of Assets

The successor trustee of your trust will become responsible for managing, and ultimately distributing to your beneficiaries, the assets that are in your trust. In addition, the executor of your pour-over will—likely the same person who is serving as trustee of your trust—should collect any assets that are held in your name individually and deposit them into the trust. This may involve opening a formal probate if the assets held outside your trust are substantial.

Within a few weeks of your passing, the trustee should begin compiling a preliminary inventory of your assets identifying each piece of real estate, bank or brokerage account, and other assets. The inventory should reflect the approximate value of the asset on the date of your death, and indicate whether or not any mortgage or other lien exists with respect to the property. Include as an asset any life insurance proceeds that will be paid to the estate or the trust. The list should be updated as more information is learned, and after two or three months should provide a clear picture of your assets. Obviously, the better records that you keep, the easier this task will be and the quicker it can be completed. Make sure that your successor trustee knows where to find the records that you maintain.

Notice to Creditors

You may recall that if your assets are subject to probate, creditors must assert any claim against your estate in a relatively short period of time; a matter of months rather than the years they may have to assert a claim if the probate process did not cut the statute of limitations short. In most states, the trustee of your trust can take steps to shorten the statute of limitations for making a claim against your assets by giving your creditors notice of your death and the administration of your trust. This is usually similar to the probate process except that it is not court supervised.

If you own your own business, or are a professional who is subject to potential claims for malpractice—such as an architect, accountant, doctor or attorney—your trustee should take all possible steps to reduce the statute of limitations for making claims against your assets. This will protect your money for the benefit of your spouse, children, and other beneficiaries.

When you pass away, your successor trustee will need to meet with an estate planning attorney to discuss proper trust administration. One of the areas to be discussed should be potential theoretical claims against your estate and whether or not it makes sense to take steps necessary to shorten the statute of limitations applicable to claims against your estate.

Estate Tax Return

Based upon the inventory prepared, your successor trustee will be able to determine whether or not it will be necessary to file an estate tax return. Generally, an estate tax return is required if the gross assets in your estate (including all assets, life insurance proceeds, property that you gave away in the three years immediately before your death, and certain other assets subject to your control) equal or exceed the amount that can be left free of tax in the year that you die ($2 million in 2007 and 2008, more in 2009 and 2010, but only $1 million in 2011). The return is due within nine months of the day that you die, and must be filed even if no tax is due (either because of deductions because assets are left to your spouse or to charity, or because the net value of the estate is reduced below the exemption amount by debts that you owe).

Your successor trustee should work with an accountant who is familiar with estate tax returns to accumulate the necessary information and timely prepare and file an estate tax return. If any tax is payable, it is due nine months after the date of your death. In a few circumstances, such as where more than 35 percent of the estate's value is derived from your family-owned business, or your estate includes a small family farm, you may have up to 14 years to pay the estate tax at a very low interest rate. The accountant and estate-planning attorney can guide you through the estate tax process.

Providing for Payment of Debts

While your successor trustee is collecting the assets that belong in your trust, he or she should also be determining the debts that you owe. After the trustee has determined whether or not estate taxes will be due, and the costs of legal and accounting advice needed to administer the trust are determined, your trustee can determine what assets will be available to pay your debts. Before any distributions can be made to your family or other beneficiaries, the trustee should make sure that there are sufficient assets available to pay your debts. If there are not sufficient assets to pay all your debts, then the trustee may choose to negotiate settlements with creditors for partial payment.

Income Tax Returns

Beginning in the year that you pass away, your trust will need to file income tax returns. If income is distributed to beneficiaries during the calendar year, the income will be taxable to the individual beneficiary on his or her personal tax return and at his or her marginal tax rate. To the extent that income is generated in the trust but not paid to beneficiaries during the calendar year, the trustee will need to make sure that the tax is paid in a timely fashion by the trust. Trust income tax law is complicated. Your trustee should work with an accountant who has experience preparing trust income tax returns.

Annual Accounting

When a trust becomes irrevocable, the trustee must provide periodic accountings to the beneficiaries of the trust. This means detailed reporting of the income and expenses of the trust, the distributions to the beneficiaries, and the assets remaining in the trust. Any beneficiary may ask the trustee to explain any entryin the accounting, or challenge any improper expense or missing income. If the trustee does not provide an adequate response, any beneficiary can file a petition in the local probate court challenging the accounting and seeking reimbursement from the trustee for improper expenses or missing income.

Distributions

Each year until the trust terminates—often upon final distribution when your child or other beneficiary reaches the age you specified when you set up the rules of the trust—the successor trustee will be responsible for distributing income and assets in the manner that you have specified. The successor trustee will be responsible for deciding the appropriate amount to be distributed to each beneficiary to meet the standard that you have set forth in the trust document. If you have required or permitted distribution for a beneficiary's health, education, support, or maintenance, it is the trustee who will decide how much money is necessary to provide an appropriate lifestyle for that beneficiary. Your successor trustee should be willing to accept input from the beneficiary, but still be strong enough to make his or her own decision even if the beneficiary is unhappy. Of course, if the beneficiary believes that the trustee has misapplied the rules you established in the trust, then he or she may petition the local probate court to correct the error. If your trust gives the trustee sole discretion to make distribution decisions, the probate court will interfere only if the trustee is clearly abusing his or her discretion.

Conclusion

The trust administration process is complex and subject to a variety of rules ranging from estate taxes, to debt payment, to beneficiary distribution. Your successor trustee should consult with an experienced estate-planning attorney at the beginning of the trust administration process and continue to consult whenever the need arises. Trust administration is streamlined when compared to court-supervised probate, but it is still complicated. A willingness to consult with experienced advisors will prevent unnecessary disputes and runaway legal fees.

The Future of the Estate Tax and Estate Planning

W hen Ronald Reagan took office on January 20, 1981, the highest marginal income tax rate for the wealthiest Americans was 70 percent. Today, the highest marginal income tax rate is 35 percent; a significant tax savings by anybody's standards.

For the last 10 years or more, Congress has been embroiled in a debate over whether to reduce the estate tax as significantly, or even whether to eliminate it altogether. Despite the fact that only 1 percent of American estates are large enough to incur any estate tax at all, emotional attacks alleging that the tax hurts families owning small businesses and farms have taken on a life of their own. Before mounting government deficits strained the federal budget, political momentum seemed sure to push through a repeal of the estate tax. In fact, Congress passed legislation that gradually increased the size of an estate that could be left free of estate tax from $1 million to $3,500,000, and then repealed the estate tax for a single year in 2010 before returning to the previous $1 million threshold. For a brief period of time, it seemed likely that Congress would repeal the estate tax permanently.

> Before mounting government deficits strained the federal budget, political momentum seems sure to push through a repeal of the estate tax. In recent years Congress has focused more on increasing the amount that can be transferred by any person free of estate taxes.

It appears now, however, that mounting federal deficits and changing political winds have reduced the talk of complete repeal of the estate tax. Instead, in recent years, Congress has focused more on making permanent a larger exemption amount—perhaps as much as $5 million—increasing the amount that can be transferred by any person free of estate taxes. At the same time, Congress has considered lowering the estate tax rate from its current 45 percent to a rate more in line with federal income tax rates. Some proposals have set the estate tax rate as low as the 15 percent capital gains rate while others have targeted a 35 percent tax rate (more in keeping with the highest marginal rates currently applicable in federal income tax law).

During the final two years of the George W. Bush administration, as a Democratic Congress looks toward the 2008 election, no clear direction appears with respect to the estate tax. What is clear, however, is that the uncertainty inherent in a system that allows $2 million or $3,500,000 to pass tax free for the next couple of years, then creates 365 estate-tax-free days in 2010, followed by a system that taxes any estate larger than $1 million, is unacceptable. Furthermore, in an age when average home prices in major metropolitan communities are approaching $1 million or more, a return to the $1 million exemption amount will be unacceptable to many voters (and the legislators who represent them).

As we approach 2010, the political pressure for change, and a return to a set rule that does not change from year to year, will result in revisions to the existing estate tax laws. Set forth below are some thoughts regarding possible changes, and a guess as to the likelihood of any particular change being incorporated into our estate tax laws.

Estate Tax Repeal

In the four or five federal elections prior to 9/11—before homeland security and the Iraq War became the dominant political issues—estate tax repeal was a major campaign issue. Particularly as the budget surpluses of the Clinton years grew, Congress seemed willing to consider abolishing the estate tax. Large majorities of the American public seem to fear the estate tax, even though no more than 1 percent or 2 percent of Americans will ever pay a penny of estate tax.

> In an age when average home prices in major metropolitan communities are approaching $1 million or more, a return to the $1 million exemption amount will be unacceptable to many voters.

Opponents of the estate tax have successfully labeled it a "death tax." In addition, they have argued that the estate tax makes it difficult for small businesses and farms to be handed down from one generation to the next.

More objectively, while the estate tax sometimes imposes a tax on the "transfer" of wealth that has previously been subject to income tax, in most cases estates that are large enough to trigger the estate are made up largely of investment assets, such as real estate, stocks, and bonds, that were purchased many years ago, and have never been subject to income or capital gains taxes since the owner has never needed to sell the asset. To simply pass the assets down to the next generation without any payment of tax is nothing more than a large loophole for the wealthiest American families. Admittedly, the 45 percent estate tax rate may be higher than necessary to close this loophole, but some tax is clearly needed.

> Estates that are large enough to trigger the estate are made up largely of investment assets that have never been subject to income or capital gains taxes. To simply pass the assets down to the next generation without payment of any tax is nothing more than a large loophole for the wealthiest American families.

In addition, most small family farms and businesses are small enough to avoid estate taxes in the first place—especially when the estate tax exemption is either $2 million or $3,500,000—and those that are subject to estate tax can often take advantage of rules permitting payment of the tax over 14 years at low interest rates. Protecting small farms and businesses does not require estate tax repeal. At most, it points toward increasing the exemption amount or crafting special provisions to reduce estate taxes for small farms and family businesses that are deemed to be beneficial to the economy.

Finally, you may recall from Chapter 7 that repeal of the estate tax will actually be a tax increase for a large number of small-business-owner families (see Figure 7-1). If the voting public catches on to the hidden tax increase, estate tax repeal will be dead once and for all.

In any event, given the anticipated budget deficits that appear likely even in a healthy economy, due in part to the substantial cost of increased homeland security and the war in Iraq, it seems unlikely that Congress will seriously consider estate tax repeal in the foreseeable future. That's not to say there won't be political maneuvering in the form of raising "estate tax repeal" as a rallying cry. However, neither party is likely to push too hard to actually make repeal happen.

Shifting from Estate Tax to Inheritance Tax

The estate tax is based on the total size of your estate and is paid by your estate before assets are distributed to your beneficiaries. Instead, it is possible to apply an inheritance tax that is imposed on each beneficiary, individually, on the amount that each beneficiary receives (rather than on your estate). An inheritance tax would allow any beneficiary to receive a certain amount tax free—say, $1 million—and anything over that amount could be subject to tax (either at a flat rate or at increasing rates depending upon the amount received). Under an inheritance tax, even the largest estate could be distributed tax free if it were divided among enough beneficiaries. If you died with $100 million in assets, and left your estate divided equally among your 100 closes relatives and friends, each would receive $1 million, and no tax would be paid by anyone. Contrast this with the current estate tax laws. A $100 million estate would result in an estate tax of around $44 million (that might be reduced by $10 million or $15 million with creative planning), no matter who inherited the money.

A carefully designed inheritance tax would increase the incentive to divide large estates into small inheritances benefiting a broader spectrum of individuals. The result would be a greater dispersion of wealth, and possibly a greater incentive for each generation of a wealthy family to be productive and create its own wealth (since the likelihood of receiving incredibly large amounts from prior generations may be reduced). It is not clear, however, whether this type of social engineering will work, or even ultimately be beneficial to society as a whole. In any event, no one in Congress has raised this idea on any serious level and there is no reason to believe that the estate tax will be replaced by an inheritance tax in the foreseeable future.

Capital Gains Recognition

One of the problems with the current estate tax system is that it looks solely at the value of your assets at the time of your death and pays no attention to whether or not you have paid income tax on the money that you have. Any individual who dies with a net value of $6 million in 2007 will pay approximately $1,800,000 in estate tax. This is true irrespective of whether the $6 million has been previously taxed.

> A carefully designed inheritance tax would increase the incentive to divide large estate into small inheritances benefiting a broader spectrum of individuals. The result would be a greater dispersion of wealth, and possibly a greater incentive for each generation of a wealthy family to be productive and create its own wealth.

Let's compare two taxpayers who invested $1 million in real estate and stocks in 1965. The first sells his portfolio of stocks and real estate in 2006, for $8 million in cash. He pays federal and state capital gains taxes of approximately $2 million, and puts the remaining $6 million in the bank. If he wants to spend the $6 million, he can withdraw it from the bank and spend it as he wishes. He paid tax on the full amount in 2006, so there no reason to make him pay a tax for taking it out of the bank.

The second taxpayer's $1 million investment has increased to $6 million as well. However, if he wants to spend it all, he must sell the assets and pay federal and state capital gains tax of between 15 percent and 25 percent, depending on which state he calls home. After tax, he will only have $4,500,000 to $5,100,000 to spend.

Although the first taxpayer has $1 million more in spendable, after-tax dollars, if they both die in 2007, each will owe the exact same estate tax of approximately $1,800,000. Taxpayer number two escaped between $900,000 and $1,500,000 of capital gains taxes.

The solution to this inequity—and a direct response to the concern that the estate tax can be imposed on previously taxed assets, that is to say, it's a "death tax"—is to replace the estate tax with capital gains tax recognition. The Canadians have been using a system like this for years, eh? Rather than a flat estate tax, under Canadian law, the estate is obligated to pay capital gains tax as if the decedent had sold all of his or her property. Under this system, taxpayer number one, who has already paid tax on every penny in his estate, can pass everything on to his heirs tax free. On the other hand, taxpayer number two, who has $5 million of untaxed growth accumulated in his assets, will be required to pay the capital gains tax. He can then leave what's left to his heirs.

> Instead of selling an asset when it make economic sense to do so—a goal in a free-market economy—many taxpayers hold onto assets for many years just to avoid capital gains taxes. A switch to the Canadian, capital gains recognition system would end this distortion of the free-market system.

The capital gains recognition system seems extremely fair, and it avoids one problem inherent in the current estate tax system. Under current law, many elderly taxpayers understand that capital gains taxes can be avoided by holding on to the asset until death so that their heirs can take over the asset with an increased tax basis (that wipes out the capital gains that have accumulated over many years). Instead of selling an asset when it make economic sense to do so—a goal in a free-market economy—many taxpayers hold onto assets for many years just to avoid capital gains taxes. A switch to the Canadian, capital gains recognition system would end this distortion of the free-market system. However, I don't see a political move toward the Canadian system until hockey becomes more popular on this country than football and basketball; and I don't see that happening any time soon.

Increased Estate Tax Exemptions

In 2006, Congress came close to permanently increasing the estate tax exemption amount. Different versions of the bill were raised in the House and the Senate. Under one House version, the exemption amount would be p e rmanently increased to $5 million (with indexing for inflation) and the maximum estate tax rate was to be lowered to 15 percent for estates valued at less than $25 million and 30 percent for larger estates. In addition, the bill allowed a widowed taxpayer to increase the $5 million by any portion of the exemption amount that his or her spouse did not use at the time of the spouse's death.

Other versions introduced into the House or Senate during 2006 incorporated exemption amounts ranging from $3,750,000 to $5 million, and tax rates ranging up to 40 percent. Although it is not clear what political climate will prevail in the Democratic Congress elected in 2006, it seems likely that this Congress will move to end the uncertainty in the current tax laws. Estate planning practitioners and their clients—all of whom are voters—are becoming uneasy as the year 2010, and especially the year 2011, approaches. Given the need to implement many estate-planning techniques several years in advance, practitioners are hoping to see clarity in the estate law by 2007 or 2008.

> It seems likely that Congress will move to end the uncertainty in the current tax laws. By the end of 2008, Congress may provide for a permanently increased estate tax exemption amount, possibly between $3,500,000 and $5 million.

In light of everything, it seems likely that by the end of 2008, Congress will provide for a permanently increased estate tax exemption amount, very likely between $3,500,000 and $5 million. Most likely, this amount will increase automatically based upon the rate of inflation, but the automatic indexing may not start until 2015 or 2020. Further, Congress appears likely to allow any unused portion of the estate tax exemption to be used by a surviving spouse, so that taxpayers who do not have trusts are treated similarly to those who do have trusts. A taxpayer with a trust will probably still be able to leave a larger combined amount to children or other beneficiaries free of estate tax, since the trust will allow the first spouse's assets to grow inside the trust and still be free of estate taxes, while the "portability" provision allowing a surviving spouse to pick up any unused exemption amount will not allow for accumulated, untaxed growth.

In addition, it seems likely that the current estate tax rate of 45 percent will disappear. While rates may drop as low as 15 percent, it seems more likely that Congress will settle somewhere between 25 and 30 percent on the first

$25 million to $50 million, with an increase to about 35 percent on larger estates.

In short, my prediction is that Congress will continue the current estate tax system with a higher exemption amount and a lower tax rate. Whatever happens, remember that the most important part of your estate plan is the personal and family philosophy that you care about. Estate tax considerations can have a serious impact on your plan, but do not ever allow them to become the driving force.

Appendix

Your Family Documentation

You:

Name: _____ Birth date _____ Soc Sec # _____

Prior Names: _____

Spouse:

Name: _____ Birth date _____ Soc Sec # _____

Prior Names: _____

Date of Marriage: _____ City of Ceremony _____

Residences During Marriage:

Current: _____ Since _____

Prior City/State: _____ From _____ To _____

Prior City/State: _____ From _____ To _____

Prior City/State: _____ From _____ To _____

Prior City/State: _____ From _____ To _____

Children of this Marriage:

Name: _____ Birth date _____ Soc Sec # _____

Address: _____ Phone: _____

Name: _____ Birth date _____ Soc Sec # _____

Address: _____ Phone: _____

Name: _____ Birth date _____ Soc Sec # _____

Address: _____ Phone: _____

Name: _____ Birth date _____ Soc Sec # _____

Address: _____ Phone: _____

Your Prior Marriages:

Prior Spouse: _____ Marriage Date: _____ Disso. Date: _____

    Child: _____ Birth Date _____ Soc Sec # _____

    Address: _____ Phone: _____

    Child: _____ Birth Date _____ Soc Sec # _____

    Address: _____ Phone: _____

    Child: _____ Birth Date _____ Soc Sec # _____

    Address: _____ Phone: _____

Prior Spouse: _____ Marriage Date: _____ Disso. Date: _____

    Child: _____ Birth Date _____ Soc Sec # _____

    Address: _____ Phone: _____

    Child: _____ Birth Date _____ Soc Sec # _____

    Address: _____ Phone: _____

    Child: _____ Birth Date _____ Soc Sec # _____

    Address: _____ Phone: _____

Spouse's Prior Marriages:

Prior Spouse: _____ Marriage Date: _____ Disso. Date: _____

    Child: _____ Birth Date _____ Soc Sec # _____

    Address: _____ Phone: _____

    Child: _____ Birth Date _____ Soc Sec # _____

    Address: _____ Phone: _____

    Child: _____ Birth Date _____ Soc Sec # _____

    Address: _____ Phone: _____

Prior Spouse: _____ Marriage Date: _____ Disso. Date: _____

    Child: _____ Birth Date _____ Soc Sec # _____

    Address: _____ Phone: _____

    Child: _____ Birth Date _____ Soc Sec # _____

    Address: _____ Phone: _____

    Child: _____ Birth Date _____ Soc Sec # _____

    Address: _____ Phone: _____

Grandchildren:

Name: _____ Child of: _____

Name: _____ Child of: _____

Name: _____ Child of: _____

Name: _____ Child of: _____

Name: _____ Child of: _____

Name: _____ Child of: _____

Name: _____ Child of: _____

Your Parents (if living):

Father's Name: _____ Address: _____ Phone: _____

Mother's Name: _____ Address: _____ Phone: _____

Spouse's Parents (if living):

Father's Name: _____ Address: _____ Phone: _____

Mother's Name: _____ Address: _____ Phone: _____

Your Siblings:

Name: _____ Address: _____ Phone: _____

Name: _____ Address: _____ Phone: _____

Name: _____ Address: _____ Phone: _____

Name: _____ Address: _____ Phone: _____

Name: _____ Address: _____ Phone: _____

Spouse's Siblings:

Name: _____ Address: _____ Phone: _____

Name: _____ Address: _____ Phone: _____

Name: _____ Address: _____ Phone: _____

Name: _____ Address: _____ Phone: _____

Name: _____ Address: _____ Phone: _____

Nieces/Nephews:

Name: _____ Child of: _____

Name: _____ Child of: _____

Name: _____ Child of: _____

Name: _____ Child of: _____

Name: _____ Child of: _____

Name: _____ Child of: _____

Name: _____ Child of: _____

Almost Family (people you may consider including in your will; for example, close friends, former in-laws, former stepchildren, former stepparent)

Name: _____ Address: _____ Phone: _____

Name: _____ Address: _____ Phone: _____

Name: _____ Address: _____ Phone: _____

Name: _____ Address: _____ Phone: _____

Charities You Support (and that you may desire to include in your estate plan)

Name: _____ Address: _____

Name: _____ Address: _____

Name: _____ Address: _____

Financial Summary Worksheet

ASSETS:

Checking Accounts:

Bank name: _____ Account No. _____ Balance _____

Bank name: _____ Account No. _____ Balance _____

Total Checking Accounts _____

Savings Accounts:

Bank name: _____ Account No. _____ Balance _____

Bank name: _____ Account No. _____ Balance _____

Bank name: _____ Account No. _____ Balance _____

Total Savings Accounts _____

Brokerage Accounts:

Brokerage name: _____ Account No. _____ Balance _____

Brokerage name: _____ Account No. _____ Balance _____

Total Brokerage Accounts _____

Certificates of Deposit:

Bank name: _____ Account No. _____ Balance _____

Bank name: _____ Account No. _____ Balance _____

Bank name: _____ Account No. _____ Balance _____

Total Certificates of Deposit _____

Money Market Accounts:

Bank name: _____ Account No. _____ Balance _____

Bank name: _____ Account No. _____ Balance _____

Total Money Market Accounts _____

Mutual Funds:

Fund Name: _____ Account No. _____ Value _____

Fund Name: _____ Account No. _____ Value _____

Fund Name: _____ Account No. _____ Value _____

Fund Name: _____ Account No. _____ Value _____

Total Mutual Funds _____

Stocks:

Stock: _____ No. of shares _____ Value _____

Stock: _____ No. of shares _____ Value _____

Stock: _____ No. of shares _____ Value _____

Stock: _____ No. of shares _____ Value _____

Total Stocks _____

Retirement Accounts:

Bank/Brokerage: _____ Account No. _____ Value _____

Primary Beneficiary _____ Alternate Beneficiary_____

Bank/Brokerage: _____ Account No. _____ Value _____

Primary Beneficiary _____ Alternate Beneficiary _____

Bank/Brokerage: _____ Account No. _____ Value _____

Primary Beneficiary _____ Alternate Beneficiary _____

Total Retirement Accounts _____

Business Interests:

Description _____ Value _____

Description _____ Value _____

Total Business Interests Value _____

REAL ESTATE

Family Residence:

Address: _____ Mortgage _____ Fair Market Value _____

Family Residence Value _____

Family Residence Mortgage _____

Rental Property:

Address: _____ Mortgage _____ Fair Market Value _____

Address: _____ Mortgage _____ Fair Market Value _____

Address: _____ Mortgage _____ Fair Market Value _____

Total Rental Property Value _____

Total Rental Property Mortgage _____

Other Real Estate:

Address: _____ Mortgage _____ Fair Market Value _____

Address: _____ Mortgage _____ Fair Market Value _____

Address: _____ Mortgage _____ Fair Market Value _____

Total Other Real Estate Value _____

Total Other Real Estate Mortgage _____

Automobiles:

Make _____ Model _____ Year _____ Value _____

Loan Balance _____

Make _____ Model _____ Year _____ Value _____

Loan Balance _____

Make _____ Model _____ Year _____ Value _____

Loan Balance _____

Total Automobile Value _____

Total Automobile Loans _____

Collectibles (valuable jewelry, antiques, or artwork):

Description _____ Value _____

Description _____ Value _____

Description _____ Value _____

Description _____ Value _____

Description _____ Value _____

Description _____ Value _____

Description _____ Value _____

Total Collectibles Value _____

Life Insurance:

Insurance Co. _____ Policy No. _____ Benefit _____

Insured _____ Cash Value _____ Loan Balance _____

Insurance Co. _____ Policy No. _____ Benefit _____

Insured _____ Cash Value _____ Loan Balance _____

Insurance Co. _____ Policy No. _____ Benefit _____

Insured _____ Cash Value _____ Loan Balance _____

Total Life Insurance Benefits _____

Total Life Insurance Cash Value _____

Total Life Insurance Loan Balance _____

Other Loans:

Lender _____ Balance Owed _____

Lender _____ Balance Owed _____

Lender _____ Balance Owed _____

Total Other Loan Balance _____

Total Assets and Liabilities Worksheet

Assets:

Total Checking Accounts	_____
Total Savings Accounts	_____
Total Brokerage Accounts	_____
Total Certificates of Deposit	_____
Total Money Market Accounts	_____
Total Mutual Funds	_____
Total Stocks	_____
Total Retirement Accounts	_____
Total Business Interests Value	_____
Family Residence Value	_____
Total Rental Property Value	_____
Total Other Real Estate Value	_____
Total Automobile Value	_____
Total Collectibles Value	_____
Total Life Insurance Benefits	_____
Total Life Insurance Cash Value	_____

Total Assets _____

Family Residence Mortgage	_____
Total Rental Property Mortgage	_____
Total Other Real Estate Mortgage	_____
Total Automobile Loans	_____
Total Life Insurance Loan Balance	_____
Total Other Loan Balance	_____

Total Liabilities _____

Net Assets (Assets less Liabilities) _____

Monthly Income and Expenses Worksheet

Asset	Monthly Income	Monthly Expense
Checking Accounts	_____	_____
Savings Accounts	_____	_____
Brokerage Accounts	_____	_____
Certificates of Deposit	_____	_____
Money Market Accounts	_____	_____
Mutual Funds	_____	_____
Stocks	_____	_____
Retirement Accounts	_____	_____
Business Interests	_____	_____
Family Residence	_____	_____
Rental Property	_____	_____
Other Real Estate	_____	_____
Automobile	_____	_____
Collectibles	_____	_____
Life Insurance – investment return	_____	_____
Total Income/Expense	_____	_____

Asset Value Test

Spouse			Children		
Asset	FMV	Debt	Asset	FMV	Debt
Residence	650,000	320,000	Life Ins.	250,00	—
Bank Acct.	70,000	—	Bank Acct.	50,000	—
401(k)	150,000	—			
Car	25,000	15,000			
Total	895,000	335,000	Total	300,000	—

Total FMV	895,000		Total FMV	300,000
Less Total Debt	335,000		Less Total Debt	_____
Net Value	660,000		Net Value	300,000

Income and Expense Test

Spouse

Asset	Income	Payment
Residence	—	1,800
Bank Acct.	300	—
401(k)	1,200	—
Car	—	450
Total	**1,500**	**2,250**

Total Income	1,500	
Plus Employment Earnings[1]	____	
Plus Pension/Social Security[2]	1,800	
Plus Other Investment Income[3]	____	
Total Aggregate Income		**3,300**

Total Payments	2,250	
Other Monthly Expenses[4]	2,850	
Total Aggregate Expenses		**5,100**

Excess of income over expenses		—
Shortfall in meeting expenses		1,800

1 Employment earning potential if you anticipate that this beneficiary will continue to be employed.

2 Pension or social security benefits anticipated, if this beneficiary is old enough to be receiving such benefits.

3 Income, if any, on any assets this beneficiary may have separate from those being inherited from you.

4 Add up all your normal monthly living expenses, such as food, entertainment, automobile operating expenses, utilities, insurance, property taxes, income taxes, etc.

Glossary

401(k) Plan. A statutorily-permitted retirement plan, often allowing contribution by both an employer and an employee.

529 Savings Plan. A statutorily-permitted, tax-deferred (and potentially tax-free) savings plan for educational expenses.

A/B Trust. A trust established in order to transfer assets to a surviving spouse, and ultimately children or other beneficiaries, without the need for probate. Also, known as a family trust, living trust, revocable trust, or inter vivos trust.

Administration. The process of accumulating the assets of, paying the debts of, and ultimately distributing a deceased person's estate, either through court-supervised probate or through trust administration.

Administrator. A court-appointed individual named to handle the probate of a decedent's estate when a person dies without a will, or with a will that does not nominate an executor.

Advance Health Care Directive. A properly-executed document setting forth a person's desires regarding health care decisions, and appointing an agent to act on the person's behalf if he or she becomes incapacitated.

Attorney-in-Fact. An individual named in a durable power of attorney to act as the agent on behalf of the person giving the power of attorney.

Beneficiary. A person named in a will or trust to receive money or property.

Bequest. A gift of money or property by will or trust.

Buy-Sell Agreement. An agreement between partners, or other co-owners of a business, contractually obligating the parties to buy or sell any interest in the business upon the occurrence of certain events, such as death, disability, termination of employment, retirement, or divorce. In addition, the agreement typically sets forth a method for determining the price for which the business interest is to be sold, and the terms of payment.

Bypass Trust. A trust used to make property or money available to one beneficiary for their lifetime (or a specified number of years), and then leave the assets to a different beneficiary without including assets in the taxable estate of the first beneficiary. This is commonly used to provide income for a surviving spouse while ultimately leaving the remaining assets to children or other beneficiaries without incurring additional estate tax.

Charitable Lead Trust. An irrevocable trust paying income to charity for a specified number of years, with the assets remaining at the conclusion of the period transferred to specified beneficiaries (often family members of the person establishing the trust).

Charitable Remainder Trust. An irrevocable trust paying income to specified beneficiaries (often the person establishing the trust and/or their family members) for a specified number of years or for the lifetime of designated beneficiaries, with the assets remaining at the conclusion of the period transferred to specified charities. There are two common types of CRTs: The charitable remainder annuity trust or CRAT (which pays a fixed dollar amount annually), and the charitable remainder unitrust or CRUT (which pays a set percentage of the value of the trust's assets each year).

Codicil. An amendment to a will, executed with the same formality as a will.

Conservator. A person appointed by a court and granted legal authority to make financial or personal/medical decisions for someone who has become mentally incapacitated. It is possible to be appointed the "conservator of the estate" (with control over financial decisions only) or the "conservator of the person" (with control over personal and medical decisions only).

Death Tax. The common name for tax imposed upon the assets left by a decedent at the time of his or her death. Also referred to as estate tax or inheritance tax.

Decedent. Refers to a person who has died.

Disclaimer. The formal rejection of the right to receive property or money under a will, trust, or probate. If made in a timely way, usually within nine months, the disclaimer can avoid unnecessary gift tax consequences.

Durable Power of Attorney. A document authorizing an attorney-in-fact to act as agent of the person granting the power of attorney and allows the authority to continue even if the person granting the power becomes legally incapacitated. A power of attorney that is not "durable" becomes ineffective when the person granting it becomes legally incompetent.

Executor. A person or organization nominated in a will, and appointed by a court, to handle the probate of an estate.

Estate Tax. A tax on the transfer of assets from a decedent to his or her designated beneficiaries or heirs. Under current law, the first $2 million or more is exempt from estate tax.

Family Trust. A trust established in order to transfer assets to a surviving spouse, and ultimately children or other beneficiaries, without the need for probate. Also, known as a living trust, A/B trust, revocable trust, or inter vivos trust.

Generation-Skipping Trust. A trust specifically designed to distribute assets directly from the trust to grandchildren of the creator of the trust, or to younger generations (or to people not related to the creator who are at least 37½ years younger than the creator).

Gift Tax. A tax applicable to gifts made during the donor's lifetime (in excess of the amount exempt from gift tax).

Grantor. The person, or people, who establish a trust. Also known as settlor.

Health Care Directive. A properly-executed document setting forth a person's desires regarding health care, and appointing an agent to act on the person's behalf if he or she becomes incapacitated.

Heir. A person, or people, entitled to inherit a decedent's assets under state law if the person dies without a will or trust designating beneficiaries.

Inheritance Tax. A tax imposed by a state government, rather than the federal government, on the transfer of assets at death.

Inter Vivos Trust. A trust established while the person creating it is alive, rather than on his or her death, often in order to transfer assets to a surviving spouse, and ultimately children or other beneficiaries, without the need for probate. Also, known as a family trust, living trust, A/B trust, or revocable trust.

Irrevocable Life Insurance Trust (ILIT). An irrevocable trust created to hold life insurance on the trust creator's life in a manner that will allow the proceeds of the life insurance policy ultimately to be distributed to his or her children (or other beneficiaries) free of estate tax. Also referred to simply as a life insurance trust.

Irrevocable Trust. A trust that is, or on the occurrence of some event has become, irrevocable and unamendable.

Issue. Refers to the group of people comprised of a person's children, grandchildren, and other lineal descendants.

Joint Tenancy. A form of ownership where two or more people own property together, usually in equal shares, in a manner such that the property automatically becomes owned by the surviving joint tenant(s) upon the death of any joint tenant.

Life Estate. A legal right to the use of property for one's lifetime, with the ultimate ownership going to a third party upon the death of the holder of the life estate.

Living Trust. A trust established during the creator's lifetime, rather than at the creator's death, often in order to transfer assets to a surviving spouse, and ultimately children or other beneficiaries, without the need for probate. Also, known as a family trust, A/B trust, revocable trust, or inter vivos trust.

Living Will. A properly-executed legal document specifying the person's desire as to whether or not he or she wishes to be kept alive by heroic measures or artificial means, if necessary. A living will does not dispose of a person's property.

Marital Deduction. Provisions in the estate tax, and gift tax, that allow an unlimited amount of money or property to pass from one spouse (except non-citizen spouses) to another without incurring tax.

No Contest Clause. A provision in a will or trust that provides that a beneficiary or heir who challenges the terms of the trust is to be disinherited and receive nothing.

Personal Representative. Refers to the executor or administrator of an estate.

Pooled Income Trust. A specialized trust, similar to a charitable remainder trust, whereby a person contributes property to a common fund managed by a charity that can avoid capital gains tax upon the sale of the contributor's assets, and provide greater lifetime income to the contributing party in exchange for the value remaining at the time of the contributor's death being distributed outright to the managing charity.

Pour Over Will. A will designed to "pour" assets held outside of a trust into a person's trust at the time of his or her death, so that the assets can be distributed according to the terms of the trust.

Power of Appointment. A power granted by a creator of a will or trust granting someone the authority to designate who shall receive the creator's property or money at some time in the future.

Power of Attorney. A document authorizing an attorney-in-fact to act as agent of the person granting the power of attorney, and allows the authority to continue only until the person granting the power becomes legally incapacitated. A power of attorney that is "durable" remains effective even after the person granting it becomes legally incompetent.

Probate. A state court procedure used to transfer property or money from a deceased person's estate to his or her heirs or beneficiaries. Probate may not be necessary if assets are held in a trust.

Qualified Domestic Trust (QDOT). A special form of trust used to leave assets to a spouse who is not a US citizen without incurring estate tax.

Qualified Personal Residence Trust (QPRT). A specialized form of trust designed to transfer ownership of a family residence or vacation home to specified beneficiaries after allowing the creator of the trust to live in the residence rent-free for a specified number of years.

Qualified Terminal Interest Property Trust (QTIP). A specialized form of trust that qualifies for the marital deduction, and defers estate tax on the assets in the trust by leaving all income to the surviving spouse, and the remaining principal in the trust to specified beneficiaries upon the death of the surviving spouse.

Residuary Estate. The balance of property and money remaining in a trust or estate after payment of all debts, expenses, taxes, and bequests of items specifically left to named individuals or organizations. This is sometimes referred to as the "residue" of the estate.

Revocable Trust. A trust that is amendable or revocable, often established in order to transfer assets to a surviving spouse, and ultimately children or other beneficiaries, without the need for probate. Also, known as a family trust, living trust, A/B trust, or inter vivos trust.

Roth IRA. A statutorily-permitted retirement account funded with after-tax dollars and accumulating earnings entirely tax-free.

Settlor. The creator of a trust.

Special Needs Trust. A specialized form of trust designed to distribute assets to supplement the needs of a person who is, or may become, entitled to receive government benefits or assistance, without reducing the government benefits available.

Sprinkling Trust. A trust that retains assets in a common fund for the benefit of two or more of the settlor's children or other beneficiaries before dividing the assets into individual shares for each beneficiary.

Term Life Insurance. Life insurance providing coverage for a specified term, usually one year at a time, with no investment or saving component (and not accumulating any cash value).

Testate. When a person dies with a will in effect.

Testator. The person who creates a will.

Transfer Tax. Refers to estate tax, inheritance tax, and gift tax.

Trustee. A person or organization who holds title to and manages the assets in a trust, for the benefit of the beneficiaries under the trust.

Will. A properly-executed legal document transferring property or money to a decedent's heirs or beneficiaries through a probate proceeding.

About the Author

The author, W. Rod Stern, is a practicing attorney with more than 20 years experience designing estate plans for individuals ranging from owners of international businesses to widows with little more than the family home and $20,000 cash in the bank. When not at the office, he can usually be found in the bleachers next to Bonita, his wife of 27 years, watching daughters Sarah and Sami (or sometimes the UCLA men's team) play basketball or softball. He holds a law degree from the University of California, Hastings College of the Law, a masters degree in taxation from New York University, and an undergraduate degree in Political Science from UCLA. Much to his dismay, he has become one of the older partners practicing in the areas of business, tax, and estate planning, with Murtaugh Meyer Nelson & Treglia, LLP, a full service law firm in Irvine, California.

Mr. Stern has been a contributing author and reviewer for leading legal publishers such as California Continuing Education of the Bar and Matthew Bender, on topics such as Selecting and Forming Business Entities, and California Limited Partnerships.

He is also a consultant to PSMJ Resources, Inc., a worldwide publisher and provider of management consulting services, and frequently participates in their seminars regarding Ownership Transition for Professional Firms and Mergers and Acquisitions of Professional Firms.

Mr. Stern participates in the Orange Coast Estate Planning Council and the Tax Section of the Orange County Bar Association. In addition, he serves on the Board of Directors of Easter Seals Southern California.

Index